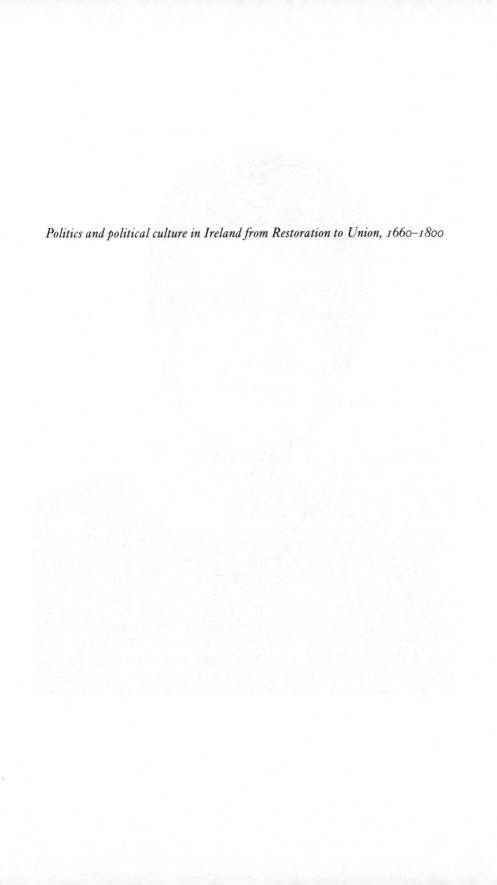

Politics and political culture in Ireland from Restoration to Union, 1660–1800

Politics and political culture in Ireland from Restoration to Union, 1660–1800

ESSAYS IN HONOUR OF
JACQUELINE R. HILL

Raymond Gillespie, James Kelly
and Mary Ann Lyons

EDITORS

FOUR COURTS PRESS

Set in EhrhardtPro 10.5pt/12.5pt by
Carrigboy Typesetting Services for
FOUR COURTS PRESS LTD
7 Malpas Street, Dublin 8, Ireland
www.fourcourtspress.ie
and in North America for
FOUR COURTS PRESS
c/o IPG, 814 N Franklin St, Chicago, IL 60610

A catalogue record for this title is available
from the British Library.

ISBN 978-1-84682-974-1

Printed in England
by Antony Rowe Ltd, Chippenham, Wilts.

Contents

Abbreviations

Add. MS	Additional manuscript
Anal. Hib.	*Analecta Hibernica*
Arch. Hib.	*Archivium Hibernicum*
BL	British Library
Cal. S.P. dom.	*Calendar of State Papers, domestic series, of the reign of Charles II, 1660–85 ...* ed. M.A.E. Green and others (London, 1860–1939)
CARD	*Calendar of the ancient records of Dublin, in the possession of the municipal corporation of that city*, ed. Sir John and Lady Rosa Gilbert (19 vols, Dublin, 1889–1944)
ch.	chapter
Chatsworth	Chatsworth House, Derbyshire
CJI	*Journals of the House of Commons of the kingdom of Ireland* (21 vols, Dublin, 1796–1802)
DCA	Dublin City Archives
DHR	*Dublin Historical Record*
DIB	*Dictionary of Irish biography*, ed. James McGuire and James Quinn (9 vols, Cambridge, 2009)
ECI	*Eighteenth-Century Ireland / Iris an dá chultúr*
edn.	edition
From patriots to unionists	J.R. Hill, *From patriots to unionists: Dublin civic politics and Irish Protestant patriotism, 1660–1840* (Oxford, 1997)
GSA	Guild of St Anne
HIP	E.M. Johnston-Liik, *History of the Irish parliament, 1692–1800: Commons, constituencies and statutes* (6 vols, Belfast, 2002)
HMC	Historical Manuscripts Commission
IADS	*Irish Architectural & Decorative Studies*
IHL Proc.	James Kelly (ed.), *Proceedings of the Irish House of Lords* (3 vols, Dublin, 2007)
IHS	*Irish Historical Studies*
Ir. Econ. & Soc. Hist.	*Irish Economic & Social History*
Ir. Geog.	*Irish Geography*
JCHAS	*Journal of the Cork Historical and Archaeological Society*
JKAHS	*Journal of the Kerry Archaeological and Historical Society*
JKAS	*Journal of the County Kildare Archaeological Society*
JLAHS	*Journal of the County Louth Archaeological and Historical Society*

MP	Member of parliament
MR	Municipal records
MS(S)	Manuscript(s)
MUN	Muniment
NAI	National Archives of Ireland
NLI	National Library of Ireland
NLW	National Library of Wales
ODNB	*Oxford dictionary of national biography* (60 vols, Oxford, 2004)
PRONI	Public Record Office of Northern Ireland
Quarterly Bull. IGS	*Quarterly Bulletin of the Irish Georgian Society*
RCBL	Representative Church Body Library
RIA	Royal Irish Academy
RIA Proc.	*Proceedings of the Royal Irish Academy*
RSAI Jn.	*Journal of the Royal Society of Antiquaries of Ireland*
SP	State Papers
TCD	Trinity College Dublin
TNA	The National Archives, Public Record Office, UK
UJA	*Ulster Journal of Archaeology*

Acknowledgments

We wish to acknowledge the support provided for this publication by the Department of History, Maynooth University and by the staff of Four Courts Press whose assistance has been invaluable. Thanks are also extended to Dr Matthew Stout for maps 1 and 1a, to Brendan Twomey, for providing assistance with the list of publications and to Dr Bernadette Cunningham for compiling the index.

Contributors

TOBY BARNARD Hon MRIA is emeritus fellow, Hertford College, University of Oxford.

VINCENT COMERFORD was formerly professor of modern history at Maynooth.

BERNADETTE CUNNINGHAM is editor of Irish History Online.

RAYMOND GILLESPIE MRIA is professor of history at Maynooth University.

DAVID W. HAYTON MRIA is professor emeritus of early modern Irish and British history, Queen's University Belfast.

JAMES KELLY MRIA is professor of history at Dublin City University.

COLM LENNON MRIA is professor emeritus of history, Maynooth University.

MARY ANN LYONS is professor of history at Maynooth University.

BRENDAN TWOMEY is an independent scholar whose research is centred on financial structures and practices in early eighteenth-century Ireland.

JONATHAN G. WRIGHT is a lecturer in the Department of History at Maynooth University.

Jacqueline R. Hill and the study of history in Ireland: a career of dedication and achievement

VINCENT COMERFORD AND BERNADETTE
CUNNINGHAM

A native of rural Devon, Jacqueline Rhonda Hill (Jackie, to her great range of friends and colleagues) graduated in history at the University of Leeds in 1969. The lecturer who introduced her to the history of Ireland was David Steele, a graduate of UCD and a specialist in the nineteenth century. Under his direction Jackie undertook her PhD, 'The role of Dublin in the Irish national movement, 1840–48', completing it in 1973. Thereafter she moved to Dublin and joined the historical community of which she has now been a dedicated and active member for almost half a century. Her point of entry was the research seminar organized by T.W. Moody, professor of modern history at TCD. After the customary round of part-time tutorial and lecturing engagements in the Dublin area and beyond, Jackie was appointed to a one-year junior lectureship in the department of modern history at Maynooth in 1976 while Tomás Ó Fiaich was head of department. Appointment to a permanent post in the department ensued in 1978, under the headship of Patrick J. Corish. Her promotion to lectureship and senior lectureship followed in due course. When in 2002 Maynooth held its first ever round of competitive promotions (as distinct from appointments) to professorial grade, two of the four successful applicants were from the history department – Jackie Hill and Colm Lennon. Jackie officially retired from the history department in 2013 but continues to teach and mentor graduate students to the present. Thus, counting from her first formal appointment in 1976, she has been on the staff over forty-five years, easily the longest service of anyone who has worked in the department, and indeed with few comparisons anywhere else in the university. However, length of service is not the explanation for Jackie's position as a uniquely popular and respected member of the university community. She achieved that status within a very short time of her arrival at Maynooth, thanks to an unfailingly tolerant, respectful and concerned attitude towards all others, across departments and faculties.

Professor Hill had contact with her largest cohort of students through the compulsory core module on the early modern history of Britain that she taught to undergraduates over several decades. In line with the evolution of historiography, what began as 'British history' became 'four nations' history. In addition, large numbers of history students over the decades had the benefit of taking one or more of the special topics and elective modules with which Jackie enriched the offerings of the department. The topics ranged from the workings of privilege in the eighteenth-century to Dublin radicalism in the 1840s, to the Protestant anniversary tradition in Ireland, and to the development of the Canadian constitution. An innovative and very successful feature of her long-running module on the Orange Order was the allocation of a session to a visit and talks by members involved in the archival and historiographical work of the society.

Jackie Hill has contributed to numerous iterations of taught research programmes and diploma courses. She has an outstanding record as a research supervisor at every level. In particular, the set of PhD theses produced under Jackie's direction is second to none in range and quality. Each of her research students had the benefit of infinitely patient guidance as to the substance and presentation of their work.

A thorough assessment of the contribution of Jackie Hill's oeuvre to historical scholarship is for another place. However, it is of major significance, ranging from her groundbreaking monograph *From patriots to Unionists: Dublin civic politics and Irish Protestant patriotism, 1660–1840* (Oxford: Clarendon, 1997) through various seminal book chapters and journal articles. In a spirit of collegiality, on behalf of *Irish Historical Studies*, she co-edited (with Cormac Ó Gráda) *'The visitation of God'? The potato and the Great Irish Famine* by Austin Bourke, which was published by Lilliput Press in 1993. On behalf of the Irish Committee of Historical Sciences, she co-organized (with Colm Lennon) the 23rd Irish Conference of Historians, at St Patrick's College, Maynooth, in May 1997. The edited proceedings of that conference were subsequently published by University College Dublin Press under the title *Luxury and austerity: Historical Studies, XXI*.

When in the late 1980s one more great effort was called for to bring the work of a New History of Ireland to a conclusion Jackie undertook the responsibility of editing the final volume of the main narrative. *Ireland, 1921–84* edited by J.R. Hill with twenty-six contributors and running to more than a thousand pages was published by Oxford University Press in 2003. In 2008 Jackie was elected to membership of the Royal Irish Academy.

From her first years in Ireland Jackie Hill stood out for the sense of responsibility combined with generosity that drove her to undertake voluntary endeavour in respect of academic and related causes. Jackie has always been not only a joiner, in the best sense of that term, but also a doer. In the 1970s and 1980s the fortunes of the NUI sector at Maynooth depended to an extent subsequently difficult to imagine on the deliberations of the Academic Staff Association. From the beginning of her time in the college Jackie was unstinting in her work for the ASA. From 1979 she was for several years one of the Maynooth representatives on the council of the Irish Federation of University Teachers. The McGrath/O'Rourke case with its implications for the future of the institution made this a tense and sometimes awkward period. It was also a time of struggling to resolve issues about salaries, employment conditions for women, and provision of teaching and library facilities. In the course of her time at Maynooth Jackie has answered the call to serve on numerous other college bodies and committees.

By the late 1970s the deteriorating imbalance in the number of women on the academic staff of third-level institutions began to receive some attention. The problem was highlighted by the rapid expansion in the number of female students, in Maynooth as elsewhere. The issue was not only one of small absolute numbers of women on the academic staff but the fact that they were located preponderantly in the lower ranks. Many of those who agreed that the situation was deplorable still believed that nothing much could be done about it. Following a discussion at a meeting of the council of IFUT on 20 January 1979 steps were taken to establish what became the IFUT Committee on Women in the University, with Jackie Hill as a founding member. It was the beginning of a long campaign which over forty years later is still not over. One of the milestones along the way was the presentation by an IFUT delegation to the Joint Oireachtas Committee on Women's Rights on 15 May 1984. Jackie Hill and her Maynooth history colleague and friend Mary Cullen were the main contributors on the IFUT side.

In 1978 T.W. Moody stepped back from the role of joint editor of *Irish Historical Studies*, a position he had held for forty years, with R. Dudley Edwards as fellow joint editor for half of that time. Moody was able to sustain his attention to the progress of the journal through a committee of management, of which he was chair until his death in 1984. The committee secretary in 1978 was Dr Jacqueline Hill. Forty-three years later, the same committee, now also incorporating the editorial committee, still has the same secretary. Accordingly, Jackie has had unrivalled exposure to the roller-coaster experiences typical of almost every academic journal that has survived the transition from the late Gutenberg age through to the current phase of the digital era. Technology apart, these have been decades of wildly fluctuating economic conditions and major change in areas such as copyright and the legal implications of published criticism of professional work. There can be few academics anywhere who have such extended and unbroken experience of this phase of unparalleled change in the history of academic publication. At *Irish Historical Studies* as elsewhere it was a story of demanding bi-annual routines punctuated by crises of every imaginable kind – financial, legal, professional – occasionally exacerbated by inevitable misunderstandings and personality clashes. (Jackie has worked with at least a dozen joint editors.) The patience, forbearance and ingenuity of the secretary of the management committee, year in, year out, have been the key to the continuity and enduring success of *IHS*. Jackie continues to campaign in support of a future for academic journals in Irish history in a rapidly changing legislative and commercial environment for academic publishing.

Survival, with greater or smaller adjustments but without much impact on public awareness (or much thanks from anyone), is the typical outcome of a successfully managed administrative glitch. However, one of the disruptions at *IHS* resulted in the emergence of a separate initiative that has become another of Jackie Hill's hallmark contributions to Irish scholarship, namely Irish History Online.

When it was launched in 1938 as the joint journal of the Irish Historical Society and the Ulster Society for Irish Historical Studies, *IHS* was intended primarily to provide students of Irish history with articles presenting the best in recent research. But the journal also aimed to provide ancillary scholarly services, including editions of documents, lists of theses in progress, and of theses completed, on Irish history in Irish universities. The second number in each year included, as a rule, the listing of writings on Irish history published in the preceding year. The expanding volume of publications from the 1960s made it necessary to put more complex arrangements in place to ensure comprehensive coverage. The double-digit monetary inflation of the late 1970s pushed the costs of publication to a critical point and in 1980 a decision was taken to abandon the publication of writings in respect of 1979. While a delay in publication was undesirable, abandonment meant the discontinuation of the painstaking system of compilation that had evolved over a number of years, involving the collaboration of university library staff. Following informal discussion, Jackie Hill and Vincent Comerford decided to take responsibility for an effort to save the project. This was possible in the first instance thanks to the willingness of two librarians (Clara Cullen and Monica Henchy) to continue their work on the project without any certainty of publication. In due course the Irish Committee for Historical Sciences provided patronship. The annual bibliographies for five consecutive years, from 1979 to 1983, edited by J.R. Hill and R.V. Comerford but hugely dependent on the work of others, were published by the ICHS in microfiche format. From 1984 to 2002 they were published in stand-alone print format, the first of those edited by Jackie Hill. The team of compilers and editors during these years included Clara Cullen, Monica Henchy, Sarah Ward-Perkins, Máirín Cassidy, Ciaran Nicholson and Bernadette Cunningham. These transitional arrangements preserved the expertise and practices that underlay the annual bibliographical project. Subsequently Jackie pursued painstakingly and with unwavering determination the transposition of Writings to the digitally enhanced product that is now Irish History Online. This resulted in the creation of an online bibliographic database that is now Ireland's national bibliography for history, freely accessible to all interested in Irish history.

In the first phase of the 'Irish History Online' initiative, Jackie secured funding from the Irish Research Council for the Humanities and Social Sciences (IRCHSS) for a three-year project, 2003–6, to create an online bibliography of Irish history. In the first phase, data was drawn from the bibliographies that had been printed annually in *Irish Historical Studies* or as separate publications issued by the Irish Committee of Historical Sciences. Jackie managed the project as principal investigator, employing two staff at NUI Maynooth, and working with Bernadette Cunningham and Mary O'Dowd on a small management team. Funding was awarded by the IRCHSS for a second three-year project, in which she again worked as principal investigator with the same management team, in 2006–9. In this new phase one editor was employed to expand Irish History Online's retrospective coverage of writings about the Irish abroad, as well as continuing to input new data contributed by the volunteer compilers, Máirín Cassidy and Ciaran Nicholson.

Jackie Hill was pivotal in establishing close collaboration with colleagues in the Royal Historical Society in London, which helped streamline the transition from print to an online bibliography. This international cooperation greatly contributed to the initial success of the Irish History Online project. In the years since Irish Research Council funding for the project ceased in 2009, Jackie has continued as convenor of Irish History Online, and has been instrumental in ensuring that the database, now hosted by the Royal Irish Academy, continues to be updated by a team of volunteer compilers. She has ensured that the longstanding commitment to the bibliography of Irish historical writing shown by the Irish Committee of Historical Sciences and *Irish Historical Studies* has been maintained through the successive incarnations of the bibliography, managing change adeptly. Irish History Online is now an essential part of the research infrastructure in the humanities in Ireland, and its continuation, despite the lack of ongoing institutional funding, is due in no small part to Jackie's personal commitment to supporting the work of the team of volunteer compilers.

By any standards Jackie Hill's research career, happily on-going, has been one of major individual scholarly achievement. That has been intertwined with one of the most impressive and sustained contributions to the collective and structural needs of our discipline that anyone of her generation or earlier has to their credit.

Introduction: Dublin and beyond

RAYMOND GILLESPIE, JAMES KELLY
AND MARY ANN LYONS

In 1973, when Jacqueline Hill completed her PhD on the politics of Dublin in the 1840s at the University of Leeds, her decision to focus on nineteenth-century Ireland must have seemed a rather esoteric, indeed probably marginal subject, in a United Kingdom context.[1] When she moved to Dublin a few years later that perspective changed dramatically. Irish history was thriving – well placed to reap the full benefits of the archive-driven approach advanced and inculcated by T.W. Moody and R. Dudley Edwards since they had assumed leadership of the profession in the 1930s.[2] There are any number of indices to which one might have recourse to measure this, but the register of publications provided on Irish History Online seems particularly appropriate in this instance, in view of the crucial part Jackie Hill played in its development,[3] and it reveals that during the years when she commenced her engagement with Irish history the number of publications (books and articles primarily) devoted to the subject rose by almost 50 per cent from 479 items in 1965 to 693 items in 1973.[4] Inputs also expanded as research students signed up in increasing number. By 1973 the list of Hill's Dublin contemporaries undertaking research degrees in history at Irish universities stretched to nine pages of *Irish Historical Studies* whereas in 1965 it had been contained in three-and-a-half, and the three theses completed in 1964–5 had expanded to twelve. The way in which the subject was developing followed patterns well established elsewhere. In the 1973 listing of theses, the ever-popular biographical studies of prominent individuals were still well represented. Those in search of more cutting edge topics in the emerging field of economic history were concentrated in the provinces, studying individual regions or even estates. Thus, theses that then were in progress included studies of the history of agriculture in Cork, the Farnham estate in County Cavan, sea fishing in County Down, the Great Famine in County Donegal and ownership of land by Galway townsmen. The most popular area of study for Jackie's Irish contemporaries, however, was political history with politics and the press in the nineteenth century, the political thought of Young Ireland, the Townshend

1 Jacqueline R. Hill, 'The role of Dublin in the Irish national movement, 1840–48' (PhD, University of Leeds, 1973). 2 See, inter alia, Ciaran Brady, '"Constructive and instrumental": the dilemma of Ireland's first "new historians"' in *idem* (ed.), *Interpreting Irish history* (Dublin, 1994), pp 3–8. 3 See R.V. Comerford and Bernadette Cunningham, 'Jacqueline R. Hill and the study of history in Ireland: a career of dedication and achievement', pp 11–15. 4 Irish History Online at https://www.ria.ie/irish-history-online.

viceroyalty, and government and opposition in the 1750s all under active scrutiny.

This approach to the study of the past inevitably mirrored the ethos and approach of the shapers of historical scholarship in the 1930s and 1940s, which was most effectively, and persuasively, articulated by G.R. Elton in his *Political history: principles and practice* (London, 1970) in which the crown, the parliament, the court and perhaps the law were the main scenes of human endeavour. This was not a view that was to remain unchallenged in the 1970s as new areas and approaches to historical enquiry, such as microhistory and cultural history, led the assault on what was perceived as a traditional and narrow approach to reconstructing the past. These new challenges emphasized the social depth of politics, finding signs of political life where none were previously thought to exist; for instance, in parishes and confraternities in the sixteenth and seventeenth centuries and in the avalanche of clubs and societies that flourished in the eighteenth and nineteenth centuries.[5] To these discoveries some applied the epithet 'popular politics', hoping to isolate these newly discovered realms from the world of 'real' political history pursed by the elite and observable only in the corridors of power of Dublin Castle and chambers of the house of parliament. The new worlds that were opened up were both complicated and enhanced by the discovery of vertical connections at lower social levels which complemented the more familiar horizontal ones. Kingship, for instance, was not simply relevant in the 'political nation' but for the whole of society. The newly discovered vertical political bonds between king and subject were, it transpired, not unrelated to the horizontal links, as it became clear that they frequently strengthened local elites just as the demands of royal government served, oftentimes, to stimulate the growth of parliament. Old well-tried ideas, including the inevitably of rebellion or the unrestrained triumph of parliament, dissolved under such scrutiny. All this required historians to think less about institutions and more about how power was distributed within society and how authority was experienced at all social levels. What was needed was not more political history but a social history with the politics put back, or so argued Patrick Collinson in his 1989 inaugural lecture as regius professor of history at Cambridge.[6] Put another way, politics needed to be understood not as a series of events but as a culture or a set of symbols (or ideas) embedded in a web of significances that give them meaning and that embraced everyday life. Thus, the members that comprised the political elite were not to be conceived

5 For works on these subjects in Ireland see Raymond Gillespie and Elizabeth FitzPatrick (eds), *The parish in medieval and early modern Ireland: community, territory and building* (Dublin, 2006); Colm Lennon (ed.), *Confraternities and sodalities in Ireland: charity, devotion and sociability* (Dublin, 2012); James Kelly and Martyn Powell (eds), *Clubs and societies in eighteenth-century Ireland* (Dublin, 2010); R.V. Comerford and Jennifer Kelly (eds), *Associational culture in Ireland and abroad* (Dublin, 2010).   6 Reprinted in Patrick Collinson, *Elizabethans* (London, 2003), pp 1–27.

of as remote figures standing outside the social order, controlling the destiny of nations, but rather as figures who have 'a deep intimate involvement ... in the master fictions by which that order lives'.[7]

In many ways Jackie Hill's work echoed and anticipated some of these developments. She was unusual in undertaking a local study of politics, as such studies were usually reserved for social and economic historians. Her scholarship also focused on what historians have come to describe as 'the middling sort' and their political lives. Subsequent work took those political actors onto the streets in articles about national celebrations and popular protest.[8] For Jackie Hill, politics has been about the articulation and exercise of power both in a symbolic and transactional way in specific local circumstances and across social boundaries. That, too, is what this volume is about. Its starting point was also Jackie Hill's starting point: the politics of the capital. Dublin in the century-and-a-half after 1660 was transformed from a fairly modest provincial centre to a city of European significance with its own distinctive and historically conditioned government. Distributing power within this organism was a delicate task that required a fine balancing act between local and national administration, the focus of her magnum opus *From patriots to unionists: Dublin civic politics and Irish Protestant patriotism, 1660–1840* (Oxford, 1997). The resulting social interactions can be observed at a number of levels. Most obviously, there were the political activities of the corporation itself. Conventionally, this has been explored through an analysis of the composition of the corporation and its relationship with the politically powerful guilds. Brendan Twomey's essay in this volume approaches the problem from a different perspective. Focusing on the financial problems experienced by the corporation during the early eighteenth century and the debates and rhetoric of Charles Lucas in the 1740s, Twomey's essay moves the 'Lucas dispute' away from the personal jealousies, inter-group rivalries and personal animus in which it has often been located, and places it instead in the recognizable realm of the financial problems occasioned by the infrastructural ambitions of Dublin Corporation. The need to provide a modern urban infrastructure, especially a water supply, to a growing city created challenges that led to an increasingly personalized debate whose participants mobilized all the tools of popular political life: the printed pamphlet, broadsheets, poems and newspapers, which were distributed among an increasingly literate and politicized populace by newspaper sellers. In this way 'popular' and 'elite' politics were firmly welded together into a set of assumptions about how the city might be managed.

This mobilization of those outside the formal institutions of political discourse could and did happen in other ways as well. The theatre, for

---

7 Clifford Geertz, 'Centres, kings and charisma: reflections on the symbolics of power' in his *Local knowledge: further essays in interpretive anthropology* (London, 1993), p. 146.   8 See the bibliography of Professor Hill's work below, pp 208–13.

instance, was an important arena in which political ideas were debated and communicated.[9] Many of those ideas were more applicable to the national arena than the inherently localized politics of Dublin Corporation, but the realms were not exclusive, and the evolution of political discourse among Lucas's supporters in Dublin within the factionalized environment of the 1750s is illustrative of the mobility of political ideas as well as of the impact of politicization across the social order. This serves to highlight the importance of the streets as a venue for political action. Chronicling street politics under the term 'popular politics' has become a significant preoccupation of historians in recent years and 'the mob', constrained by the rules of the 'moral economy', has become an increasingly important presence in describing politics from the bottom up. Yet, what is equally clear is that the strategies employed at street level were not invariably expressions of protest or demands for change from below. Popular rituals, processions, disturbances, the power of printed libels and powerful oratory, all of which feature prominently in Jackie Hill's work, could all be pressed into service in maintaining the status quo as well as changing it.[10] This was certainly the case when such forms were deployed by the state in days of celebration, such as the rituals surrounding the celebrations marking the delivery from the rebellion of 1641 on 23 October.[11] Bonfires, sermons and parades could all contribute to a stabilization and enhancement of the existing political order.[12] If that is true from the perspective of the nation it is equally correct from a local perspective. As Mary Ann Lyons's essay demonstrates, political culture in the city was also expressed by the actions and activities organized and executed by the guilds in the city. The guilds – active and powerful players in city politics in the seventeenth and eighteenth centuries – invested considerable sums of money in sustaining traditional rituals such as the processions and feasts accompanying the Riding of the Franchises, the annual march to Cullenswood and the marshalling of the citizens at locations such as St Stephen's Green and Oxmantown Green. The rituals surrounding these events acted as both markers of inclusion, drawing Dubliners together into a common sense of the city while at the same time reminding many of those who observed these events that they

---

9 See, for example, Raymond Gillespie, 'Political ideas and their social contexts in seventeenth-century Ireland' in Jane Ohlmeyer (ed.), *Political thought in seventeenth century Ireland* (Cambridge, 2000), pp 107–30; H.M. Burke, *Riotous performances: the struggle for hegemony in the Irish theatre, 1712–1784* (South Bend, IN, 2003). 10 See, in particular, 'National festivals, the state and "Protestant ascendancy" in Ireland, 1790–1829', *IHS*, 24 (1984–5), 30–51; '"Allegories, fictions and feigned representations": decoding the money bill dispute, 1752–6', *ECI*, 21 (2006), 66–88. 11 T.C. Barnard, 'The uses of 23 October and Irish Protestant celebrations', *English Historical Review*, 106 (1991), 889–920. 12 James Kelly, '"The Glorious and immortal memory": commemoration and Protestant identity in Ireland, 1660–1800', *RIA Proc.*, 94C (1994), 25–52; idem, 'The emergence of political parading, 1660–1800' in T.G. Fraser (ed.), *The Irish parading tradition: following the drum* (Basingstoke, 2000), pp 9–26.

were no less excluded from the elite world of the guild than they were from the still-more visibly elevated realms of parliament by existing assumptions about hierarchy. As such these public-facing rituals both confirmed but also potentially disrupted social order, even as they displayed the realities of power within the city in a very visible way.

Once released from the long dominant preoccupation with the institutional contexts of parliament and council chamber, historians have discovered that arguments about the distribution and exercise of power featured in many contexts, of which the street was only one. Colm Lennon's essay, for instance, identifies the parishes of the established church as an important pressure point in which competing ideas about civic authority and civic order contested for ascendancy. As the basic unit of local government, the Church of Ireland parish was a place where all elements of a locality met. The parish graveyard contained the bodies of all parishioners, rich and poor, Catholic and Protestant, while wealthier churches contained vaults where several generations of families might be buried. Indeed, while it was unusual, Catholics might share in the administration of the parish by acting as senior officials, such as churchwardens. More commonly, Catholics might be found as sidesmen or collectors of the parish cess. Yet, the religious rites performed in those churches, and the financial support for those rites provided by the parish cess, alienated many from their parish church. Colm Lennon identifies these tensions in the parish of St Audoen, with its surviving, wealthy pre-Reformation chantry of St Anne, and, in particular, the tensions generated by the obligation to provide for the poor. As his essay demonstrates, both Catholic and Protestant poor were relieved from the guild income suggesting that, in this parish at least, accommodations could be reached between Catholics and Protestants on certain issues. The parish served as a site for negotiation of the distribution of power and the exercise of authority among the communities resident within the parish. The process is only partly reconstructable and was not expressed in street protest or pamphlet wars but its results are still observable in the evidential record. In some areas of political life, the culture that the exercise of authority created, particularly that identifiable at local level, may have wanted for dramatic expression but it was present nonetheless and, as Lennon's sensitive reconstruction attests, can be revealed by patient historical investigation.

If these essays relocate political activity away from the centralized political institutions of the state into the streets and localities of the city, two other essays take the argument further by suggesting not just that a diversity of places in the city were sites of political action but that the city itself constituted a political statement. Raymond Gillespie's and James Kelly's essays argue that the idea of the city came to have a political meaning that was expressed in the manner in which the political culture of the place was revealed in the actions of its residents. For Mark Quin, Gillespie argues, his personal identity and that of the city became so closely intertwined that when, in the 1670s, the factional politics of the city created rifts in the social fabric, Quin saw his carefully constructed persona as a civic father being threatened. That situation had come about as a consequence of the opportunities for social mobility that accompanied the expansion of Dublin in the late seventeenth and early eighteenth centuries. That rapid social mobility swept Quin from humble beginnings to the lord mayoralty in the space of a generation, without the usual attributes of self-worth, such as honour, 'credit' or lineage, that characterized those at the pinnacle of the political elite. Mark Quin compensated for this by aligning himself with the institutions of the city that allowed him to demonstrate his civic loyalty and provide him with a sense of self-worth. When those institutions failed him in 1671–4, it not only caused him to question his relationship with them but also his very reason for being, which led to his suicide.

A second way in which the city as artefact could shape the political culture of the place is explored in James Kelly's essay. As Dublin expanded physically, economically and demographically during that late seventeenth and eighteenth centuries, it was transformed from a town of wooden buildings to structures of brick and stone. In this process, the image of the town acquired tangible form and its power structures were given expression in the architecture of public buildings and the layout of streets and squares. This was not a random process as much earlier urban development had been. Rather, its development reflected the power structures of the city, the predominance of the mercantile interest of the early part of the century yielded to landed developers and the politically shaped Paving Board and the Wide Streets Commission. The Dublin administration was also more concerned to brand public buildings with iconographical statements that served to give the citizenry an increasing sense of belonging to an improving space, aided by topographical artists, such as James Malton, who assisted the process by providing idealized versions of the landmark buildings they captured in their editions of views and vistas.[13] The aim of all these bodies was to foster an underlying sense of modernity and belief in the value of the culture of improvement in the city, driven by the political elite who had the power to give effect to the desire to change the face of the city. As a result, Dublin itself became a political statement, a reflection of local identity and a demonstration of the orderly values of the elite in the same way that the image of the seventeenth-century city served to define a persona for Mark Quin as he gravitated from one set social arrangements to another.

The popular politics of Dublin described in these essays were unusual in an Irish context. The city itself was by far the largest and most complex urban entity in Ireland. It had a well-developed social structure and the presence in the seventeenth century of a printing house and, in the eighteenth century, of a

13 Edward McParland, 'Malton's views of Dublin: too good to be true' in Brian P. Kennedy and Raymond Gillespie (eds), *Ireland: art into history* (Dublin, 1994), pp 15–25.

vibrant newspaper press created an increasingly well-informed population eager to think in political terms. Moreover, the presence of a national parliament served to sharpen popular political awareness on the streets as well as in the clubs and coffee houses that shaped the city's unique political culture. Beyond Dublin, the position is less clear. In Belfast, the economic powerhouse of Ulster, for instance, the picture was different. The corporation was controlled during the eighteenth century by one family, the Chichesters, and the strict enforcement of religious conformity ensured that that the corporation was moribund. There were, however, similarities with the Dublin situation. As Jonathan Wright's essay demonstrates, the same considerations of urban improvement that occupied grandees in Dublin were also in the mind of John Black of Belfast, who urged social reform with the various groups in the town, fulfilling what he regarded as their political obligations in the exercise of authority. For Black, the buildings of a town were important as a manifestation of its status and civility, and proof of its enlightened and improving image.

Important as figures such as John Black were, the shaping of local political cultures was a process that transcended the thoughts or actions of individuals. The similarities between Belfast and Dublin in the distribution and exercise of power mask the very real regional effects of the operation of politics. David Hayton's essay, atomizing events around Ballentoy in north Antrim in 1716, suggests that a three-level approach may be necessary if we are to understand how local political cultures were formed and how power was distributed. There was clearly a national context, represented in this case by religious differences played out in parliamentary conflict between High Churchmen (whom some viewed as Jacobites) and Dissenters, and a regional context, reflected in the changing balance of the religious demography of County Antrim. Finally, there was a parochial context in which local friendships, relations with the landlord and patterns of sociability, served to sharpen tensions. In themselves, these variables do not fully account for the political complexion of Ulster in the early eighteenth century which is Hayton's focus. Rather, it was the changing balances between the elements shaped by the rapid dissemination of information and ideas that promoted new configurations of political culture at local and regional level that were contested and argued out under the guise of national political concerns. Thus, the dramatic influx of Scottish Presbyterian radicals into County Antrim in the late seventeenth century served to destabilize regional relationships and to create the conditions that produced the Ballentoy episode.

These changing balances of ideas and beliefs were shaped into a recognizable political culture by the immediate circumstances of the local parish and it is these micro variables that serve as the focus for Toby Barnard's atomization of the Munster town of Dungarvan during the election of 1758. This episode emphasizes the agency of Dungarvan voters who, like the inhabitants of Ballentoy, in a different way, were active participants in the political process.

The manner in which they did so, however, reveals the very real differences that existed between the political cultures then obtaining in Ulster and Munster. Whereas Presbyterianism shaped ways of thinking in Ulster, it was Catholicism that exerted a compelling influence on the manner in which politics played out in Dungarvan at election time. Both functioned, of course, within a world in which the landed elite was the primary repository of power, though this too assumed different forms. In Dungarvan, the power of the local landlord, the Boyle family, was very real, whereas in County Antrim, the earl of Antrim's influence was more muted. In shaping political cultures, local decisions about the distribution of political power, and the consequences of the way it was expressed, were of vital importance.

Taken together, these essays argue for a way of thinking and engaging with politics and political culture in the seventeenth, eighteenth and early nineteenth centuries not, as was once the case, in terms of a select body of national institutions but rather as an argument about the expression of power and its impact on the social order. Drawing on, and shaped by the insights provided in Jackie Hill's work over some four decades, these essays stress the importance of regional political cultures, reflected and shaped in turn by religious and social structures, which were manifest on the streets, in local communities, through actions such as processions as well as through abstract thought about social structure and the desire to bring about improvement. Perhaps most importantly they highlight the roles of real people in specific places, in Dublin and beyond, in shaping how their world might be arranged.

'The receiver-general is not in cash to pay …': the financial travails of Dublin Corporation, 1690–1760 – causes, actions and political impact

BRENDAN TWOMEY

The publication in 1997 of *From patriots to unionists: Dublin civic politics and Irish Protestant patriotism, 1660–1840* established Jacqueline Hill as the preeminent scholar of Dublin Corporation during its heyday as an exclusively Protestant institution.[1] As she reminded us, 'Irish Protestantism was as much an urban as a landed phenomenon'.[2] Since then, Hill has further explored the complex politics of Dublin and shed much-needed light on the city's administrative and financial history.[3] Building on these foundations this essay explores aspects of the interaction between the administrative and financial history of Dublin Corporation and the political history of Dublin during the period from the Hanoverian succession in 1714 through to what Hill has termed the 'challenge to oligarchy' in the 1740s.[4]

Narratives of this 'challenge' have traditionally centred on the colourful and patriotic rhetoric of the apothecary Charles Lucas, the self-proclaimed 'Last free citizen of Dublin'.[5] However, the Lucas 'challenge' did not appear out of nowhere. The populist sentiment tapped into by Lucas, the traction he secured with elements of the freemen of Dublin, the governance, administrative and financial issues that he foregrounded, and the animosity that he aroused within the aldermanic cadre of the Dublin patriciate, were more than just a response to his torrent of words. Rather it is argued here that Lucas, for all of his rhetoric of personal sacrifice, his lengthy enforced exile following his proclamation for seditious libel, and the many pamphlets he ushered into the public sphere, was but the highest profile manifestation of what were long-standing, highly politicized but also instrumental issues and concerns.[6] Lucas also tapped into

1 The quotation in the chapter title is taken from *CARD*, viii, 276, 10 Feb. 1738. Jacqueline Hill, *From patriots to unionists: Dublin civic politics and Irish Protestant patriotism, 1660–1840* (Oxford, 1997). 2 Ibid., p. 3. 3 See the bibliography of Jacqueline Hill's works for a listing of her works on Dublin civic life from the mid-seventeenth century through to the mid-nineteenth century. 4 Hill, *From patriots to unionists*, pp 79–111. 5 Charles Lucas, *An appeal to the commons and citizens of London* (London, 1756); Sean Murphy, 'The Corporation of Dublin, 1660–1760', *DHR*, 38:1 (Dec. 1984), 22–35; idem, *A forgotten patriot doctor: Charles Lucas, 1713–1771* – Centre for Irish Genealogical and Historical Studies, 3rd edn., http://homepage.eircom.net/~seanjmurphy/epubs/lucaspatriot.pdf [accessed 28 Mar. 2020]; see also David Dickson, *New foundations: Ireland, 1660–1800* (Dublin, 2000), pp 95–7, 143–4, 152–8 for an assessment of the role of Lucas in eighteenth-century Irish politics. 6 A proclamation for apprehending Charles Lucas, apothecary, *Dublin Journal*,

deep-seated interpersonal rivalries and populist political practices whose origins can be traced over several decades. The financial stresses resulting from the corporation's ambition to provide an adequate supply of 'pipe water' to the citizens of Dublin was one such ongoing issue. The resultant fiscal stresses on the city's always-precarious finances were such that in 1738 the city assembly was informed that 'there are demands on the city of about £3,000 ... and ... the receiver-general is not in cash to pay them'.[7]

Pamphlet wars prompted by parliamentary and mayoral elections, or public outcries in respect of security, the management of gaols, trading standards and the price of essentials such as coal and bread, were a recurring feature of Dublin civic politics in the first half of the eighteenth century. These were among the quotidian issues that required active intervention by the lord mayor and the corporation. David Hayton has argued that the by-times violent street politics of this period, and the associated heated and intemperate *ad hominem* rhetoric, can be seen as manifestations of a 'city in crisis'.[8] These controversies engendered vigorous debate in the public sphere and provided experience of direct political action on the part of the citizenry. That in turn shaped what Timothy Watt has called the 'complex and often incongruous relationship [that] existed between rulers and the ruled in Dublin' and prefigured the better known events of the 1740s, described by T.C. Barnard as 'this more excitable phase of politics'.[9]

I

Between the late seventeenth and the middle of the eighteenth century the population of Dublin city grew from *c*.50,000 to *c*.140,000.[10] During this period Dublin Corporation was the principal body charged with the provision of a broad range of municipal services for most of the built-up area of the city.[11] The Dublin elite relished this responsibility for, as Jonathan Swift's long-time friend Sir William Fownes, a former lord mayor and MP, proudly proclaimed in 1733, Dublin city was the 'second in his majesties dominions'.[12] In the

16 Dec. 1749 in James Kelly with Mary Ann Lyons, *The proclamations of Ireland, 1660–1820* (5 vols, Dublin, 2014), iii, 379–80.   7 *CARD*, viii, 276, 10 Feb. 1738.   8 David Hayton, 'Swift and the politics of Dublin, 1727–33' in Janika Bischof, Kirsten Juhas and Hermann J. Real (eds), *Reading Swift: papers form the seventh Münster Symposium* (Paderborn, 2019), pp 479–96, p. 479.   9 Timothy Watt, 'The corruption of the law and popular violence: the crisis of order in Dublin, 1729', *IHS*, 39:153 (May 2014), 1–23, 2; T.C. Barnard, *The kingdom of Ireland, 1641–1760* (Basingstoke, 2004), p. 90.   10 Patrick Fagan, 'The population of Dublin in the eighteenth century with particular reference to the proportions of Protestants and Catholics', *ECI*, 6 (1991), 121–56.   11 The politics of the independent liberties in Dublin and their interaction with the politics of the wider city are not addressed in this chapter.   12 Sir William Fownes, *A letter to the Right Honourable Humphry French, Esq.; present lord mayor of the city of Dublin* (Dublin, 1733), p. 3.

decades between the resumption of Protestant control of the city's affairs in
the summer of 1690, and the reforms that were enacted in 1760, the governance
of Dublin Corporation was determined by a set of arrangements known as the
'new rules' of 1672.[13] While these governance structures functioned reasonably
well, the self-perpetuating nature of the twenty-four man aldermanic board
and the perceived concentration of power within their hands gave cause
for on-going public concern. There were repeated charges of aldermanic
oligarchy and pandering to vested interests, which Charles Lucas denounced
as 'infringements on the rights, and liberties of the commons and citizens of
Dublin'.[14] The services overseen by Dublin Corporation, such as the regulation
of trade, security, street cleaning, the disposal of domestic sewage, street paving
and lighting, and especially the provision of 'pipe water', were central to the
lived experience of the citizens of Dublin. Success in the provision of these
services was an important yardstick by which the management of the civic elite
was judged by the increasingly well-informed 'free' citizens of the city.

In the early decades of the eighteenth century the provision of an adequate
supply of pipe water was perhaps the greatest, and certainly the most expensive,
infrastructural challenge facing Dublin Corporation.[15] In 1721 a report to the
city assembly acknowledged that 'in a dry season the city is in want of water,
though at other times it runs much to waste'. Following consultation with the
surveyor general Captain Thomas Burgh, proposals were developed to source
water from the Dodder, and for the construction of a basin to facilitate the
distribution of pipe water through an expanded network of wooden pipes.
A scheme to install a water mill at Dolphin's Barn was also proposed at this
time.[16] In the early 1720s, faced with the pressing need to generate cash to
fund such investment, the corporation made determined efforts to improve the
collection of the 'pipe water revenue' and to collect fines from those who drew
water from 'concealed' pipes.[17] However, despite the expansion of the system,
and the introduction of a more rigorous collection regime, pipe water rents,
which totalled £1,853 in 1725, had only increased to £2,654 by 1758.[18] The
costs involved in the expansion of the water supply, along with other financial
pressures, caused repeated cash flow problems for the corporation. For example,
in 1727 the city needed an immediate loan of £500 from the Blue Coat School

---

13 33 George II, c. 16, *An act for the better regulating the Corporation of the city of Dublin, and for
extending the power of the magistrates thereof, and for other purposes relative to the said city*; see Hill,
From patriots to unionists, pp 46–58; *CARD*, i, 56–67; Murphy, 'The Corporation of Dublin',
pp 24–5 for details of this complex and often contested governance structure.   **14** Charles
Lucas, *A remonstrance against certain infringements on the rights and liberties of the commons and
citizens of Dublin* (Dublin, 1743).   **15** Following the establishment of the Ballast Office in
1707, a body that had its own revenue stream and borrowing capacity, the significant expense
involved in the construction of city quays and the South Bull Wall were no longer part of
the annual accounts of Dublin Corporation.   **16** *CARD*, vii, 152–5, 21 Apr. 1721.   **17** Ibid.,
178–9, 18 Jan. 1722.   **18** Ibid., 302, 16 July 1725; x, 367–70, 20 July 1759.

'to pay for a quantity of timber that is daily expected for the use of the city pipe water'.[19]

In 1731, and again in 1733, both the current MP for the city, Samuel Burton, and the recent incumbent John Rogerson made unsuccessful attempts to secure parliamentary support for Dublin pipe water legislation.[20] In 1733, during the mayoralty of Swift's friend Humphry French, Sir William Fownes declared: 'if our City wants a new supply of water, I am of opinion that by help of a mill plac'd above Bloody Bridge, very good water may be raised out of the river to supply the north side or great parts of it.'[21] However, problems with the provision of pipe water persisted and in 1735 the city assembly ordered 500 copies of two reports on the issue to be printed, one by the leading surveyor Gabriel Stokes and the other by the up-and-coming architect Richard Castle.[22] Also in the mid-1730s the corporation consulted with the city's leading physicians, Dr Richard Helsham (a close friend of Swift) and Dr Bryan Robinson, on the health issues involved in the various schemes proposed. In 1737, as an expression of gratitude for services provided, Dr Helsham was granted the freedom of the city.[23] By the late 1730s, these initiatives notwithstanding, no sustainable technical or financial solution had been implemented and in 1738, as noted above, the city assembly was forced into the embarrassing admission that 'the receiver-general is not in cash to pay'.[24] As a short-term crisis management measure the assembly decreed that the receiver-general could not issue any payment in excess of the modest sum of £10 'unless the same be examined on oath and certified by five of the committee to be appointed'.[25] Furthermore, in order to raise cash immediately, the assembly agreed to sell a life assurance annuity of £100 per annum to Ruth Corker, the widow of a leading city merchant, for the sum of £1,000. The accounts for 1738 also record that cornet Richard Stevenson advanced the city £1,500 'at interest'.[26]

Finally, in August 1741, in a bold move, having acknowledged that 'the inhabitants of this city have of late been very badly supplied with water' and following a review of the previous reports, the corporation agreed to pay £3,500 to purchase the mills at Island Bridge on the Liffey and to install a water engine.[27]

19 Ibid., vii, 395, Aug. 1727. 20 Irish Legislation Database; https://www.qub.ac.uk/ild/?func=simple_search [accessed 1 Nov. 2020]. A Dublin pipe water bill was finally passed in 1775, 15/16 George iii, c. 24, *An act for the better regulating the pipe water of the city of Dublin.* 21 Fownes, *A letter to Humphry French*, pp 20–3. 22 *CARD*, viii, 171–2, 18 Apr. 1735. Gabriel Stokes, *A scheme for effectually supplying every part of the city of Dublin with pipe-water, without any charge of water-engine, or any water-forces, by a close adherence only to the natural laws of gravitation and principles, rules and experiments of hydrostaticks* (Dublin, 1735); Richard Castle, *An essay towards supplying the city of Dublin with water* (Dublin, 1735). 23 *CARD*, viii, 182, 18 July 1735, 262–3, 6 Sept. 1737. 24 Ibid., 276, 10 Feb. 1738. 25 See Robert Hume, 'The value of money in eighteenth-century England: incomes, process, buying power, and some problems in cultural economics', *Huntington Library Quarterly*, 77: 4 (2015), 373–416 for a discussion on the real purchasing power of money in this period. 26 *CARD*, viii, 276, 10 Feb. 1738, 299, 31 July 1738. 27 Ibid., ix, 32–4,

Since the corporation did not have the cash to fund this purchase, it was agreed to issue 'an obligation under the city seal to the said Mr Darby for the aforesaid sum of £3,500, at five per cent.'[28] However, this new scheme got off to a bad start; less than a year later the assembly was informed that the mills were in a 'very ruinous and leaky condition' and required 'immediate works'.[29] It was this expensive, and supposedly game-changing, decision to purchase the Island Bridge mills that became the central *cause célèbre* of Lucas's twenty-year anti-aldermanic campaign. Lucas objected to nearly every aspect of the project: the chosen location, the price paid, and especially the role of alderman Nathaniel Kane whom he accused of a corrupt conflict of interest in the transaction.

II

While the accounts and the minutes of the corporation meetings are available for this period, these can be a problematical source and, as noted by Hill, an understanding of what transpired has, on occasion, 'to be constructed from tantalizingly brief and occasional references'.[30] Reports are often summarized with a managerial briskness that elides a clear understanding of the underlying administrative processes and that can hide deep-seated political and inter-personal rivalries. Specifically the corporation's accounts, although based on double entry accounting, are a *mélange* of cash-based income and expenditure information, intermixed with other data using accrual accounting principles.[31] Nonetheless, some tenable conclusions in respect of income and expenditure, and the financial health of the corporation, can be extracted from these data. A brief analysis for the year ended Michaelmas 1758 will serve to illustrate.[32] The reported income for that year totalled £14,213 0s. 8d. and expenditure, identified as 'Discharge', totalled £15,114 19s. 9¼d. The difference of £901 19s. 1½d., in this instance an excess of expenditure over income, was recorded as the 'Balance due to the accountant from the city'.[33] The largest income item of £4,275 16s. 9½d. was described as 'arrears of rent due Michaelmas 1757':

14 Aug. 1741. By 1758 (see Table 1) the seller Jonathan Darby had reduced his exposure to the corporation to £1,500. There is no reference in the assembly records to his selling/assigning his bonds to others: see Michael Corcoran, *Our good health: a history of Dublin's water and drainage* (Dublin, 2005). **28** *CARD*, ix, 50, 15 Mar. 1742. **29** Ibid., 62, 25 June 1742. **30** Jacqueline Hill, 'Dublin Corporation and the levying of tolls and customs, *c.*1720–*c.*1820' in Michael Brown and Seán Patrick Donlan (eds), *The law and other legalities of Ireland, 1689–1850* (Abingdon, 2016), pp 187–208, 188. **31** 'Italian' bookkeeping texts were available; William Webster, *An essay on book-keeping. according to the true Italian method of debtor and creditor, by double entry* (Dublin, 1734). **32** The principal components of annual income and expenditure of the corporation and the management issues arising therefrom changed relatively slowly over the period under review. **33** *CARD*, x, 367–70, 20 July 1759: see Hill, 'Tolls and customs', *passim* for a more detailed discussion of the sources of

modern accounting practice would treat this as a balance sheet item. A further twenty-nine sources of income were recorded, most under the rubric of 'cash from'. The largest of these sources was £2,654 for the 'rents and fines of the pipe water'. Expenditure was recorded under six headings of which 'arrears of rent due to the city at Michaelmas, 1758' totalling £4,367 6s. 2½d. constituted the largest item. The other items of expenditure included 'casual expenses' (£5,011 15s. 8d.), 'debts of the city' (£2,835 12s. 9¾d.), and 'annual expenses' (£1,887 13s. 4d.). A final expense of £496 11s. 9d. was identified as 'poundage of £9,931 15s. 10d. money paid at 12d., per pound'; that is, the 5 per cent commission paid to the treasurer for managing the books and for acting as a short-term banker to the corporation. If the 'arrears of rent' are excluded from both the income and expenditure side, the income for 1758 was £9,937 3s. 10½d. and expenditure was £10,741 13s. 6¾d., that is, a deficit of £810 9s. 8¼d. (The difference from the reported deficit of £901 19s. 1½d. is the increase of £91 9s. 5d. in the arrears of rent, which today would be accounted for through the profit and loss account and the balance sheet.) In line with contemporary practice, the city treasurer John Hornby financed the deficit and, since the corporation did not have the cash to reimburse him, in January 1760 he was granted a bond (that is, he made a loan to the corporation) for £901 19s. 1½d.[34]

While the corporation incurred a deficit in most years, this was not the universal experience; so, for example, when in 1752 it ran a surplus, it was agreed that £1,000 would be 'applied to discharge so much of the city debt as pays interest'.[35] The corporation financed its recurring deficits by recourse to borrowing and the debt of the city increased from nearly £20,000 in 1735 to over £33,000 in 1758. The favoured borrowing modality was the issue of bonds secured 'on the seal of the city'.[36] In the absence of balance sheets, and of a loan ledger, it is difficult to establish a clear picture of the total debt outstanding at any particular point in time, or to confirm the identity of all of the lenders. Yet, data extracted from the annual accounts and periodic reports prepared for the city assembly provide some insights into the outstanding quantum of debt, the proposals advanced for the management (that is, reduction) of the interest costs, as well as proposals for securing alternative sources of finance and for other administrative reforms. One such effort to manage the cost of borrowing occurred in 1758 when the city estimated that its debt was '£33,000 and upward, at an interest of £4, per cent'.[37] The accounts ledger that year recorded total payments of £2,835 12s. 9¾d. under the heading of debts of the city, of

revenue for Dublin Corporation in this period.   34 *CARD*, x, 399, 18 Jan. 1760.   35 Ibid., 79, 7 June 1753.   36 As these debts were not secured on land there was no requirement/ incentive to record them in the Registry of Deeds. It is likely that the maturity date for these bonds was one year from the issue date. However, in line with contemporary practice, such debts were treated as open-ended loans and typically these loans were not redeemed until either the bondholder asked for repayment or the borrower was able to make an out of course payment.   37 *CARD*, x, 318–19, 7 Apr. 1758.

which £1,641 16s. 0d. can be identified as payments of interest on loans.[38] In
that year there were 35 individual payments covering twenty-one separate loan
transactions involving a total principal amount of £33,390.[39] The lenders and
the amount of their loans is shown in Table 1.

Table 1. Lenders to Dublin Corporation 1758

Lender	Size of loan to Dublin Corporation £	Background details of lenders
Individual Lenders	**£**	
Executors of Alderman John Adamson	500	In October 1755 the widow of alderman Adamson's (decd.) and also her sisters were granted relief on account of being 'greatly distressed'. *CARD*, x, 184, 17 Oct. 1755. Adamson and his son John held extensive rental property from the corporation in Baldoyle. *CARD*, x, 340, 20 Oct. 1758.
Executors of Mr James Bowden	200	
Mr Mathew Broughton	500	Mathew Broughton was a member of the common council of the city and served on the board of the Ballast Office and on the audit committee. *CARD*, x, 116, 18 Jan. 1754.
Mr Valentine Browne	4200	Sometime before April 1757 the brewer Valentine Browne had purchased outstanding loan bonds from Rev. John Grattan (£500) and the executors of alderman Nathaniel Pearson (£1,000). *CARD*, x, 266, 22 Apr. 1757. The details of his acquisition of other bonds from other creditors are not recorded in *CARD*.
Jonathan Darby Esq.	1500	Darby sold the Island Bridge mills to the corporation in 1741. *CARD*, ix, 50, 15 Mar. 1742.
Alderman Daniel Falkiner	1500	Daniel Falkiner was a partner in the failed bank of Burton and Falkiner. Falkiner was lord mayor of Dublin in 1739.
Assignees of Thomas Finlay	600	Returned as a member of the common council for the Trinity Guild, 1741-44-47-50. *CARD*, ix, 449–58. Member of the board of the Ballast Office, 1744. *CARD*, ix, 155–6, 18 Jan. 1745.
Rev. Mr Gasper Galliard	200	
Assignees Mrs Ann Hamilton	200	
Alderman Henry Hart	850	A member of the board of the Ballast Office and of the committee to acquire new furniture for the Mayoralty House in Dawson Street. *CARD*, x, 120, 18 Jan. 1754 and 142, 19 July 1754.
Mr Edward Hendrick	1000	Member of the common council. In 1749 he was nominated unsuccessfully for the office of sheriff. *CARD*, x, 458, 14 Apr. 1749.
Percival Hunt Esq.	2240	Lord mayor 1755. *CARD*, x, p. 461, 11 Apr. 1755. Hunt's debt was repaid in full in 1759 by the issue of four bonds of £500 and one for £240. *CARD*, x, 376, 20 July 1759.

38 The other items listed under this heading included rental payments and other short-term liabilities of the city.   39 See DCA, Book of Accounts, C1/Treas/01/03, 1758, pp 7–8. While there are frequent references in *CARD* to the acceptance of new loans, changes in loan terms, and transfers of the liability from one creditor to another, this record is incomplete.

Table 1. Lenders to Dublin Corporation 1758 *(continued)*

Lender	Size of loan to Dublin Corporation	Background details of lenders
Individual Lenders	£	
Richard Mathews Esq.	2000	
Executors of Alderman Nathaniel Pearson	2000	Pearson was member of the alderman board for many years. He was lord mayor in 1730 and also receiver-general of the revenue of the city in 1730. *CARD*, vii, 494, 1 June 1730.
Ann Pearson and Executors of Mrs Ann Pearson *	1000	Widow of Alderman Nathaniel Pearson.
Mrs Ann / Hanna Skellern **	1000	This debt was assigned to her in 1740. Prior to that the debt had been due to alderman Dawson and before him to alderman Percival Hunt. *CARD*, ix, 95–6, 1 Feb. 1743.
Executors of Charles Powell	800	Debt to Charles Powell was to be laid out at interest to support charitable donations to be made by the corporation. *CARD*, ix, 318, 20 Oct. 1749.
Mrs Jane Stephenson	1500	
Theobald Wolfe Esq.	3000	Member of the common council and in 1757 appointed to the committee to 'enquire into city leases near expiring'. *CARD*, x, 289–92, 14 Oct. 1757.
Total of Individual Lenders	**24790**	
Institutional Lenders		
The Blue Coat Hospital	5100	The board of the Hospital and Free School of King Charles II (know as the Blue Coat School or Hospital) was controlled by members nominated by the corporation. The hospital had provided loans to the corporation from at least 1719: *CARD*, vii, p. 90, 3 Mar. 1719. In the early decades of the century Daniel Wybrants acted as the accountant/bookkeeper for both the hospital and also for Dublin Corporation.
The Incorporated Society in Dublin for Promoting English Protestant Schools in Ireland	2000	This loan from the society was redeemed in July 1761. *CARD*, xi, 24–5, 17 July 1761.
George Reynolds Esq. Master of Trinity Guild	1500	The corporation had borrowed from the Trinity Guild (the most powerful guild in the commons) as early as 1725. *CARD*, vii, 303–4, 16 July 1725.
Total of Institutional Lenders	**8600**	
Total debt of Dublin Corporation 1758	**33390**	

* Payments to Mrs Ann Pearson and the executors of Mrs Ann Pearson have been combined into a single entry
** Payments to Mrs Ann and Hanna Skellern have been combined into a single entry.
Source: Dublin City Archives, Book of Accounts, C1/Treas/01/03 (formerly MR/37).

Nearly three-quarters of the loans taken out by the corporation, as measured by value, were made by individuals, including at least ten lenders who were either a serving alderman, a former lord mayor, a member of the common council, or executors of former members of the city assembly. Four of the lenders were female or their executors. The three institutional lenders were longstanding providers of credit to the corporation; for example, the Blue Coat Hospital had granted a loan of £1,000 to the city as far back as 1719.[40] The long-term financial relationship between the Blue Coat Hospital and the corporation was facilitated by the fact that Bartholomew Wybrants (d.1739) was the agent (that is, the bookkeeper and financial manager) for the Hospital from 1694 until 1730. He was also the bookkeeper for the corporation, from whom he received an annual salary of £10.[41] The corporation had borrowed from the Trinity Guild since at least 1725 when Nathaniel Kane was the accounting master of the guild. At the same time Kane paid two of the city's obligations, totalling £900 due to Gabriel Cannsilles, and he offered to lend the city a further £100 to 'complete the sum of £1,000'.[42] The interest paid on these bonds was typically one per cent below the current legal rate; these loans were seen as low risk, and they had none of the legal or administrative costs associated with the secured person-to-person lending practice that, aside from Irish government debt, constituted the only other viable lending alternative in Ireland at this period.[43]

As the level of debt grew over time, the officers of the corporation sought to identify various means either to reduce the interest cost or to secure alternative sources of finance. In April 1758, on 'being informed that some persons were willing to lend such a sum of money at an interest of three and half per cent', the city assembly proposed to swap the old debt for new debt at the reduced rate. Success in implementing such a policy would yield an annual saving of £165 in interest costs.[44] However, the city's institutional lenders rejected this approach and in July the Incorporated Society in Dublin for Promoting English Protestant Schools in Ireland requested repayment of its £2,000 loan.[45] The corporation relented and resolved 'that the said sum of £2,000, should be continued at £4 per cent'. At the same meeting the Trinity Guild, pleading that 'the revenue of the said guild was decreased, prayed that the said sum of £1,500, may be continued at £4 per cent': this request was also acceded to.[46] In October the Blue Coat School secured a similar concession on the grounds

40 *CARD*, vii, 90, 3 Mar. 1719.   41 Ibid., 395, 25 Aug. 1727, 509, 16 Oct. 1730; *Daily Gazetteer (London)*, 21 Mar. 1739; Lesley Whiteside, *A history of the King's Hospital* (Dublin, 1975), p. 37.   42 *CARD*, vii, 303–4, 16 July 1725.   43 See Brendan Twomey, 'Personal financial management in early eighteenth-century Ireland; practices, participants and outcomes' (PhD, TCD, 2018).   44 *CARD*, x, 318, 7 Apr. 1758.   45 Ibid., 325, 21 July 1758. A 'Bond of the city of Dublin' for £2,000 was recorded as an asset in the society's accounts for 1757. *A sermon preached at St Anne's Church, Dublin, on the 9th of April, 1758, before the Incorporated Society, for Promoting English Protestant Schools in Ireland* (Dublin, 1758), p. 27. 46 *CARD*, x, 325–6, 21 July 1758.

that 'the interest of the said sum of £5,100, is part of the standing revenue of the said hospital'.⁴⁷ Individual lenders were not afforded the same indulgence. In April 1759 Mary Broughton, a widow, on 'being informed the city would give only an interest of £3 10s. per cent., prayed that the said principal sum of £500 with interest for the same might be paid to her': the assembly agreed to do so.⁴⁸ On this occasion the entire exercise proved futile since in January 1760 the corporation was forced to concede that 'the present scarcity of money and a parliamentary loan at five per cent will oblige your honours to raise the interest payable to their several creditors to five per cent.' However, having noticed that the city's paper was frequently transferred by assignment, or by inheritance, from one lender to another, the committee submitted for consideration whether 'by giving obligations to the said creditors for £100, each, for their respective debts, will not create a greater circulation of the said securities and thereby enhance their interest'. This proposal was carried.⁴⁹

This was not the first attempt to restructure the city's debt. More than twenty years earlier, in 1735, when the total debt of the city stood at £19,838 18s. 11d., a committee recommended: 'the taking up of money on annuities (like to that of the Mercer's Company in London), will be the most likely means of clearing or paying off the same'.⁵⁰ In January 1737 a detailed proposal for a scheme to take securities of £50,000 in order to support the launch of a scheme to raise £25,000 by offering annuities to widows was presented to the assembly. It was also proposed to pledge the city's annual rent roll of £1,328 15s. as security.⁵¹ In December 1741, at a time when the corporation was in the process of issuing new debt of £3,500 to finance the purchase of the water mills at Island Bridge, it was agreed to expand the proposed annuity scheme to £30,000.⁵² However, owing to legal concerns in respect of 'making a legal conveyance of the part of their estate for the security of the subscribers' and the difficulty in collecting rents due to the corporation from tenants who 'file bills in chancery to protract the time', the launch date was repeatedly postponed, and in the end the scheme was abandoned.⁵³

47 Ibid., 342, 20 Oct. 1758.   48 Ibid., 361, 27 Apr. 1759.   49 Ibid., 415, 18 Apr. 1760. Contemporary practice was that on the assignment of the loan to another party the original bond was surrendered and a new bond was issued to the new creditor.   50 Ibid., viii, 180–2, 18 July 1735.   51 Ibid., 180–1, 18 July 1735, 227–32, 21 Jan. 1737, 246–9, 22 July 1737. The Mercer's scheme was an early example of a life assurance/annuity initiative targeted at clergy widows; see William Assheton, *A full account of the rise, progress, and advantages of Dr. Assheton's proposal (as now manag'd by the Worshipful Company of Mercers, London) For the benefit of widows of clergymen, and others; By settling jointures and annuities at the rate of twenty per cent, with directions for the widow how to receive her annuity, without delay, charges, or deductions* (London, 1730) for one of the seven editions/versions of this scheme and Geoffrey Clarke, *Betting on lives: the culture of life insurance in England, 1695–1775* (Manchester, 1999).   52 *CARD*, ix, 41, 7 Dec. 1741.   53 Ibid., viii, 277–9, 10 Feb. 1738, 291, 5 June 1738, 300, 21 July 1738, 308–9, 20 Oct. 1738.

As noted earlier, in 1738, when facing yet another of its periodic cash flow crises, the assembly agreed to a proposal from a

> Mrs Ruth Corker, widow that she will pay to this city £1,000, sterling, in consideration of your honours perfecting a security to her for the payment of an annuity of £100, per annum, during her life, which proposal we recommend to your honours as a fair one, and will be of service to the city towards discharging the present debts'.[54]

The assembly minute does not record any debate in respect of the long-term financial risks/benefits associated with this transaction. It may have been the case that the dire financial situation facing the corporation was so urgent that the need for an immediate cash injection trumped any detailed consideration of these risks.[55] However, given the close business and family ties between members of Dublin's civic elite, it is certain that committee members would have known that Ruth Corker was the widow of the leading, and recently deceased, Dublin merchant Thomas Corker. Corker was a representative for the Trinity Guild on the assembly between 1717 and 1726 and he had been a member of the board of the Ballast Office.[56] He had been proposed for the office of city sheriff in 1721 and again in 1723.[57] Corker's business affairs with leading figures included his purchase in April 1732 of a mortgage for £800 from the estate of the Dublin banker Joseph Damer and in November 1733 he advanced £1,000 by means of a secured mortgage to Richard Wingfield of Powerscourt.[58] In 1733 Corker was appointed as one of the committee of creditors seeking to recover money from the failed Burton and Falkiner bank.[59] Ruth Corker also had strong family ties with the aldermanic and business elite in her own right. She was the daughter of Richard Falkiner, a brother of the banker Daniel Falkiner. After the death of her father, her mother married the banker Joseph Kane, the brother of alderman Nathaniel Kane. Her birth date is not known, but she married in 1715 and her will was proven in 1772. On the assumption that she was married in her early twenties, Mrs Corker would have been in her mid/late 40s in 1738. At the then legal rate of 6 per cent, a 10 per cent annuity would have been priced at an implied maturity of between 14 and 15 years. The corporation's financial

54 Ibid., 276, 10 Feb. 1738. The £1,000 was duly received by the corporation and appeared on the revenue side of the next set of accounts – see ibid., 299, 21 July 1738.   55 Expertise in respect of annuity pricing, life tables, and compound interest/present value calculations was readily available in this period: see Abraham de Moivre, *Annuities upon lives: or, the valuation of annuities upon any number of lives; and also, of reversions* (Dublin, 1731) and John Castaing, *An interest-book four, five, six, seven, eight percent* (Dublin, 1724).   56 *CARD*, vii, 575; viii, 470–1, 477.   57 Ibid., vii, 402, 21 Apr. 1721, 408, 30 May 1723.   58 Registry of Deeds, 73 158 50307; *Dublin Journal*, 20 June 1732; Registry of Deeds, 75 64 52164.   59 *Dublin Journal*, 14 Aug. 1733; *Dublin Evening Post*, 7 Aug. 1733. The same notice appeared in various Dublin newspapers for a two-month period in the autumn of 1733.

records show that the £100 annuity was paid to Mrs Corker up to 1764 (at which point she may have been over 70 years old), with a three-quarters payment recorded for 1765. It would appear, therefore, that Mrs Corker got the better bargain. While not referenced by Lucas, this transaction is an example of the insider transaction that he railed against. This was not the only occasion when the corporation granted such annuities in return for an up-front cash injection. For instance, in 1741 Thomas Gillam paid the city £300 for an annuity of £30.[60] The recurring financial difficulties faced by Dublin Corporation, driven in large part by the costs associated with the expansion of the pipe water system, were just one part of the highly contested world of civic politics in early eighteenth-century Dublin. These financial pressures presented the city's civic leaders with significant administrative and management challenges and the decisions taken formed the backdrop to the regular cut and thrust of the city's politics. In time, they informed and energized the more radical political anti-oligarchic and constitutional challenge from Charles Lucas.

III

The historiography of the polemical *oeuvre* of Charles Lucas is usually set within the Irish patriot constitutional tradition that places him in a line of succession linking Molyneux, Swift, and Grattan.[61] However, in addition to constitutional themes, his writings were laced with specific, often *ad hominem* attacks on individuals from within the Dublin aldermanic elite. These attacks foregrounded specific events, in what Lucas maintained was the decades-long flawed and corrupt governance of Dublin city. In his pamphlets Lucas accused named individuals of nepotism, fraudulent preference, insider dealing, mismanagement, and both petty and significant corruption. He contended that these abuses reduced the corporation's revenues, resulted in its failure to deliver on important infrastructural projects, and thereby diminished the ancient political rights and freedoms of the citizens of Dublin.[62] His criticism of Alderman Nathaniel Kane, and his acolytes and relatives, and especially of Kane's role in the controversial purchase of the Island Bridge mills, was central to these attacks.

However, Lucas's by-times hyperbolic pamphlets were not the first in which political controversies, ideological disputes, management failures and the interpersonal rivalries of those involved in Dublin civic politics, were argued out in print. As far back as 1713 Swift's friend Sir William Fownes stood

60 *CARD*, ix, 36, 16 Oct. 1741.   61 See Ian McBride, *Eighteenth-century Ireland: the isle of slaves* (Dublin, 2009), pp 282, 299; James Kelly, 'The life and significance of Charles Lucas (1713–1771)', *Irish Journal of Medical Science*, 184:1 (2015), 1–5.   62 Hill, *From patriots to unionists*, p. 9 and ch. 3, pp 79–111; Charles Lucas, *An appeal to the commons and citizens of London by Charles Lucas* (London, 1756).

unsuccessfully as a Tory parliamentary candidate in Dublin in a hotly contested, and at times violent, election campaign that saw the publication of numerous such squibs.[63] A second round of pamphleteering occurred 1729 during the by-election that took place following the death of anti-oligarchic MP William Howard.[64]

The concept of political density has been used to understand the means through which the eighteenth-century populace obtained and then acted upon political information. Conduits of transmission included a broad range of media such as the press, toasts, petitions, public celebrations, the production of memorabilia, shop and tavern names and signs, ballads and street protest.[65] In any society there were moments of more vigorous political activity than others; in the case of early eighteenth-century Dublin periods of such activity included the mayoral dispute of 1712–15 and, especially, the Wood's Halfpence and the economic improvement debates of the 1720s. This was followed by a relatively quiet period until the 1740s when the advent of the campaigns of Charles Lucas gave rise to Barnard's 'more excitable phase of politics'. The broadsheet *A poem occasion'd by the lord mayors's reducing the price of coals, &c.*, from 1729, is an example of the lesser-studied, but nonetheless impactful, effusions of these genres.[66] In that year, following three years of bad harvests, Dublin was traumatized by serious rioting, social tensions and an influx of beggars that provided the background to and the impetus for the production of Swift's notorious pamphlet, *Modest proposal*.[67] While the narrative of the anti-Wood's Halfpence campaign from the mid-1720s has traditionally centred on Swift's *Drapier's letters*, the controversy gave rise to at least 80 other printed items.[68] Moyra Haslett has identified eighteen printed street songs/ballads on the affair, some of which carried an extra political charge by their setting of new words

63 *Advertisement. Whereas a sham letter was privately dispersed last night late; the original of which is said to be directed to Sir William Fownes* (Dublin, 1713); *All which consider', I leave every impartial man to judge who was the authors of this riot* … (Dublin, 1713); *Case of Sir William Fownes, Kt. and Martin Tucker, Esq; with relation to the late election of members of parliament for the city of Dublin* (Dublin, 1713); *A reply to the aspersions cast on Sir William Fownes and Martin Tucker, Esq; in a paper intituled, An answer to D. Clayton's letter* (Dublin, 1713); *Sir Will. Fownes's and Tucker's friends vindication or, a truer account of the bloody and barbarous murder committed at the Tholsel on Friday the 6th of this inst. Novemb. 1713, than that published under the Rose* (Dublin, 1713). For a detailed examination of this election see Gerard McNamara, 'Crown versus municipality: the struggle for Dublin 1713', *DHR*, 39:3 (June 1986), 108–17. **64** See Hayton, 'Swift and Dublin politics', for a full rehearsal of Swift's several interventions in this by-election and later in the selection of the recorder of the city in which Swift supported the candidacy of his friends, Eaton Stannard and Sir William Fownes. **65** Nicholas Rogers, *Crowds, culture, and politics in Georgian England* (Oxford, 1998) and *idem*, 'Popular protest in early Hanoverian London', *Past & Present*, 79 (May 1978), 70–100. **66** *A poem occasion'd by the lord mayors's reducing the price of coals, &c.* (Dublin, 1729). **67** Ian McBride, 'The politics of *A modest proposal*: Swift and the Irish crisis of the late 1720s', *Past and Present*, 244 (Aug. 2019), 89–122. **68** Sabine Baltes, *The pamphlet controversy about Wood's Halfpence (1722–25) and the tradition of Irish constitutional*

to the airs of loyal songs, thereby transforming them into tools of opposition.[69] In October 1733 the London *Gentleman's Magazine* reported that 'we have received four very good Pieces from Dublin, in praise of their late active Lord Mayor, Humphry French, Esq; who used very frequently to visit the markets, bakers-shops, prisons, &c. in person'.[70] In the same year a two-page broadsheet entitled *A full vindication of the behaviour of Humphry French, late lord-mayor of the city of Dublin* (Dublin, 1733) addressed his achievements and supported his candidature in the upcoming by-election of an MP for Dublin city.[71] Despite the quantum of such material it is difficult to gauge the response of the 3,000 plus voters in Dublin to these effusions into the public sphere. However, it is worth noting that French's activist approach lived long in the memory and in October 1748 an anonymous author, signing himself Philopolites, cited French as 'that worthy Man' and 'one of the best Lord Mayors that ever ruled the City'.[72] Swift became embroiled in these electoral contests in 1729 and again in 1733. At the heart of Swift's advocacy of Humphry French, both as lord mayor and as a candidate for MP, was that, as an independently wealthy man, he would not be beholden to vested interests or to those who wielded the power to grant preferment or other favours.[73] French duly won the seat following a campaign in which he highlighted that he had done so 'without a Penny Expense'.[74] Swift's endorsement of his friends French, Stannard and Fownes cannot, however, be taken as unambiguous proof of their financial probity. In 1712 Fownes had been involved in an unseemly dispute in respect of his previous role as an agent for payment of the soldiers of the Innishillings.[75]

These texts and other manifestations of increasing political density such as loyal toasts, bonfires to celebrate the Drapier's birthday, and taverns named after

nationalism (Frankfurt am Main, 2002), p. 4.   **69** Moyra Haslett, '"With brisk merry laws": songs on the Wood's Halfpence affair' in Janika Bischof, Kirsten Juhas and Hermann J. Real (eds), *Reading Swift: papers from the seventh Münster Symposium* (Paderborn, 2019), pp 199–222. In this article she also discusses the use of songs in several other political disputes. See also Sean Moore, *Swift the book and the Irish financial revolution: satire and sovereignty in colonial Ireland* (Baltimore, 2010) for a discussion of the role of print in the creation of an Anglo-Irish public sphere.   **70** *The Gentleman's Magazine or, Monthly Intelligencer*, Oct. 1733, pp 542–3.   **71** The text of *The lamentation of the poor of the city of Dublin, after the late lord mayor, with a work of advice to the freemen, &c. of said city* (Dublin, 1733), *Astraea's congratulations. An ode upon Alderman Humphry French on being elected representative for the city of Dublin, on account of his wise and just administration during his late mayoralty* (Dublin, 1733); *A full vindication of the behavior of Humphry French, late lord-mayor of the city of Dublin* (Dublin, 1733) is typical of the hyperbolic praise that was heaped on French both during and after his term as lord mayor.   **72** Philopolites, *The freeman: being his first letter of honest advice to the free-men and free-holders, of the city of Dublin* (Dublin, 1748), p. 7.   **73** Jonathan Swift, 'Advice to the free-men of the city of Dublin in the choice of a member to represent them in parliament' in David Hayton and Adam Rounce (eds), *Irish political writings after 1725; A Modest Proposal and other works* (Cambridge, 2018), pp 279–87.   **74** *The historical register, containing an impartial relation of all transactions, foreign and domestic. With a chronological diary ...* (London, 1736), p. 56.   **75** *The Inskillingers complaint against Sir William Fownes for*

the Drapier, provided Lucas with a wealth of metaphors, colourful rhetorical flourishes, and arguments to support his political objectives.[76] In addition, these experiences facilitated the development of a politically informed local audience and provided numerous precedents as to how the print media could be used to achieve political ends.

In December 1741 Charles Lucas became a member of the common council of Dublin Corporation as a representative of the barber-surgeons guild and in January 1742 he was nominated to both the pipe water and the watercourse committees.[77] Other members of these committees included Lucas's soon to be principal target Nathaniel Kane, and other influential figures including alderman Nathaniel Pearson, the banker Daniel Falkiner, Kane's relatives Joseph and Mathew Weld, and Lucas's erstwhile ally James Digges La Touche. In 1743 Lucas was nominated for the audit committee, again in the company of Kane, Joseph and Mathew Weld, and La Touche.[78] His participation in these committees alerted him to the minutiae of the issues that he would later foreground as evidence of mismanagement and corruption. For instance, in October 1742 he would have been aware of the detailed report submitted by the pipe water committee that advised of the immediate need to borrow £600 to pay for imported wooden pipes, the urgent need for repairs to the water wheel at Island Bridge, the requirement to replace decayed lead pipes in Cork Street at a proposed cost of £700, and the trouble encountered by Darling the water rates collector, which necessitated a resolution to proceed to law 'for the recovery of the arrears due'; it can be reasonably assumed that he was not impressed.[79]

In 1743 Lucas went public with his campaign when he published a lengthy pamphlet the full title of which encapsulated his agenda viz.: *A remonstrance against certain infringements on the rights and liberties of the commons and citizens of Dublin. Humbly addressed to the Right Honourable the Lord Mayor, the recorder, the board of aldermen, the sheriffs, commons, and citizens of the said city. By Charles Lucas, one of the said commons, in behalf of himself, and the other representatives and freemen of the Corporation of Barbers and Chirurgeons, Apothecaries and Perukemakers, of Guild of St. Mary Magdalene within the said city.*[80] Approximately half of this pamphlet was assigned to a deep trawl of the ancient charters of Dublin dating back to King John. The second half addressed contemporary events where Lucas pointed out, inter alia, as an example of the malpractice that lay at the heart of his campaign, that the charter of the Blue Coat School forbade 'any Governor's being a Tenant to the said corporation'.

detaining their pay (Dublin, 1712).   **76** In 1732 Swift noted, perhaps with some self-serving exaggeration, the existence of 'two or three dozen sign-posts of the Drapier in this city'; Swift, Dublin to Charles Wogan, London, 2 Aug. 1732, David Woolley (ed.), *The correspondence of Jonathan Swift* (5 vols, Frankfurt am Main, 1999–2014), iii, 517.   **77** *CARD*, ix, 42, 45, 22 Jan. 1742.   **78** Ibid., 90, 21 Jan. 1743.   **79** Ibid., 83–5, 21 Oct. 1742.   **80** Charles Lucas, *A remonstrance against certain infringements on the rights and liberties of the commons and citizens of*

In 1749 Alderman Kane was rather shamefacedly forced to admit that he held leases on a number of properties from the hospital. He pleaded that he was unaware of such a restriction and declared that he was more than willing to have any interested party 'take this much-envied bargain of my hands'.[81] Lucas's central contention was that 'the *Estate* of the City was not a little injured by the powers assumed by the few is too evident, from its having been cantoned out in *Fee-Farm*, or other *long* leases, for *trifles*, to *aldermen*, and their *friends* and *dependents*'. He concluded with an appeal to the better nature of the alderman, declaiming 'your *remonstrant*, from his personal knowledge of some of the *aldermen*, and the general characters of other, believes them to be strenuous *advocates* for *liberty*, *freedom*, and *truth*'.[82]

Despite increasing acrimony between Lucas and the aldermanic leadership, Lucas and his allies did achieve some minor victories. For example, in July 1743 a motion that it 'would be for the advantage of the city, that the accounts should be forthwith printed' was passed and implemented.[83] However, in 1744 Lucas experienced a serious setback when the aldermanic veto on the choice of members of the common council (one of the abuses highlighted by Lucas) ensured that he was not re-selected. However, by this stage the genie was out of the bottle and the controversies in respect of not only governance issues but also financial mismanagement or even malpractice were very much in the public domain. To further his campaign, Lucas unsuccessfully took his case to court and in April 1746 the assembly approved a payment of £200 to reimburse Robert King for defending a suit brought by La Touche and Lucas in the court of King's Bench against 'George Ribton, alderman, thereby striking at the power the aldermen have in the electing of aldermen'.[84]

While the purchase of the Island Bridge mills was referenced by Lucas in the mid-1740s, it was only in 1748–9, when Lucas began his campaign to be elected MP for Dublin during which he rehearsed his accusations against Kane in detail, that the controversy entered the broader public domain.[85] He accused Kane and a group of four other alderman of having a power that 'made them a *Majority* of *twenty-four Aldermen*' and 'they ruled the whole *Board*, and the *Board* ruled the whole *City*'. He repeated his perspective on the technical issues surrounding sourcing and supplying water, his accusations of corruption in respect of the debt that had been incurred, and his assertion that the site had been offered for sale to all comers for a fraction of the finally agreed purchase price. Throughout, Lucas maintained that he was not motivated by personal animus by pointing out that, prior to his appointment to the committee in January 1742, he did know Alderman Kane.[86] He also added the accusation that one of the committee 'had

Dublin (Dublin, 1743).   81 Ibid., p. 19; Nathaniel Kane, *Address to the freemen and freeholders of the city of Dublin* (Dublin, 1749), p. 14.   82 Lucas, *A remonstrance*, pp 28, 37.   83 *CARD*, ix, 569, 28 July 1743.   84 Ibid., 200, 11 Apr. 1746.   85 Charles Lucas, *An eighteenth address to the free-citizens and free-holders of the city of Dublin* (Dublin, 1749), pp 39–51.   86 Ibid., pp

a large mortgage on them or at least to whom the proprietor owed a considerable sum of money'.[87] Kane was forced to resort to print to deny these accusations, initially by releasing the correspondence between himself and Lucas, and then in an *Address to the freemen and freeholders of the city of Dublin*, where he set out his position in what he termed 'a natural, true, and just light'. Kane denied that his bank had a financial interest in the site as security or that a debt was due to the bank by any of the selling parties whom he claimed not to know personally.[88]

As the dispute became more riven by inter-personal animus, Kane was not alone in refuting Lucas's charges. During the debate in the House of Commons on the censure of Lucas, the speech by Eaton Stannard, provocatively entitled *The honest man's speech*, was printed in three editions.[89] Stannard labelled Lucas, inter alia, as 'weak, mistaken, insidious, deluded, immoral, licentious and seditious'.[90] Samuel Davey issued three short pamphlets in which he accused Lucas of the sort of malfeasance that he so readily imputed to others, highlighting the resolution 'Mr Lucas to be receiver of the three-penny customs' under which, Davey alleged, he would use the authority of the aldermen to 'levy money on his fellow subjects'. Davey concluded: 'if it proceeded not from selfish views I leave it to the world to judge.'[91] The three-penny toll was an ancient, complex, and by-times contentious, port tax that was levied on certain goods imported and exported by certain merchants. As late as 1730 it yielded the not-inconsiderable sum of £130 19s. 4d.[92] In July 1731 the corporation, having been informed of difficulties in collecting this tax, acceded to a proposal by Stearne Tighe (a leading member of a well-connected Dublin aldermanic family) to pay £200 per annum for a 21-year lease on this revenue source.[93] In July 1732 the assembly noted that its collectors were experiencing difficulties in collecting this tax and how 'of late many Popish merchants now absolutely refuse to pay any such custom, composition, or the arrears due on account thereof'.[94] Some months later, Tighe reported that the legal expense involved in providing a covenant to the city to demonstrate and preserve its title to this charge was prohibitive, and he withdrew from the arrangement.[95] By the early 1740s, despite several legal opinions from the recorder, and a recommendation from the solicitor general in April 1745 to appoint special

39, 42, 44–5.   **87** Urbanus, *Mr. C – s L – s's speech to the corporations of the city of Dublin, in a letter from a gentleman in this city, to a friend in the country* (Dublin, 1748), p. 15.   **88** *Genuine letters between alderman Nathaniel Kane and Mr. Charles Lucas concerning the purchase of the mills at Island Bridge* (Dublin, 1749) (two editions priced at 1d.) and Nathaniel Kane, *Address to the freemen and freeholders of the city of Dublin* (Dublin, 1749).   **89** Anon. (Eaton Stannard), *The honest man's speech* (Dublin, 1749).   **90** Ibid., *passim.*   **91** Samuel Davey, *A view of the conduct and writings of Mr Charles Lucas, Number I* (Dublin, 1749), p. 11; idem, *A view of the conduct and writings of Mr Charles Lucas, being an answer to some passages in the eighteenth address of C. Lucas, P. 13, 25, 28, reflecting on the late Sir Samuel Cooke, Number II* (Dublin, 1749); idem, *A view of the conduct and writings of Mr Charles Lucas, Number III* (Dublin, 1749).   **92** Hill, 'Tolls and customs', pp 194–5.   **93** *CARD*, viii, 21, 23–4, 16 July 1731.   **94** Ibid., 64, 21 July 1732.   **95** Ibid., 79, 19 Jan. 1732.

collectors for this tax, the three-penny tax no longer featured as a separate line item in the corporation's accounts.[96] Despite his previous conflicts with the aldermanic board, in February 1748 the city approved a proposal that Lucas would pay £200 per annum, with a reduction to £5 for the first three years, to collect and receive the three-penny custom. As part of the transaction, Lucas agreed that he would vigorously 'assert and prosecute the city's right and title to the said three-penny custom at his own proper costs and charges.'[97]

Lucas's motivation for offering the significant sum of £200, which he probably could ill afford, in order to collect the disputed three-penny custom, is unclear. Was he trying to shame the leading figures within the aldermanic elite by seeking to prove that he could make a success of asserting an ancient right of the city that the existing leadership were signally failing to do? Or did he see it as a business opportunity? His detractors were quick to challenge him. In October 1748 an anonymous author, signing himself as Philopolites, challenged Lucas to explain 'his application for, and acceptance of, a lease of the *Three-penny* Customs to one (for the Lord-Mayor is an ALDERMAN –) of those very Persons against whom he spends himself railing'.[98] Lucas was forced to defend his actions. In his 'reported' speech to the corporation in 1748 he recounted the ancient origin of the tax and how the 'aldermen are so ignorant' and that 'so little is all this known, that it was given up, and never sued for since the Year 1731'. He admitted that the lease would offer 'a prospect I have of recovering this for the City with some advantage to my self'. However, he also made the argument that under his agreement with the corporation he would have access to the records of the city for which 'I was obliged to pay for this Liberty, was but a trifle, compared to the opportunity this will give me'.[99] Shortly afterwards, Lucas was exiled from Dublin for over a decade. Notwithstanding the legal and collection difficulties that he faced, and the likelihood that he never collected anything on foot of his lease, the accusation of bad faith retained some currency. In the election campaign of 1761, following his return from exile, an anonymous broadsheet rehearsed this issue. Lucas was accused of duplicity, of being a 'usurper', and of being unable to display the required level of 'disinterestedness' in seeking to collect a tax that would be 'centred in the Doctor's pocket'.[100] In 1764, three years after his election as an MP for Dublin city, he was 'discharged from all rent and arrears of rent due by him to the city for the three-penny custom'.[101] During this surrender process Lucas published a self-serving memorial in which, for the most part, the older and perhaps somewhat wiser man managed to eschew *ad hominem* criticism, though he could not resist recounting how he had persuaded the then recorder of the city (Eaton Stannard) to change his view on the legal status of the toll.[102]

96 Ibid., 161, 26 Apr. 1745, 199, 11 Apr. 1746.   97 Ibid., ix, 258–9, 5 Feb. 1748.   98 Philopolites, *The freeman*, pp 6–7.   99 Urbanus, *Mr. C – s L – s's speech*, pp 13–14.   100 *QUERIES Addressed to all FREE-ELECTORS, and lovers of the Trade of the City of Dublin by a FREE WEAVER* (Dublin, 1761).   101 *CARD*, xi, 182, 20 Jan. 1764.   102 Charles Lucas, *To the*

In 1760 (at the third attempt) the demand for governance reform finally bore some fruit when the Irish parliament passed an act 'For the better regulating the corporation of the city of Dublin, and for extending the power of the magistrates thereof, and for other purposes relative to the said city.'[103] The act removed the aldermanic requirement of a double return from the guilds for nominations to the common council; it also increased the oversight and decision-making function of the commons. Not surprisingly, Lucas was not satisfied; he referred to the reforms as 'a pitiful palliative, for some abominable oppressions in the city, agreed upon to silence the clamour of the abused citizenry'.[104] However, following his return to Dublin and the reversal of his disenfranchisement, Lucas could no longer be considered an outsider. In 1763 he was one of the commons who prepared the loyal address to the king on the conclusion of the peace that signified the end of the Seven Years War.[105] His funeral in 1771 was an elaborate affair that would be expected for any pillar of society. But even in his newfound insider position, Lucas, with the backing of his supporters, could find ways to aggravate the aldermanic oligarchy. In 1766, and again in 1770, in a gesture that was perhaps designed to fail, the commons of Dublin Corporation petitioned that an annual stipend of three hundred and sixty-five pounds should be granted to Doctor Charles Lucas 'with a public testimony of the city's approbation of his conduct': not surprisingly, this proposal was 'unanimously rejected by the said Lord Mayor and Board of Aldermen'.[106] Even this late in his career, Lucas could use the management of the financial affairs of the city to challenge and provoke the aldermanic elite.

IV

In the early decades of the eighteenth century recurring budget deficits, and the escalating costs involved in the expansion of the pipe water supply, led to frequent cash flow problems for Dublin Corporation. The corporation repeatedly resorted to borrowing, often at short notice, to pay for imported wooden pipes and other necessary supplies. This credit was provided by a well-connected group of insiders, or by institutions that were intimately linked to the aldermanic group that controlled the civic life of the city. In the 1740s the campaigns of Charles Lucas on behalf of the 'free citizens' of Dublin to reform

right honorable the lord mayor, sheriffs, commons, and citizens, of the city of Dublin, the memorial of Charles Lucas, M.D. (Dublin, 1763).   **103** 33 George II c. 16. An earlier attempt in 1755 had been spearheaded by Thomas Adderley MP for Charlemont and an ally of Lucas. Two attempts in 1758 and 1759 led by Sir Edward King MP for Boyle were rejected by the Irish privy council.   **104** Charles Lucas, *Seasonable advice to the electors of members of parliament at the ensuing general election* (Dublin, 1760), p. 26.   **105** *CARD*, xi, 133–4.   **106** Ibid., 472–3. This action was reported on, unfortunately without comment as was the practice of the period, by several London newspapers. See, for example, *British Evening Post*, 25 Jan.

the oligarchical stance of the aldermanic board foregrounded these financial and management issues and what he saw as endemic financial mismanagement and corruption. However, as Jacqueline Hill has demonstrated, the tensions so colourfully and voluminously highlighted by Lucas were a feature of Dublin politics for generations; there was nothing new in public challenges to aldermanic hegemony, or controversy in respect of financial affairs.

This essay has argued that many elements of the polemical neo-populist politics, and the reforming impulses that are associated with the campaign of Charles Lucas from 1741 onwards, predated his entry into Dublin civic politics, and were, therefore, not solely dependent on the arrival of Lucas and his allies. The pamphlet controversies linked to elections in 1713, 1729 and 1733 were manifestations of these long-standing trends and are illustrative of the rich political density of Dublin civic politics throughout this period.[107] However, it must also be recognized that the fraternal liberties being claimed by Lucas for the 'free-born' citizens of Dublin were limited; they were confined to the Protestant freemen of Dublin. Lucas's crusade, while perhaps innovative in the extent of his use of print as a vehicle to advance his message, and as a means to arouse popular commitment, was socially and politically conservative. For example in the 1760s, from his new-found position of power and influence as an MP and as a member of the common council of the city assembly, Lucas was associated with several, in essence backward looking, attempts to legislate for the re-imposition of quarterage fees for Catholics in the urban guilds.[108] As Barnard has observed, his programme was one that 'sought adjustments in the way that those benefits were distributed, but not their cancellation'.[109]

The dispute between Lucas and the elite of Dublin Corporation, and with alderman Nathaniel Kane in particular, which formed such a central part of the Lucas controversies throughout the 1740s, may not have started out as an interpersonal battle. However, over time it became one with *ad hominem* accusations of bad faith, incompetence and corruption being levelled by both sides. Lucas was an outsider who was not accepted by the coterie of vested interest of the aldermanic elite. They closed ranks against him in the 1740s and succeeded in 1749 in forcing him into exile. But Lucas returned in triumph, his banishment was reversed, he was elected MP for the city and he served once again on the common council of the corporation. However, the financial issues that he campaigned on had not gone away and the troubled finances of Dublin Corporation continued to be matters of on-going public concern into the second half of the century.

1766, *Lloyd's Evening Post*, 27 Jan. 1766, *Public Advertiser*, 28 Jan. 1766. **107** See David A. Fleming, *Politics and provincial people: Sligo and Limerick, 1691–1761* (Manchester, 2010) and David Dickson, *Old world colony: Cork and South Munster, 1630–1830* (Cork, 2005) for details of popular politics in other Irish urban settings in this period. **108** Dickson, *New foundations*, pp 152–3. **109** Barnard, *Kingdom of Ireland*, p. 91.

The politics of pageantry: the participation of Dublin guilds in public-facing ceremonial and celebratory events, 1660–*c*.1770

MARY ANN LYONS

The expression of political culture in late seventeenth- and eighteenth-century Dublin was reliant upon an expanding array of media ranging from the press and pulpits to streets, theatres and taverns; through each, political ideas, ideologies and propaganda reached a widening audience.[1] This culture encompassed both formal and informal activities, some conducted behind closed doors while other forms of 'out-of-doors politicking' took place in full view of the general populace.[2] In common with cities such as Newcastle and Norwich, Dublin's political, civic and religious calendar provided regular occasions for the demonstration of elite grandeur, paternalism, largesse and legitimacy. As Kathleen Wilson and James Kelly have shown, national and local political anniversaries, from the monarch's birth and accession days and guild days to corporation election day; Anglican fast and feast days; the opening of fairs and erection of new public buildings and other landmark events prompted purposeful ceremonial displays, marked by processions of the aldermen, common council, clergy and minor officers, all dressed in their robes and regalia.[3]

According to Kelly, the enthusiasm of Irish Protestants for commemorative celebration reached its peak when George III ascended the throne in 1760. In total, twenty days were given over in whole or in part to this purpose each year in the mid-eighteenth century. However, only the festivals of 1 July, 23 October and 4 November were major events and it was in the evenings, when the day's work was done, that the populace joined in the celebrations.[4] While dignitaries

---

1 In this essay, political culture is understood to mean the sphere encompassing political values and ideologies, the forms of their expression and the mechanisms of their dissemination and transformation. This is the definition adopted by Kathleen Wilson in *The sense of the people: politics, culture and imperialism in England, 1715–1785* (Cambridge, 1998 edn.), p. 12. My thanks to Hugh Murphy, Head of Collections and Content, Maynooth University Library for assistance in accessing material for this essay. 2 Wilson, *Sense of the people*, p. 21. 3 Ibid., p. 295; James Kelly, '"The Glorious and Immortal Memory": commemoration and Protestant identity in Ireland, 1660–1800', *RIA Proc.*, 94C (1994), 25–52. 4 These were – in chronological order – the queen's birthday (18 Jan.); the anniversary of the martyrdom of Charles I (30 Jan.); St Patrick's Day (17 Mar.); the duke of Cumberland's birthday (15 Apr.); the anniversary of the battle of Culloden (16 Apr.); the restoration of the monarchy (29 May); George III's birthday (4 June); the anniversaries of the battles of Dettingen (16 June), the Boyne (1 July), Aughrim (12 July), Enniskillen (28 July), and the relief of the siege of Derry

44

and invited guests attended Church of Ireland services, banquets and plays, all of the city's residents were encouraged to join 'demonstrations of public joy' on such occasions including street processions, fireworks displays, bonfires, illuminations, bell ringing and artillery bursts, and on very special occasions, to partake of free meat and alcohol to toast the monarch's health.[5]

While the number of such events decreased over the course of the eighteenth century in Dublin as in England's provincial cities, as late as the 1770s the city's chief officers still kept up a busy civic ceremonial programme and lavish entertainments.[6] These ceremonies at which the lord mayor, sheriffs, aldermen and occasionally representatives of the city's guilds presided were intended to give public expression to the corporation's privileges, dignity and authority. Highlights include showy street displays intended to impress upon the population the growing prestige of the office of lord mayor. The ceremonial swearing-in of the lord mayor saw the corporation proceed in a cavalcade to Christ Church cathedral and a grand reception, hosted by the new lord mayor, took place that evening. By the 1700s the most spectacular street ceremony was the triennial Riding of the Franchises in which the mayor, accompanied by three hundred citizens on horseback, and followed by the city's guilds, paraded around the city's boundaries to reassert the corporation's immunity from royal, ecclesiastical and seigneurial authorities, and afterwards enjoyed lavish entertainment.[7] Such events were integral to the fabric of Dublin's civic and political culture during this period when the importance of socializing and hospitality was acknowledged by the corporation. In 1760, the lord mayor's budget for hospitality was increased from £1,350 to £2,000 so as to keep the officeholder in the 'splendour and hospitality necessary to preserve respect and conciliate the good affections of the citizens by promoting a social and friendly intercourse between them and their magistrates.'[8]

Through their public participation in such high-profile events, Dublin city's twenty-five guilds manifested their appreciation of ceremony, pageantry and hospitality in maintaining amicable relations and cohesion among the citizenry

---

(31 July); the Hanoverian succession (1 Aug.); the prince of Wales's birthday (12 Aug.); the anniversaries of George III's coronation (22 Sept.), of the surrender of the city of Cork to the Williamite army (29 Sept.), of the outbreak of the 1641 Rebellion (23 Oct.), of George III's accession to the throne (25 Oct.), of King William's birthday (4 Nov.) and of the discovery of the gunpowder plot (5 Nov.); Kelly, "'The Glorious and Immortal Memory'", 42–3; see also T.C. Barnard, 'The uses of 23 October and Irish Protestant celebrations', *English Historical Review*, 106 (1991), 889–920. **5** Kelly, "'The Glorious and Immortal Memory'", 28–31; S.J. Connolly, *Religion, law, and power: the making of Protestant Ireland, 1660–1760* (Oxford, 1992, 1995 ed.), p. 136; James Kelly, 'The emergence of political parading, 1660–1800' in T.G. Fraser (ed.), *The Irish parading tradition: following the drum* (Basingstoke, 2000), pp 9–26; Ian McBride, *Eighteenth-century Ireland: the isle of slaves* (Dublin, 2009), pp 306–8. **6** Wilson, *Sense of the people*, p. 295. **7** Jacqueline Hill, *From patriots to unionists: Dublin civic politics and Irish Protestant patriotism, 1660–1840* (Oxford, 1997), p. 44; David Dickson, *Dublin: the making of a capital city* (London, 2014), p. 232. **8** *CARD*, x, 433.

and in projecting and preserving the privileged status of citizenship. Ceremony and recreation were intermixed and fulfilled significant political functions for the guilds. Both their members and the city's municipal authorities understood the importance of being seen to participate in festival activities, and processions and worship helped reassert political authority within the city and reinforced bonds within the Protestant ruling elite. The guilds engaged in an array of elaborate public rituals and ceremonies that placed them at the heart of the city's associational and political culture. Many of their celebratory dinners in the city's taverns, processions and rituals brought them directly into contact with the ordinary people of Dublin. Designed to attract the attention of the general public and impress upon them the ancient lineage, strength of numbers, prestige and importance of the guilds, their processions were vitally important displays of the guild system's role not only within Dublin's commercial and industrial sphere but also in the city's political structures and culture.

In common with their equivalents in London, York, Preston, Nottingham, Bristol and Coventry, Dublin's guilds were important observers of the political calendar that aimed to convey to the general public a particularized version of Ireland and England's political heritage and the benefits of the current regime. Within the privacy of their halls, the guilds paid homage to monarchs and commemorated landmark events through their extensive collections of portraits, arms and statues.[9] As several of the guilds let their halls for public exhibitions and meetings, the city's better-off residents had opportunities to view these impressive collections.[10] But it was through their involvement in public celebrations of pivotal historical events, when liberty, moderation and loyalty triumphed over despotism or intolerance, that the guilds played a prominent role in the 'popularization of the historical and political principles which legitimized current constellations of power in the state'.[11]

For centuries, guilds were an integral part of Dublin life, regulating trade, administering property, conducting charitable work and providing public entertainments. Their early history has attracted some scholarly attention.

9 William Cotter Stubbs, 'The weavers' guild, the guild of the Blessed Virgin Mary, Dublin 1446–1840', *RSAI Jn.*, 44:1 (1919), 64–5; Henry F. Berry, 'The records of the feltmakers' company of Dublin, 1687–1841: their loss and recovery', ibid., 41 (1911), 31; *idem*, 'The merchant tailors' gild – that of St John the Baptist, Dublin, 1418–1841', ibid., 48 (1919), 29, 46; Charles T. Keating, 'The guild of cutlers, painter-stainers and stationers, better known as the guild of St Luke the Evangelist, Dublin', ibid., 30 (1900), 137; Henry S. Guinness, 'Dublin trade gilds', ibid., 52 (1922), 156; Hill, *From patriots to unionists*, p. 11.   10 Guinness, 'Dublin trade gilds', 158. Certain guilds also sponsored the public statues of monarchs. In 1750 the weavers adorned the doorway of their newly constructed hall in the Coombe with a gilt statue of George II by Van Nost – see Constantia Maxwell, *Dublin under the Georges, 1714–1830* (London, 1936; repr. 1979), p. 226.   11 Wilson, *Sense of the people*, p. 22; Jacqueline Hill, 'National festivals, the state and "Protestant ascendancy" in Ireland, 1790–1829', *IHS*, 24 (1984–5), 30–51.

Yet, as Jacqueline Hill has noted, although the guilds retained an important place in civic life down to 1841, little interest has been shown in their activities after 1700.[12] This essay focuses on the Dublin guilds' public-facing rituals and ceremonies on the city streets and roadways, in parks and taverns from the Restoration of the monarchy in 1660 until *c.*1770. On such occasions the ordinary people of Dublin were generally relegated to the status of observers. However, from the 1730s onwards, the parades had the potential to provoke rare, hostile reactions from those denied the rights and privileges the guilds enjoyed. These ceremonies, therefore, embodied the chasm between the enfranchised citizenry and the disenfranchised public, the 'two nations' (to evoke Kathleen Wilson's phrase), in a particularly pronounced fashion. To varying degrees, and in a variety of forms (verbal and non-verbal, in actions and artefacts), these events constituted sites and contexts for impressing upon the ordinary people the power that the guilds wielded in their city. This study shows how the guilds' most important theatrical and conspicuous demonstrations of authority and community made a significant contribution to the political culture of Dublin by sustaining a civic polity permeated by hierarchy, paternalism and privilege, even while it grudgingly recognized the entitlements of the capital's labouring population as the eighteenth century wore on.[13]

For most of this period the wealthier merchants and master craftsmen of Dublin supplied the majority of members of the civic governing bodies, thereby dominating the city's political and commercial life.[14] Yet, as the decades passed, they experienced growing challenges to that dominance in both spheres. In the context of these developments, this essay explores the extent to which the guilds' involvement in public-facing rituals, ceremonies and celebrations serves as a barometer for their dominance in Dublin's commercial and political life and the onset of decline in their traditional influence from the mid-1700s.

FOUNDATION STONES OF THE POLITICAL EDIFICE

Originally conceived as mutual benefit associations, Dublin's guilds were intensely hierarchical, political and competitive. The oldest and most prestigious, the guild of merchants which was possibly operating in 1190, regulated commerce. From the early 1400s artisans working in various crafts combined to form their own guilds; the last, the apothecaries guild, was established in 1747, bringing the total to twenty-five. These trade and craft guilds were established either under royal charter or civil charter issued by the Dublin city assembly.

12 Hill, *From patriots to unionists*, p. 24.   13 Ibid., p. 297.   14 Janet Redmond, 'Sir Daniel Bellingham, Dublin's first lord mayor, 1665' in Ruth McManus and Lisa-Marie Griffith (eds), *Leaders of the city: Dublin's first citizens, 1500–1950* (Dublin, 2013), p. 65.

Guild members had the exclusive right to practise a craft or to engage in commerce within the city's franchises or boundaries.[15] Honorary membership, or freedom of the guild, was conferred on prominent figures.[16] The guilds also played a fundamental role in politics as, on completion of an apprenticeship, each newly qualified craftsman was entitled to the franchise or freedom of the city and acquired the right to vote in municipal and parliamentary elections. Moreover, guilds determined the membership of the council of the corporation. As a result, guild membership was prized as 'an essential first step for anyone contemplating a career in municipal politics' since members of the common council were eligible for election to the offices of city sheriff, alderman and, ultimately, lord mayor.[17]

All of the city's guilds were acutely conscious of the supreme importance of three factors in determining their status and influence, namely their ancient lineage, their place in the overall guild hierarchy, and their strength of numbers. This rank had its most meaningful expression in their 96-strong representation on the common council, the lower house of the corporation where the order of precedence was determined by the antiquity of the guilds. Thus, the oldest, the merchants, occupied first place and had the largest council membership (31).[18]

During the Restoration era (1660–85), when a sympathetic government promoted the foundation of new guilds, the system of trade corporations expanded and strengthened.[19] The fact that eleven of Dublin's twenty-five guilds were founded during the period 1660–1747 reinforced the dominance of qualified Protestant craftsmen, their acute awareness of their need for collective representation, and their determination to exert influence in municipal and, increasingly, national politics.[20] The popularity of the guilds also shows that these corporations met members' needs in a host of meaningful and practical ways, affording them real protection, influence, access to networks of contacts, and career opportunities in politics as well as industry and commerce. Furthermore, they contributed to the upkeep of the city and its population by organizing the militia, administering charity, making financial contributions to the city and the Church of Ireland,[21] and improving the streetscape and infrastructure through building and renovating houses and proto-factories.

15 Mary Clark and Raymond Refaussé (eds), *Directory of historic Dublin guilds* (Dublin, 1993), p. 12.   16 Ibid., p. 11.   17 Ibid., p. 121; Hill, *From patriots to unionists*, pp 28–30.   18 Ibid., p. 43.   19 James Kelly with Mary Ann Lyons (eds), *The proclamations of Ireland* (5 vols, Dublin: IMC, 2014), i, 265–9, 270–4, 274–8, 279–83, 283–9, 290–2; Edward Whelan, 'The guilds of Dublin and immigrants in the seventeenth century: the defence of privilege in an age of change', *Ir. Econ. & Soc. Hist.*, 39 (2012), 27.   20 Sheermen and dyers (no charter but represented in the city assembly's common council from 1660 onwards); coopers (est. 1666); feltmakers (est. 1667); cutlers, painters, and stationers (est. 1670); bricklayers and plasterers (est. 1670); hosiers and knitters (est. 1688); tanners (est. 1688); curriers (est. 1695); brewers and maltsters (est. 1696); joiners, ceylers and wainscotters (est. 1700) and apothecaries (1747).   21 Keating, 'Cutlers', 145.

PROGRAMME OF CELEBRATORY EVENTS

Each guild organized a programme of celebratory events annually. This included post-meeting dinners on assembly and quarter days when members were required to appear in gowns.[22] All guilds celebrated the feast day of their patron saint; this was generally, though not always, the day on which the swearing-in ceremony for new brethren was held. While many of these celebratory events took place behind closed doors in their halls, or in churches or chantry chapels to which the guilds were affiliated, many took place in taverns and all involved a street procession in which the brethren, dressed in their gowns, distinctive coloured hoods or livery, appeared in full view of the public.[23] As such, their observance of traditional civic culture provided important sites and contexts for raising political awareness among the public. For example, every year, on 24 June the brethren of the tailors' guild celebrated their patron St John the Baptist's feast day by processing from their hall (originally in Winetavern Street and from 1706, in Back-Lane) to St John's church. After new members were sworn in and the congregation heard the minister's sermon, they once again processed through the streets to a nearby tavern where they dined.[24] In addition to lending colour and ceremony to city life, the guilds' processions and celebrations on their patron saints' days were important occasions for conveying their antiquity and commitment to perpetuating a time-honoured tradition.[25] The guilds took full advantage of the ritual surrounding the swearing-in of new brethren to impress upon the city's leading officials and the general public their pivotal role as gatekeepers to the civic franchise.

While the most spectacular of these colourful displays of the guilds' standing in the city's body politique was the triennial Riding of the Franchises which is discussed below, they capitalized on other events in the political and religious calendar to assert, publicize and legitimize their position in municipal life and political culture. Traditionally, the military forces of the city were mustered and exercised four times a year, at Oxmantown among other locations, on Easter Monday, May Day, Midsummer's Eve and St Peter's Eve, while the cavalry were mustered on Shrove Tuesday.[26] In the mid-1650s, two of these ancient customs were revived by mayors of the city, and throughout the period under review, members of the guilds regularly participated in both. The first, the Black Monday march, which took place on Easter Monday, saw all of the city's guilds march from the Tholsel to Cullenswood (south of Ranelagh). This was to commemorate the massacre in 1209 of a number of citizens by raiders from Wicklow in what was known as the Bloody Fields. Members of

22 Berry, 'Feltmakers', 32; *idem*, 'Merchant tailors', 56. 23 *idem*, 'The records of the Dublin gild of merchants, known as the gild of the Holy Trinity, 1438–1671', *RSAI Jn.*, 5th ser., 10:1 (1900), 46. 24 *idem*, 'Merchant tailors', p. 52; Maxwell, *Dublin under the Georges*, p. 227. 25 Hill, *From patriots to unionists*, p. 44, n. 9. 26 Walter Harris, *The history and antiquities of the city of Dublin* (Dublin, 1766), p. 151; Berry, 'Gild of merchants', p. 61.

the guilds aged between 16 and 60 were summoned to muster at seven o'clock on Easter Monday morning, fully armed and equipped and, bearing their distinctive colours, to parade to Cullenswood. Each guild member was ordered to wear a decent feather, according to the colours of the guild. Those who failed to participate were subjected to heavy fines; some were even committed to prison for contempt.[27] The other revived custom that guilds were expected to participate in was the celebration of May Day when the lord mayor and corporation attended a ceremony in St Stephen's Green.[28] The guilds were represented in these military parades by bowmen and drummers. Certain guilds spent substantial sums on hospitality at these events. In 1703, for example, the feltmakers bought drinks for the bowmen and drummers at Lucas's tavern and footed the bill for drinks at St Stephen's Green for the bowmen's dinner to the tune of 11s. 7d.[29] The tailors added to the pageantry that characterized these parades by sponsoring a scene from the Garden of Eden, featuring Adam, Eve and the serpent surrounded by green boughs; they also paid over £25 for dinner and associated costs.[30] With the city's two military guilds (St Edmund and St George) long defunct, the guilds' purpose in participating in these military parades was clear: inspired by civic duty, they stood ready to respond to any summons to defend the persons, property or privileges of the people of Dublin.[31] Through their celebration of key events in the political and religious calendar in taverns, the guilds publicly displayed their loyalty to the crown and established church and reinforced the historical and constitutional legitimacy of their privileged position in the political sphere.

Throughout this period, the guilds clearly felt the burden of expectation to organize and fund busy annual programmes of events. The extent of the combined input of the city's twenty-five guilds into the political and religious culture of the city may be gleaned from reviewing the calendar of one guild – the tailors. In addition to marking significant dates in their own year (feast day of their patron saint, John the Baptist, Baskin day, assembly, quarter, station, election and swearing-in days), they held dinners, suppers and smaller celebrations at various taverns for Prince's day, Easter Monday (one of three 'scarlet days' when the members wore robes of that colour), Childermas, the feast of St Barnabas, muster days, the King's day, Shrove Tuesday, Ascension day, All Saints' Eve and Gunpowder Treason day.[32] The political events commemorated and celebrated by the guild in taverns – King William's birthday (4 November), the anniversary of the Battle of the Boyne (1 July), the outbreak of the 1641 rebellion (23 October), the defeat of the Scots at Culloden (Thanksgiving day, 1745) and British success in taking Louisburgh, Canada in 1757 – served as occasions for public displays of loyalist triumphalism,

27 Harris, *The history and antiquities of the city of Dublin*, p. 153; Berry, 'Gild of merchants', 61.   28 Henry F. Berry, 'The goldsmiths' company of Dublin', *RSAI Jn.*, 31 (1901), 129.   29 Berry, 'Feltmakers', 33.   30 Berry, 'Merchant tailors', 52.   31 Clark and Refaussé (eds), *Directory*, pp 41–2.   32 Berry, 'Merchant tailors', 29, 52–3.

which were vital in forging Irish Protestant identity by perpetuating an active memory of key men and events in their history, affirming their links with the wider Protestant community in England and Scotland, and fostering devotion to the British monarchy.[33] King William's birthday, first celebrated in 1690 with a procession and a dinner in Dublin Castle for leading citizens, remained a highpoint in the calendar down to the early 1800s and was marked by (among others) the brethren of the tailors' guild: on 4 November 1767 they assembled in the Phoenix tavern on Werburgh's Street to drink to the king's memory, each member having been issued with a summons 'to appear with an orange cockade in his hat, or [incur] a forfeiture of a bottle of wine, agreeable to a bye-law made for that purpose'.[34] In addition to marking these key dates for Irish Protestants, the tailors were expected to attend multiple charity sermons, to participate in religious ceremonies, including processing behind the civic sword to St Patrick's cathedral on Ash Wednesday, and, of course, to turn out for the Riding of the Franchises.[35]

The guilds' custom of holding their celebratory dinners in city taverns made these important sites for heightening political awareness among the general public. Depending on a guild's size and means, these could vary in scale. In 1698, for example, forty-four members of the guild of cutlers, painter-stainers and stationers dined at the Duchess' Head in Dame Street.[36] The following year, after the election of officers at St Audoen's Arch, and having heard a sermon at St Michael's church, they adjourned to the Cock tavern on St Werburgh's Street for dinner.[37] In 1699 the goldsmiths' company marked its feast, All Saints' day, with 'a good' dinner, towards which the guild made a contribution of £10 on condition the celebration was held in a tavern.[38] On 28 October 1726 the guild of shoemakers dined at the Bull's Head in Fishamble Street to mark the feast of St Crispin (25 October).[39]

Across the city, ordinary patrons of taverns were clearly well accustomed to witnessing large parties of these finely dressed guild members celebrating, often very lavishly, proposing toasts, delivering speeches and reciting specially composed poems in their local hostelry.[40] This is borne out by the example of the feltmakers' guild which spread their patronage widely across the city's many taverns. They held events during the 1690s in the Crown, and the Three Tuns (St Michael's Lane) (1691); the 'Change (1694); the Fountain, the King's Head, the Lion, the Nag's Head, and the Ram (1695–6). The year 1700 was

33 Ibid., 29–30; Hill, *From patriots to unionists*, pp 11, 69; Kelly, '"The Glorious and Immortal Memory"', 25; Raymond Gillespie, 'Political ideas and their social contexts in seventeenth-century Ireland' in Jane H. Ohlmeyer (ed.), *Political thought in seventeenth-century Ireland. Kingdom or colony* (Cambridge, 2000), p. 127; Toby Barnard, 'Conclusion: Restoration Ireland' in Coleman A. Dennehy (ed.), *Restoration Ireland: always settling and never settled* (Aldershot, 2008), p. 181.   34 F.E. Dixon, 'The Dublin tailors and their hall', *DHR*, 22:1 (1968), 151.   35 Berry, 'Merchant tailors', 29, 53.   36 Keating, 'Cutlers', 145.   37 Ibid. 38 Berry, 'Goldsmiths', 129.   39 *CARD*, i, 70.   40 Guinness, 'Dublin trade guilds', 151.

especially busy with events held at the Cock, the Duke's Head (Castle Street), the Golden Lion, the Ram and Lamb, and Robinson's Head. Between 1703 and 1706, they patronized the Duchess' Head, the George (Cornmarket), the Bull (Fishamble Street) and the Crown (Essex Street). In 1707, forty years after the guild's foundation, the feltmakers celebrated often and widely, frequenting the Bull's Head, the Cock (Werburgh Street), the Custom House, the Doctor's Head (Crane Lane), the Rose and Crown, the Sun (Nicholas Street), the Swan, the Three Tuns (Fishamble Street) and the Tun (1707). Their finances no doubt substantially depleted, the following year, they chose the Bear (Crane Lane).[41]

The guilds were by no means exceptional in holding their celebrations in the city's taverns. In the late 1750s, for instance, the revitalized Friendly Brothers of St Patrick – a Protestant society – celebrated the 17 March in virtually the same way that the Boyne and Aughrim Societies commemorated the victories of the Williamite armies. It was their practice to assemble at the Rose tavern in Castle Street and walk in procession to St Patrick's cathedral to hear a sermon, after which they returned to the Rose tavern for dinner.[42] However, the guild members' fondness for ostentatious dining in taverns occasionally drew stinging criticism and damaged their reputation in the eyes of the public. In 1726, for example, a lampoon castigated them for their gluttony and excess on such occasions:

> Now the sermon being ended,
> And the minister descended,
> To the 'Castle' or the 'Rose',
> Or whatever place you've chose.
>
> Now the dinner's in the table,
> Each one eats as fast as able,
> Each one eats as much as ten,
> For the Lord knows when again.[43]

From at least the 1620s, the officers of certain guilds, accompanied by a number their brethren, conducted 'walking day' processions in full view of the public, which symbolically demonstrated the extent of their authority by traversing the municipal boundaries. During these 'walks', traders (particularly journeymen) working illegally in the city were sought out.[44] On such occasions, the guild officers used powers invested in them through by-laws to seize the goods of these so-called intruders. In the 1670s and 80s, for example, the feltmakers publicly burned hats seized from illegal hat-makers during their

41 Berry, 'Feltmakers', 33.   42 Kelly, "'The Glorious and Immortal Memory'", 42.
43 Quoted by Sir John T. Gilbert, in Berry, 'Gild of merchants', 48.   44 Berry, 'Merchant tailors', 29.

'walks' while in 1698 officers of the weavers' guild endeavoured to confiscate illegally produced woollen cloth.[45] There was also a consciously symbolic dimension to some intruders' attempts to ingratiate themselves with the city's guilds. On a number of occasions in the early eighteenth century, illicit traders paid their fine by presenting portraits of Queen Anne (1708), King William (1720) and King George I (1720) to the exclusively Protestant guild of cutlers, painters-stainers and stationers.[46] The same was true of intruders applying for admission to the guild: in 1698 Martin Skinner was admitted on presenting a painting of King William.[47] On a more modest level, but in the spirit of the Riding of the Franchises, certain guilds made formal annual excursions to their properties outside the city. Throughout this period, the tailors paid an annual visit to survey their land at Baskin in north County Dublin where they were entertained at considerable cost to the tenant.[48]

THE PRICE OF PARTICIPATION

Surviving sources indicate that it was not only the medieval guilds such as the merchants, tailors and barber-surgeons that participated actively in such events. Recent foundations, such as the feltmakers (est. 1667) and the cutlers, painter-stainers and stationers (est. 1670), keen to embrace the trappings of the ancient guild system, processed in public parades, including the Riding of the Franchises, and organized their own programme of festivities throughout the year.[49] Routine parades were often a very substantial drain on a guild's resources. In 1656 the merchants paid £55 7s. 6d. to meet the cost of its participation in a single Easter Monday (Black Monday) parade. For the smaller and more recently established feltmakers' guild, the bill for the same parade came to £12 in 1670: in addition, they paid £4 10s. to cover other expenses associated with parading, including a fee for a drummer, gunpowder, a beadle's cloak, stockings, a hat and a tent in which the party of guild members dined on such an occasion.[50] Guilds went to great lengths at this point to ensure that members, their clothing, flags, musical instruments, vehicles, horses, furnishings and other accessories were turned out to the highest standard. They also insisted upon members' participation in these gatherings, fining anyone who refused to do so. This demonstrates the guilds' consciousness of how important these ceremonies were for impressing upon the lord mayor, aldermen, bailiffs, sheriffs and the general public their importance as a united, ancient and fundamental element in their city's distinguished political institutions, traditions and culture.

---

45 Berry, 'Feltmakers', 33; Whelan, 'Guilds', 31. 46 Keating, 'Cutlers', 137. 47 Ibid. 48 Dixon, 'Tailors', 151. 49 Keating, 'Cutlers', 136–47; Berry, 'Feltmakers', 31–3. 50 Berry, 'Gild of merchants', p. 61; *idem*, 'Feltmakers', 32–3.

THE RIDING OF THE FRANCHISES AND POLITICAL CULTURE

Throughout the late seventeenth century and down to 1782, in compliance
with Prince John's grant in 1192 to the citizens of Dublin 'both within and
without the walls' to have their boundaries 'perambulated on oath by good men
of the city', in early August every third year, a ceremonial event known as the
'Riding of the Franchises' took place in which the mayor of Dublin, escorted
by 300 citizens on horseback and representatives of all of the guilds, marked
the boundaries of the city's jurisdictions.[51] This was by far the most spectacular
display of the guilds' role in Dublin's civic, political and commercial life. Their
main contribution to the procession, a series of what would now be called
floats, was 'a mixture of entertainment and self-advertisement, which blended
classical, biblical, and folk themes, and drew on the tradition of the mystery
plays that the guilds had acted down to Elizabethan times.'[52]

By the mid-seventeenth century it was usual for the guilds to accompany the
lord mayor in formation, each member wearing the appropriate guild colours,
typically as a cockade in his hat. At that time, the date for the Riding of the
Franchises was not fixed; later it would routinely take place during the first week
in August. In 1649 the master of the goldsmiths' company was served with a
warrant from the mayor, dated 3 September, to be in attendance and suitably
turned out with horse and arms, at 4 a.m. on the 10th of the month, at Christ
Church meadows. Guild members subscribed to cover the costs, including a
dinner, and two yards of broad ribbon in the guild's colours (yellow and red) for
each representative who attended. On that occasion, the master did not ride but
appointed a deputy who, as captain, led a party of 16 men, six of whom belonged
to other guilds but chose to ride with the goldsmiths 'as loving brothers in our
company'.[53]

In the eighteenth century, the ceremony evolved into a more elaborate
procession with each guild exhibiting its wares. As a result, the event became
a major attraction, allegedly drawing visitors from Britain and Continental
Europe.[54] However, some contemporary accounts undoubtedly exaggerated its
importance and appeal, including the report on the 1755 procession, published
in *Faulkner's Dublin Journal*, 12–16 August:

> Last Tuesday the Liberties and Franchises of this city were ridden and
> perambulated by the Rt. Hon. The Lord Mayor, Sheriffs and Corporations,
> in the most grand and elegant manner, each body riding with the other
> in Pageantry, fine horses, rich furniture and cloaths, all which made a

---

51 Originally envisaged as an annual event, from 1606 the city assembly ruled that it should
take place every third year. See Lennox Barrow, 'Riding the Franchises', *DHR*, 33 (1979–80),
135; *idem*, 'The franchise of Dublin', ibid., 36 (1982–3), 68–80.   52 Hill, *From patriots to
unionists*, p. 44.   53 Berry, 'Goldsmiths', 127–8.   54 Clark and Refaussé (eds), *Directory*,

finer figure than ever was known upon a like occasion, which was not only pleasing to all citizens in general, who are true lovers of Liberty, but to the many thousands of people who came from England, many other parts of Europe, and even from America to see so grand a procession, which greatly surpasses the Lord Mayor's Show of London; the carrying of the Host or Corpus Christi at Paris: or the Wedding of the Sea by the Dodge of Venice. These franchises are of the greatest use and service to the public as they bring vast numbers of strangers to this Kingdom, and cause large sums of money to be spent in this Metropolis, by which all Tradesmen whatever benefit.

Typically in July of the year when the ceremony took place, the mayor or (post-1660) lord mayor issued a summons to each of the twenty-five guilds represented on the common council, instructing them to participate. This afforded the master and members time to decide whether they would comply with the summons or opt not to turn out and instead pay a fine; it also allowed them time to approve a budget and carry out the necessary preparations.[55] Each participating guild member paid a fee: in July 1713 the barber-surgeons paid 4s. In 1703, when the weavers' guild received their summons to attend the lord mayor with 'complete arms and furniture [harness]', those members who had become freemen during the preceding three years had to contribute 10s. or pay a fine of 10s. which was the standard fee imposed on individuals who refused or failed to turn out.[56]

We are provided with an insight into the process by which guilds decided on their participation in the triennial ceremony in the example of the goldsmiths' company. On 24 July 1764, having been served the lord mayor's warrant and an order of assembly dated the 20th of the month, the master convened a hall meeting. After both documents were read, a motion was tabled and seconded that members should be balloted on whether the guild would comply with the warrant. A second motion was tabled and seconded on the question of whether the goldsmiths would ride the franchises in a public or private manner; in the ballot that followed, the majority (16:14) voted in favour of public participation. The meeting also agreed to assign the master 'a sum not exceeding thirty pounds to defray the expense'.[57] This reflected general practice whereby guilds imposed caps on expenditure for major events, including swearing-in ceremonies for masters and wardens. Only limited funds were to be collected for specific ceremonies; beyond that, each participating guild member was

pp 12–13.   **55** Keating, 'Cutlers', 145.   **56** Cotter Stubbs, 'Weavers', 67, 71; Henry F. Berry, 'The ancient corporation of barber-surgeons, or gild of St Mary Magdalene, Dublin', *RSAI Jn.*, 33 (1903), 232.   **57** Company of Goldsmiths of Dublin, MS 21 Minute Book, P93, 1 May 1760–8 June 1779. My thanks to Dr Alison FitzGerald for this reference.

expected to cover any additional costs he incurred.[58] On 28 July the master and three wardens of the goldsmiths' company issued a warrant to the company brethren, notifying them

> To appear at the master's house in Skinner-row, Dublin, on Tuesday the seventh day of August next, at seven of the clock in the morning, on horseback, with complete arms and furniture, a plain hat with a gold button and loop, a cockade with the corporation colours, which are, yellow, white and red, and buff-colour gloves, to attend the sword, and ride the franchises according to the custom of the city, whereof you are not to fail, on the penalty of five shillings and five pence to be paid the master, provided you pay said fine two days before the day of riding; if not, afterwards to pay a fine of eight shillings and three half-pence.[59]

While participation was expected, it could not be assumed. Records of fine payments prove that on occasion, guilds or individual members chose not to turn out. This trend is also suggested by patchy references to participation in surviving guild records: for instance, the barber-surgeons' archive contains only two records of the guild's involvement, in 1713 and 1731. However, this was not the full story as a *Faulkner's Journal* report of 1 August 1767 describes the barbers' guild members perambulating. At times, a guild's decision not to comply with the warrant stemmed from its inability to meet the anticipated outlay. When the cost of participation (£60–£80) was prohibitive for the guild of cutlers, painter-stainers and stationers, they elected to pay the £10 fine.[60] In 1773, 1776 and 1779, financial disarray prevented the tailors from turning out.[61] In the event of an emergency, a guild could request an exemption. Thus, when in 1742 the master of the weavers' guild died, his brethren presented a memorial to the lord mayor, sheriffs and commons requesting that the guild be excused from Riding the Franchises which was due to take place a few days later.[62] Equally, individuals were required to account for their absence. Any master who was unable to attend was required to notify formally the lord mayor and nominate a deputy to officiate in his stead.[63]

Occasionally guilds received a public and humiliating reminder that the invitation to join the lord mayor and corporation in Riding the Franchises was not a thing to be taken for granted but a time-honoured privilege issued only to those citizens of the city who earned the honour by conducting their business in a manner that befitted their office and standing. Failure to do so could result in temporary exclusion from participation. This was the case in July 1782 when the lord mayor was requested not to permit the tailors to join the procession the

58 Cotter Stubbs, 'Weavers', 69.   59 Douglas Bennet, *The goldsmiths of Dublin: six centuries of achievement* (Dublin, 2018), p. 19.   60 Keating, 'Cutlers', 145.   61 Berry, 'Merchant tailors', 54.   62 Cotter Stubbs, 'Weavers', 72.   63 Berry, 'Goldsmiths', 127–8.

following month owing to recent trouble with the guild involving combination of journeymen tailors.[64]

Participating in this triennial event was expensive. The fact that so many turned out on a regular if not constant basis is testimony to the high premium placed on the procession as a means to impress upon the city's municipal leaders and the general public their centrality in the political and commercial life of the city. The ceremony was an occasion for posturing and positioning by guild freemen who entertained commercial and political ambitions. In the words of the memoirist, judge and MP, Jonah Barrington (1756/7–1834), 'the gayer they appeared on that great day, the more consideration would they be entitled to throughout the ensuing three years!'[65] Outshining other guilds was a key concern: an anonymous mock heroic poem (*c.*1716) describing 'the glorious cavalcade', which was reissued throughout the eighteenth century whenever the procession took place, emphasized how

> The chief contention and the only care
> Is, who shall best equipt and arm-d appear.[66]

The lengths to which the guilds went is illustrated by the cutlers, painter-stainers and stationers whose outlay on hiring horses and trappings, paying musicians' fees, and buying drinks for the lord mayor's servants, amongst other costs at various Riding of the Franchises, ranged from £60 to £80.[67] Others may have spent less. In July 1701 the goldsmiths voted £20 for the charges associated with their public participation in the ceremony. In preparation for the procession, having recently purchased two silver trumpets, the goldsmiths ordered two new trumpet banners and issued a directive for the guild standard and staff to be painted.[68]

The amount of money, time and attention to detail invested in preparation for participation in the parade is illustrated by the following franchise account entry in the cutler, painter-stainers and stationers' archive. Provision was made for a bomb cart, under the charge of a man on horseback, which was conveyed by a team of twelve horses, six clad in field cloaks. A vulcan, riding a horse adorned with a black feather, and accompanied by an attendant, carried the guild's armour. The centrepiece of the guild's 'float' was a carriage on which

64 Berry, 'Merchant tailors', 54; Imelda Brophy, 'Women in the workforce' in David Dickson, *The gorgeous mask: Dublin, 1700–1850* (Dublin, 1987), pp 57–8; Hill, *From patriots to unionists*, pp 207–8. 65 Jonah Barrington, *Personal sketches of his own times* (2 vols, Philadelphia, 1827), i, 159. 66 'From: The Cavalcade: A Poem On the RIDING THE FRANCHISES' in Andrew Carpenter (ed.), *Verse in English from eighteenth-century Ireland* (Cork, 1998), p. 104. 67 Keating, 'Cutlers', 145. 68 Berry, 'Goldsmiths', 129; see Alison FitzGerald, 'The business of being a goldsmith in eighteenth-century Dublin' in Gillian O'Brien and Finola O'Kane (eds), *Georgian Dublin* (Dublin, 2008), pp 132–3.

compositors operated the stationers' printing press. In preparation, the carriage had to be fitted up and painted; the press had to be cleaned and repainted. Ironworks, woodscrews, girts and tinpins were mended. Six horsemen, a coachman and a postillon were charged with transporting the carriage which was also attended by two pressmen, a compositor, three figures representing the author, the printer and the devil who wore a pair of black stockings. Outfits for the carriage men had to be supplied. Two peelmen were to walk in the procession. Reams and twelve quires of paper were required for printing 2,250 copies of poems that were distributed to the crowd. The party included musicians – three men on horseback, one playing the kettle-drum, the other two playing trumpets. A fourth man led the drum-horse while others played French horns. A beadle paraded on horseback with harness. The master rode a horse adorned with a silk bradong bridle and harness; a horse and servant attended him. Several wardens, displaying silver coxcombs in their cockades, rode horses wearing silk bradong bridles. The coronet and quarter master wore silver coxcombs in their cockades and a loop in their hats; each of their horses wore a silk bradong bridle and a distinctive black feather. The expense did not stop there as the guild also incurred ancillary costs. These included the cost of 200 freemen's summonses and a similar number of quarter-brother summonses; fees to officers of the commons for the franchise warrant; the price of six pairs of gloves, ribbands for those leading the cavalcade, riding gear and dressings. The guild also paid carriage fees incurred before and after the pageant. It covered the cost of coach hire to transport provisions to the Charter School on the Strand, and paid the servants who attended the group as they dined there. The cost of hiring horses and buying drinks for the workmen and servants both before and after the procession also had to be met by the guild.[69]

The Riding of the Franchises ceremony afforded guilds opportunities to impress the city's dignitaries, other guild members and the general public with shows of lavish hospitality. At various points in the parade, the party stopped for refreshments. The goldsmiths' company was renowned for its entertainment. In 1656, having returned from the procession, thirty members assembled at the George tavern on Thomas Street were treated by the guild to a feast of roast and boiled beef, lamb, cauliflour and other vegetables, lamb pie, fruit, leg of mutton, rabbit, the best quality white bread, sack, claret and tobacco. The guild also paid for white wine, sugar and butter to be used by the cook who was paid 3*s*. for preparing the meal, and the George was paid 1*s*. 7*d*. for firing.[70] In 1673 the feltmakers paid Michael Banes in Francis Street for supplying beer, bread and meat, and dressing it. During the Riding in 1691 they paid for dinner and wine served at Blackrock and the Strand as well as a meal at the Crown tavern. For the parade in July 1755, they supplied 30 lbs of round beef, ham, eighteen fowl,

69 Keating, 'Cutlers', 146.   70 Berry, 'Goldsmiths', 128–9.

four dozen sheeps' tongues, six penny loaves, tea, coffee, sugar, along with wine at breakfast and both wine and malt served at the Strand.[71]

GROWING CHALLENGES TO THE GUILDS' MONOPOLY OVER TRADE, INDUSTRY AND ADMISSION TO THE FRANCHISE

The guilds were at their most influential during the early to mid-eighteenth century. During the 1720s and 1730s they and the city corporation were active in urging the administration to modify the navigation acts so as to promote the interests of Irish merchants. Many guild representatives also supported demands for reform of the corporation and for the aldermanic monopoly to be broken; a significant breakthrough came in the 1740s when two members of the city assembly's commons council, Dr Charles Lucas (representing the guild of barber-surgeons) and James Digges La Touche (representing the merchants' guild), vigorously challenged the corporation's oligarchy, defending the rights of the commons.[72] In the 1750s the weavers' guild took up the issue of foreign imports with parliament and in the 1760s the brewers' guild petitioned parliament on matters relating to the excise. That said, down to the 1760s, when the pattern began to change, guilds exhibited a low level of interest in purely political affairs.[73]

In the 1660s, because the modern division between manufacturers and retailers had not yet come about, the guilds spoke for the majority of the city's manufacturing and retail trade. Apart from a single interlude of Catholic supremacy during the reign of James II, the guilds and municipal officers successfully defended their economic privileges and Protestant dominance from the Restoration to the early 1840s.[74] As the merchants and artisans got on with negotiating commercial and industrial challenges, they did so confident that the freemen of the guilds would exercise their authority and influence to 'preserve the established order from the threat of the rising Catholic middle class and the journeymen's clubs.'[75] According to Hill, there are strong indications that the guilds continued to exercise some sort of control over the handicraft and retail trades in Dublin down to the mid-eighteenth century. During the 1750s many guilds, including the goldsmiths, brewers, weavers, barber-surgeons, tanners and chandlers, were still acting on the powers invested in them by their charters. In the 1760s, certain guilds, including the smiths and stationers, adopted by-laws that relaxed guild control over trades, indicating that hitherto control had been exercised or at least aspired to. Others reaffirmed their control: in 1769 the

71 Berry, 'Feltmakers', 32.   72 Clark & Refaussé (eds), *Directory*, p. 13; Hill, *From patriots to unionists*, ch. 3.   73 Hill, *From patriots to unionists*, pp 26–7.   74 Kelly with Lyons (eds), *Proclamations*, ii, 190; Hill, *From patriots to unionists*, pp 20–3, 26–8.   75 Mel Doyle, 'The Dublin guilds and journeymen's clubs', *Saothar*, 3 (1977), 6.

saddlers introduced a new by-law reaffirming regulation of manufacturing and retailing.[76]

However, during the eighteenth century the guilds in Dublin, as in other cities throughout the country, faced mounting internal and external challenges that would test the unity, authority and ultimately undermine the very viability of the guild system. During this period of growth, the city's population rose from around 10,000 in 1600 to possibly 40,000 in the 1660s and to 180,000 by 1800.[77] Within Dublin's burgeoning economy, the textile industries dominated in terms of employment, providing a livelihood for a third of the expanding population.[78] The problem of growing numbers of interlopers – 'intruders' – who endeavoured to operate outside the guild system escalated as the city's economy diversified, making it difficult for the guilds to exercise effective control. The rapid growth of the city's four liberties (those of Christ Church cathedral, St Selpuchre, St Patrick's cathedral, and Thomas Court and Donore) which, following the Restoration, stridently asserted their independence from the municipality, compounded the guilds' difficulties. It was there that much of the city's population increase and economic expansion occurred, especially as the liberty of Thomas Court became increasingly industrialized with the introduction of 'new draperies', and there that growing numbers of intruders conducted their business, exempt from the control of the guilds.[79]

Furthermore, there were serious rifts between and within several guilds as it proved increasingly difficult for guilds from the late seventeenth century to enforce rules and regulations governing the conduct of their journeymen. In 1674 and 1707 respectively the journeymen tailors and journeymen brewers openly defied their guilds. In 1719 the authority of the feltmakers was challenged when journeymen quit work without due notice and sought employment with masters who paid better wages. In retaliation, the feltmakers banned their re-employment within their jurisdiction. Disaffected journeymen turned away from the guilds and formed clubs and societies to represent their exclusive interests. In the 1720s, the Society of Journeymen Tailors, first noted in 1674, held annual ceremonial events in the month of July, processing through the city in their finest attire to St John's church to hear a sermon and then on to dine in the King's Inns

> where all that sees, do by experience know
> That meats are plenty, tides of liquor flow.[80]

76 Hill, *From patriots to unionists*, pp 27–8.   77 Ibid., pp 19–22; for an overview of Dublin's development in this period, see Dickson, *Dublin*, chapters 2–4.   78 Ibid., pp 20–1; Connolly, *Religion, law, & power*, p. 45.   79 Whelan, 'Guilds', 28, 29, 32; Hill, *From patriots to unionists*, p. 21; Patrick Fagan, *Catholics in a Protestant country: the papist constituency in eighteenth-century Dublin* (Dublin, 1998), p. 26.   80 Doyle, 'Dublin guilds', 7–9; Patrick

By mid-century combination of journeymen posed a serious problem to the guild system, which struggled to assert its authority in the face of 'the evil tendency and iniquity of all such unlawfull combinations'.[81] The authorities were obliged to take steps to curtail violent attacks by journeymen: in November 1747 the lord lieutenant and council issued a proclamation offering a reward for the apprehension of journeymen broad-weavers involved in a recent violent assault on a broad-weaver operating in the earl of Meath's liberty.[82]

In a pragmatic response to the challenge posed by illicit traders, the guilds insisted that any intruder pay a fee and recognize the guilds' authority and rights; the city's aldermen supported that policy of licensing non-guild artisans and craftsmen.[83] They approached the growing problem of Catholic 'infiltration', which was causing heightened anxiety among corporations throughout Ireland, in a similar fashion. From 1650 to the reign of James II (1685–8), the government and civic elite reserved guild membership to Protestants and following the Treaty of Limerick (1691), Roman Catholics were prevented from becoming full members, though they were admitted as quarter-brothers. The guilds required Catholic artisans to pay quarterage and admitted Catholic merchants, tradesmen and craftsmen as quarter-brothers of guilds; however, they were to have no political rights and few commercial privileges.[84] By the early 1700s quarterage had become an entrenched feature of the guild system.[85] According to Hill, the quarterage system is 'best regarded not as a means of excluding Catholics from trade, rather the contrary; it was designed to facilitate some degree of guild control over all substantial tradesmen, including Catholics, and it reflected the guilds' ability to adapt to changing conditions.'[86] It was not until 1793 that the freedom of the guilds was opened to Catholics. Even then, 'admission was "resisted on avowed principles of sectarian distinction" ... [and] Protestants sympathetic to Catholic claims or advocates of "liberal or popular principles' were similarly excluded'.[87]

In their efforts to withstand the challenges of intruders, journeymen combinations and Catholics demanding greater rights and privileges, the guilds could generally count on the backing of the city's lord mayor and aldermen. When illicit traders refused to comply with guild by-laws, the lord mayor had the power to send them to the quarter sessions.[88] While on the one hand the

---

Walsh, 'Club life in late seventeenth- and early eighteenth-century Ireland: in search of an associational world, *c.*1680–*c.*1730' in James Kelly and Martyn J. Powell (eds), *Clubs and societies in eighteenth-century Ireland* (Dublin, 2010), pp 44–7.   81 Resolutions passed by the warden and Brethren of the Barber-surgeons, 10 Oct. 1757 in John J. Webb, *The guilds of Dublin* (Dublin, 1929), p. 243; see also John Swift, *History of the Dublin bakers and others* (Dublin, 1948), pp 170–1.   82 Kelly with Lyons (eds), *The proclamations of Ireland*, iii, 357–8.   83 Whelan, 'Guilds', 34.   84 Hill, *From patriots to unionists*, pp 31–2.   85 Ibid., p. 32.   86 Ibid., pp 38, 40, 41, 130–1, 134–5, 171, 202–3, 231, 249, 268.   87 Doyle, 'Dublin guilds', 6; Jacqueline Hill, 'The politics of privilege: Dublin Corporation and the Catholic Question, 1792–1823', *Maynooth Review*, 7 (1982), 17–36.   88 Berry, 'Merchant tailors', 20.

patricians and guilds displayed a flexibility towards immigrant traders and artisans that proved essential in enabling the city's economic and demographical expansion, on the other they were united in repeatedly condemning all immigrants, irrespective of geographical origin or religion, who sought to operate outside the ambit of the guild system and thereby excluded themselves from the civic franchise. The aldermen recognized that if unlicensed artisans were permitted to trade without becoming citizens, the guilds' traditional role in qualifying candidates for admission to the civic franchise, which was so central to their raison d'être, would be fundamentally undermined. 'This in turn would have grave consequences for municipal administration, which depended heavily both on the financial contributions of citizens and on their obligatory service as unpaid municipal officials.'[89] The guilds' participation in the Riding of the Franchises, therefore, was of more than mere ceremonial significance. Rather, it was an important show of unity, staged by the city's entire ruling elite – lord mayor, aldermen, sheriffs and city assembly commons – in full view of the public, including traders in the liberties, aimed at reinforcing the demarcation between the four liberties and the rest of the city where merchants, craftsmen and artisans were subject to their regulation.

SHIFTING PRIORITIES AND WANING ENTHUSIASM FOR PARTICIPATION IN THE RIDING OF THE FRANCHISES

Throughout the period 1660–*c*.1770, the involvement by individual guilds in the Riding of the Franchises waxed and waned. From the start of the eighteenth century there were signs of increasing disengagement from the Riding of the Franchises ceremony. The archives of the tailors,[90] feltmakers,[91] weavers[92] and cutlers, painter-stainers and stationers[93] all feature multiple records of fines paid by guild brethren who failed to turn out. A substantial number of tailors paid fines of 8*s*. 1*d*. By 1719, such was the level of disengagement that the fine had to be raised to 10*s*. 10*d*. per individual. The problem clearly persisted: in 1756, a total of twenty-nine tailors were fined amounts ranging from 3*s*. 10*d*. to 8*s*. 1½*d*. The availability of money and a willingness to spend it on the pageant were important determinants. In 1722 the tailors cut a dash by having a man on horseback, dressed as a huzzar and carrying a large sword, lead their party. In 1737 they put on an elaborate display which once again featured a huzzar, dressed in a specially made goat-skin coat and cap and bearing a great sword. A coat and hat were also purchased for the beadle. An array of silver and other ribbons, gold fringe and white serge pieces were ordered for distribution to onlookers. A trumpeter provided the music for the tailors, many of whom were

89 Whelan, 'Guilds', 28, 32, 37.   **90** Berry, 'Merchant tailors', 53.   **91** Berry, 'Feltmakers', 31.   **92** Cotter Stubbs, 'Weavers', 67.   **93** Keating, 'Cutlers', 145.

on horseback. But the spectacle cost them dearly – the horses, harnesses, dinner and the trumpeter's fee alone ran to £36 with a result that next time around, the expenses were capped at that amount.[94]

They were not alone in this. From the end of the seventeenth century there were signs that some of the guilds were experiencing financial strain and this forced them to keep a tight rein on expenditure on ceremonial and recreational activities, including the triennial procession. In 1699 when the tailors guild was in dire financial straits, all unnecessary expenses had to be suspended; what little money they did have was to go towards relieving the poor and rebuilding their guild hall. In 1739, 1765 and 1769, because the guild's financial reserves were again very low, expenditure on celebratory events was severely curtailed once more. It was not until 1795 that the guild was solvent.[95] In the early 1700s and 1710s the tailors and the goldsmiths were on a par in terms of their corporate donation for their members to Ride the Franchises, both approving a sum of no more than £20 for costs.[96] Keeping a cap on expenditure was very necessary: whereas the tailors approved a maximum spend of £20 on the 1716 parade, three years later, the cost of the dinner, horses, decorations and other items ran to £34 17s. 6d. Yet, notwithstanding its attendant costs, the tailors remained committed to subsidizing their participation. Even in 1739, when funds were especially depleted, the guild approved a maximum spend of £39 on the parade; the same sum was approved in 1755. Later, in 1770, when their accounts were in complete disarray, the tailors undertook to pay a subscription to ensure their involvement in the event.[97]

By then, the guilds were becoming increasingly politicized. Whereas in the early decades of the eighteenth century the guilds appear to have played no significant part in parliamentary elections, from the 1720s by-laws dealing with the regulation of trades and industries yielded to politically controversial resolutions, addresses to members of parliament and to parliamentary candidates, as well as votes of censure on municipal representatives. From the late 1720s guild meetings were canvassed by candidates standing for election to parliament and, in another new departure, the guild of barber-surgeons pioneered the practice of issuing instructions to parliamentary representatives in 1744.[98] Furthermore, the guilds continued to press for reform of civic governance. In the 1750s, a group of merchants and traders protested to the king against the excessive powers invested in the lord mayor and aldermen. When nothing came of this, in 1753 a group styling itself the 'Merchants, Traders and Citizens of Dublin' requested that the king would one day give consideration to 'this great metropolis' and its administration.[99] 'By the 1760s the oligarchic grip on corporate life in Dublin had been undermined, while the guilds and the city

94 Berry, 'Merchant tailors', 53–4. 95 Ibid., 52–3. 96 Ibid., 52; Berry, 'Goldsmiths', 129.
97 Berry, 'Merchant tailors', 53, 54. 98 Hill, *From patriots to unionists*, pp 108–9. 99 Ibid., p. 122.

commons component of the corporation were beginning, cautiously, to adopt the part of guardians of the constitution, and were implementing reforms in order to protect and enhance that role'.[100] That decade saw a consolidation of gains achieved through the Dublin Corporation Act (1760), evident in a new willingness by the guilds and city commons to pass resolutions on constitutional matters; a move towards greater internal democracy, and a wish to defend recent gains by reasserting corporate privileges and by continuing to advance the civic reform programme that had been in train for several decades. Arising from the 1760 Act, the importance of guild representation on the city commons increased and the triennial elections became the subject of much interest to the press.

'A MATTER OF THE UTMOST CONSEQUENCE TO THE ESTATE AND FRANCHISE OF THIS CITY'

During the 1760s, against a backdrop of heightened anxiety among city officials and guilds regarding the escalating threat to the guilds' regulatory authority over commerce and industry in the city and to their role as gatekeepers to the city franchise, their participation in this major triennial event assumed particular political significance. Key to the guilds' response to corporation reform were their efforts to confirm or recover corporate privileges, most especially to reassert their rights in controlling trade. While they were prepared to relax some of their control, they were not yet willing to abandon it entirely: by the late 1760s a drive to reassert control through a statutory instrument to confirm the quarterage system was in train.[101] Facing mounting pressure and animated by an imminent threat to the rights and privileges of the municipal authorities, including the guilds, the city assembly's commons council issued all masters and wardens with a sharp reminder of their obligation to participate in the Riding of the Franchises and its very real function in regulating the commercial and political life of the city.

In 1761 certain members of the commons expressed concern that the Liberties had been encroached upon and lost to the city by the intrusion of illicit traders, 'which mischief', they declared, 'can only be remedied by carefully tracing and perambulating the city franchises'. At the same time they had, 'with the greatest concern', heard that several of the city guilds, whose members were represented on the common council, did not intend to attend the lord mayor in Riding the Franchises on 18 August, 'contrary to their duty as citizens'. The commons targeted the ambivalent guilds where they knew it would hurt most – their representation on its benches. All masters and wardens were served with an order that any guild neglecting to attend the chief magistrate throughout

100 Ibid., p. 113.   101 S.J. Connolly, *Divided kingdom: Ireland, 1630–1800* (Oxford, 2008), pp 393–4.

the entire perambulation would have its representation cut to just one on the common council and their remaining places distributed among the other guilds.[102] When the time for the next parade came around, in 1764, members of the commons once again emphasized to their brethren that the Riding of the Franchises was 'a matter of the utmost consequence to the estate and franchise of this city … [and] an indispensable part of the duty of every citizen'.[103] They threw down the gauntlet to all of the city's elected representatives, including the guilds, by insisting that

> It is the duty of the corporation to attend the right honourable the Lord Mayor, agreeable to ancient custom, in Riding the Franchises of this city on 7 August next, that it is the indispensable duty of the citizens at this time to show themselves unanimous and resolute to support all their legal rights and liberties which both seem to be in great danger from the combination against quarterage.[104]

The Assembly strongly supported this stance and ordered that

> the master, wardens and brethren of every corporation of this city be obliged to attend the Lord Mayor in such rising or perambulating, under the severest penalties that are in the power of the corporation to inflict (except such private brethren as are excused on paying the usual fines imposed by their respective corporations,) and that the masters and warden of the several corporations be served with a copy of this order.[105]

While the level of guild participation in the 1764 Riding of the Franchises is not known, it is clear that this anxiety to protect the rights and privileges of the guilds had escalated significantly by the time the next parade was staged, in 1767. In the interim, on 3 February 1766 the Dublin council joined the councils of Cork, Waterford, Drogheda, Youghal, Clonmel, Limerick, New Ross and Wexford in petitioning parliament for legal confirmation of the rights of guilds to impose quarterage on non-freemen. The Catholic merchants of Dublin in turn presented a petition signed 'the non-freemen of Dublin' to parliament on 14 February 1766, protesting the proposed quarterage bill. Petitions from their counterparts in Cork, Limerick, Drogheda and Clonmel soon followed and parliament responded by appointing a committee to inquire into the quarterage issue. On 3 November 1767 Dr Charles Lucas, who had been re-elected as a representative for the barber-surgeons' guild to the common council of the corporation in 1762, introduced heads of a bill for the better regulation of the trades, arts and manufactures in Dublin city in the House of Commons. For Lucas, the freemen's contribution to commerce, the arts, and liberty justified

102 *CARD*, xi, 30–1.   103 Ibid., 221.   104 Ibid., 220.   105 Ibid., 221.

and necessitated their special privileges. The following February, the non-freemen of Dublin presented a long petition opposing Lucas's initiative.[106]

Viewed in this context, the scale and splendour of the 1767 parade, which took place on 4 August, three months before Lucas's initiative in the commons, combined with the guilds' particularly strong participation, represented a significant show of strength at a time when the guilds' position was under real threat. Far from being a mere pageant, this was serious business for the guilds, a vital element in their armoury at a critical juncture in their effort to bolster their position within the political system.

'THE MOST MAGNIFICENT AND SHOWY PROCESSION': THE RIDING OF
THE FRANCHISES (1767)

Sir Jonah Barrington, who witnessed the cavalcade during his youth, declared it 'the most magnificent and showy procession', which 'made such a strong impression upon my mind, that it never could be obliterated'.[107] On the morning of Tuesday 4 August 1767, when the lord mayor, aldermen, sheriffs, and commons, all in their robes and paraphernalia, together with representatives of the city's twenty-five guilds, assembled at the Customs House and set out to ride the franchises, they did so in line with time-honoured tradition. In the procession, which was accompanied by bands playing music, the masters of the guilds rode on horseback while their journeymen and apprentices made their way on foot. A large number of servants followed the cavalcade. The guilds processed according to the order of precedence on the common council, each displaying its band and colours. First came the merchants in blue and yellow, followed by the tailors, wearing saxon blue and white, the smiths in black and white, then the barber-surgeons in purple, cherry and white and so on until at the end, the apothecaries displayed their signature colours – purple and orange. Reflecting precedence, some guilds such as the merchants and the shoemakers were represented by two masters and two wardens as compared to the usual one master and two wardens.[108] Patron saints joined the procession – St Crispin with his last, St Andrew with his cross, St Luke with his gridiron.[109] Numerous other gods and goddesses, saints, devils, and satyrs also featured.[110] For some guilds, such as the cutlers, painter-stainers and stationers who created the great sword of state which its master proudly displayed when Riding the Franchises,

---

106 Maureen Mac Geehin, 'The Catholics and the quarterage dispute in eighteenth-century Ireland', *IHS*, 8:30 (1952), 104–6; James Kelly, 'Lucas, Charles' in *DIB*, *sub nomine*; Hill, *From patriots to unionists*, p. 131; Fagan, *Catholics in a Protestant country*, pp 160–1; David A. Fleming, *Politics and provincial people: Sligo and Limerick, 1691–1761* (Manchester and New York, 2010), pp 132–3; McBride, *Eighteenth-century Ireland*, p. 126.   107 Barrington, *Personal sketches*, i, 158; James Quinn, 'Barrington, Sir Jonah' in *DIB*, *sub nomine*.   108 *CARD*, xi, 485–8.   109 Barrington, *Personal sketches*, i, 160.   110 Ibid.

the processions not only displayed their skilled craftsmanship but also gave symbolic public recognition to their prized role in municipal governance.[111]

Each guild had an immense carriage with a high canope and a wide platform. The carriages were usually drawn by six or eight horses decked out and caparisoned, their flag and signature colours flying in all directions. On the platforms, tools of the trade were on display and experts from the guild demonstrated their craft throughout the entire perambulation, which generally took two hours to pass, and lasted between eight and nine hours in total. Some exhibits were exceptionally elaborate and popular with the crowd.

The merchants or Holy Trinity Guild led the way. Their exhibit typically featured a large ship on wheels, drawn and manned by real sailors and they displayed a giant-sized shamrock in honour of the Holy Trinity. According to Barrington, the crowd was always eager to see the tailors who generally borrowed the best horses from their customers for the event. However, since they were not used to riding horses, the scene was 'highly ludicrous' as 'a troop of a hundred and fifty tailors, all decked with ribbons and lace and every species of finery, on horses equally smart, presented a spectacle outvying description'.[112] Following directly after the tailors, the smiths presented the most spectacular – in Barrington's view, gaudy – exhibit. It featured a forge, in full working order, and a sporty, light carriage, drawn by horses decorated with flowers and streamers, carrying Venus who was dressed 'as nearly as decency would permit; a blue scarf, covered with silver doves, was used at her discretion'. She was attended by four or five cupids who aimed bows and arrows at the ladies in the windows. On one side rode Vulcan on a large horse, dressed in black armour and waving an immense smith's sledgehammer, on the other, his rival, Mars, on a tawdy caparisoned horse, in shining armour 'with an immensity of feathers and horse-hair, and brandishing a two-edged glittering sword six or eight feet long.'[113] Behind the carriage came Argus wearing an enormous peacock's tail.[114] The millers and bakers dressed up as wheatsheaves. The butchers wore hides and long horns and brandished great knives and cleavers as they passed. The shoemakers' display featured a prince and princess dressed in gold and silver robes, attended by two pages bearing a crimson velvet cushion on which rested a golden slipper. The saddlers were singled out for particular praise in the mock-heroic poem:

> Next march the Saddlers, glorious to behold,
> On Sprightly Beasts, their Saddles shine with Gold:
> A war-like Steed most proudly walks before,
> Richly attir'd, led by a Black-a-moor.[115]

---

111 Keating, 'Cutlers', 137. 112 Barrington, *Personal sketches*, i, 160. 113 Ibid., 159–60.
114 Maxwell, *Dublin under the Georges*, pp 228–9. 115 'From: The Cavalcade: A Poem On

In the cooks and vintners display, the latter had a carriage carrying a Bacchus decorated in ivy and vine-leaves. Tanners and skinners dressed in sheepskins and goatskins. The weavers, who wore large wigs of wool of various colours, wove ribbons, which they threw to the crowds or tossed patterns of the material that they were making into the air. As has been mentioned, the centrepiece of the display by the cutlers, painters, paper-strainers, printers and stationers was the printers' printing-press from which they printed handbills, songs and odes in honour of the lord mayor that they threw to the people as they passed. The hosiers' carriage had a loom weaving stockings. On the last carriage in the procession, the apothecaries made up and distributed pills and boluses. Their exhibits included pestles and mortars which, when used to grind medicines, sounded like bells pounding out a popular tune.[116]

When all participants were assembled and ready, the lord mayor led the cavalcade to Essex Street, Temple Bar and then onwards to the east end of Lazers Hill (now Townsend Street). From there, they rode across the Strand to Ringsend where they stopped for refreshments. They then proceeded to the Water-mark where, according to the ancient custom, one of the water bailiffs was called upon and told to ride as far into the sea eastward as possible (the water being at low level), and from there to cast a spear as far eastwards as he could. The point where the spear landed was taken to be the boundary of the franchises of the south side of the river Liffey and harbour of Dublin.

The party then processed to Blackrock (the modern Merrion Road) and headed westwards, passing through precisely named gardens and fields before heading for Simmonscourt. From there, they crossed more fields to emerge on the road to Bray and travelled southwards for a time before again crossing fields to join the road to Clonskeagh opposite a mill on the river Dodder at Donnybrook. From there they continued on to Clonskeagh Bridge, passed under its most easterly arch, and passed Clonskeagh mill. Next they went to Milltown Road before turning northward and crossing the fields to Donnybrook Road. They proceeded northwards along the road and having passed through a house and garden, arrived on Patrick Street. When they reached a house displaying a sign of King William and Queen Mary on the west side of the street, they proceeded along the Coombe towards Crooked-Staff and took the road to Dolphin's Barn. From there they travelled along the watercourse to the malthouse at the west end of Dolphin's Barn. Turning northwards, they crossed gardens and fields before reaching Cut Throat Lane (now Brookfield Road). They then proceeded to Bow Bridge, passed under the most central arch, and crossing the Kilmainham hospital fields, headed towards the Deer Park wall.

the RIDING THE FRANCHISES' in Carpenter (ed.), *Verse*, p. 106.   116 Barrington, *Personal sketches*, i, 160; Deana Rankin, 'The emergence of English print and literature, 1630–1730' in Jane Ohlmeyer (ed.), *The Cambridge history of Ireland*; ii, *1550–1730* (Cambridge, 2018), p. 458.

Having passed over the wall, they made their way to a corner of the wall near the dog kennel on the north side of the park. Once again they crossed the wall and travelled northwards alongside it until they arrived at the first half-round on it. There, they turned eastward and having once again passed through fields and several gardens, they reached Stoneybatter. There, they processed through two houses en route to Grangegorman Lane. More gardens were traversed before the party arrived at the sign of the coach and horses in Ballybough Lane. They then headed northwards along Ballybough Lane to Ballybough Bridge, crossing the river on the west side of the bridge, and proceeded along the Strand to Clontarf. There, they processed to the Sheds before heading for the mill in Raheny. The final leg of the itinerary was a further 130 perches (0.65 kilometers) northward until they arrived at a small brook which marked the end of the liberties of Dublin city.[117]

Traditionally, the cavalcade returned to the city centre by riding westwards along the Liffey, passing the south wall of St Mary's Abbey. Having made their way down Abbey Lane and the street at Oxmantown, they re-formed in the correct order, crossed the bridge and rode to the Mayor's door. There, every member of the party blessed the King's Majesty, bid farewell to the mayor and departed.[118]

> Then homewards steer their Course without Delay,
> And fall to drink, the business of the Day;
> Next Morning send their Horse and borrow'd things away.[119]

DISPLAYING THE GUILDS' PARTICIPATION IN PATRIOT POLITICS

Far less spectacular but nonetheless important for the guilds' increasing assertion of their patriot credentials in the political arena from the mid-eighteenth century onwards were presentation ceremonies at which they conferred honorary freedoms on eminent men whom they wished to distinguish.[120] Readers of the city newspapers' extensive coverage of these events were kept abreast of the guilds' growing participation in patriot politics, notably when several guilds conferred freedoms on MPs who had led the defence of parliament's rights during the money bill dispute in the 1750s. Among these was the guild

---

117 *CARD*, xi, 489–91; Barrow, 'Riding the Franchises', 138; Colm Lennon, *That field of glory: the story of Clontarf from battleground to garden suburb* (Sandyford, 2014), pp 146, 155.   118 Barrow, 'Riding the Franchises', 135–8.   119 'From: The Cavalcade: A Poem On the RIDING THE FRANCHISES' in Carpenter (ed.), *Verse*, p. 107.   120 Hill, *From patriots to unionists*, p. 130; Martyn J. Powell, 'Civil society, *c*.1700–*c*.1850' in James Kelly (ed.), *The Cambridge history of Ireland*; iii, *1730–1880* (Cambridge, 2018), p. 467; Damian Collins, 'The production and supply of gold and silver boxes in late Stuart and Georgian Dublin' in Alison FitzGerald (ed.), *Studies in Irish Georgian silver* (Dublin, 2020), pp 26–63.

of cutlers, painter-stainers and stationers, which asserted its patriot stance in 1755 by conferring an honorary freedom on James FitzGerald, twentieth earl of Kildare. In addition to his patriot credentials, confirmed during the money bill dispute, the earl was a prominent employer of craftsmen, his magnificent seat in Dublin – Kildare (Leinster) House – having been built in the 1740s.[121] In their address, which together with the freedom of the guild was presented to Kildare in a gold box, the guild master, wardens and brethren commended the earl for his 'distinguished love of his country' and for his 'support of Honest Liberty and Rational Constitution'. They declared: 'while you exert the manly virtue of assisting the poor and upright … Britons must love you, for, as Brethren, they are equally engaged in the same measures.'[122] That year, at the Riding of the Franchises, when guild members wore Irish-manufactured hats and gloves, they publicly celebrated their association with the country's leading peer, paying for drinks for 'the earl of Kildare's servants'.[123] They were also extremely keen to draw upon their privileged access to Kildare in order to enhance their cavalcade in the grand procession. No sooner had they granted him freedom of the guild than the brethren asked Kildare to lend his support for their participation in the event. He replied graciously:

> … There is not anything that I have … the day that you ride the Franchises, but that you may command. If you should have any carriage on the occasion, my long-tail horses are at your service, or any other thing that will answer your purpose. Bere can inform you what things I have which you may want, and I shall order him to let you have them. I am, Sir, your most humble servant – KILDARE.[124]

Not unsurprisingly, other patriot orientated guilds were also keen to demonstrate their support for Kildare: in 1768, two years after his elevation to duke of Leinster, Sir Charles Lucas's guild – the barber-surgeons – conferred its freedom on him.[125] Furthermore, during a by-election the previous year, several of the guilds, including the Goldsmiths, and a majority of the city commons (though not the aldermen) were prepared to consider the duke's 18-year-old son William FitzGerald, marquis of Kildare, as MP for the city.[126]

Although the merchant guild supported John La Touche, the majority of the tailors backed FitzGerald; it was in their hall that his supporters gathered. Kildare won the by-election by 137 votes but did not return from his continental travels to take up his seat on this occasion. However, that did not prevent the

121 Hill, *From patriots to unionists*, pp 132–3.   122 Quoted in Keating, 'Cutlers', 144; see Alison FitzGerald, *Silver in Georgian Dublin: making, selling, consuming* (Abingdon, 2017), p. 165.   123 Ibid., p. 145.   124 Ibid.   125 James, twentieth earl of Kildare, was created duke of Leinster in 1766; see Berry, 'Barber-surgeons', 234; FitzGerald, *Silver in Georgian Dublin*, p. 166.   126 FitzGerald, *Silver in Georgian Dublin*, p. 185 n. 51.

guilds from proceeding with the traditional chairing ceremony to celebrate publicly their candidate's victory. Deputizing for Kildare, John St Leger, MP for Doneraile, was carried in a procession of the guilds, with bands, from the Tholsel to parliament house, scattering money to the crowds as he passed. The tailors were among several guilds who showed their appreciation to the duke of Leinster for allowing his son to be elected, presenting both father and son with the freedom of the guild and a gold thimble each. (During the same period, the guild of bricklayers and plasterers presented the marquis with an ornamental silver trowel.)[127] In 1768 the marquis was returned at the general election on which occasion he was present and dined with several guilds. In 1769 the tailors paid a portion of the cost of the 'public breakfast' that was held in his honour and that of Dr Lucas at the music hall.[128]

The twenty-eight toasts proposed at the tailors' dinner which took place in the Phoenix tavern on Werburgh Street at 4 p.m. on 26 October 1767, while the by-election was in progress, reveals much about the guild's patriot priorities and increasing preoccupation with parliamentary politics. They began by toasting the king, the queen, the prince of Wales and the rest of the royal family, the lord lieutenant and the prosperity of Ireland, and the 'glorious memory of the great King William'. Next they saluted the duke of Leinster, the marquis of Kildare (to whom they wished a safe journey home and success in the election), the duchess of Leinster ('patroness of Irish manufacturers'), and the Dowager Lady Kildare ('may she live many years to see this city represented by her grandson in parliament.') They then toasted the minority of the weavers at their hall and 'the Irish cooks that cannot relish French sauce' (possibly referring to their opposition to rival French silk weavers). Next they saluted the lord mayor and board of aldermen and the recorder of the city of Dublin. They then toasted the 16 October 1767 and the majority of the commons – the occasion being the presentation of the freedom of the city and 20-guinea gold boxes to the duke of Leinster and the marquis of Kildare.

They then broadened their range, proposing praise and denunciation to allies and opponents in the political arena. They proposed a toast to the success of the Septennial bill and to 'attempts for obtaining a law for establishing a reasonable quartering'. They wished success to those guilds who supported the duke of Leinster and hoped that 'their public spirited example [might] influence the free electors of the city of Dublin'. Separately, they expressed a wish that 'the city of Dublin [may] never want a representative of consequence, sufficient to obtain the beneficial laws it stands in need of.' They then saluted Dr Charles Lucas, MP for Dublin, before toasting that all promises made to candidates would be understood to relate only to them alone and that 'all badger [may] be hunted into their holes.' They hoped that the press would preserve its liberty

127 Dixon, 'Tailors', 149; FitzGerald, *Silver in Georgian Dublin*, pp 166, 185.   **128** Berry, 'Merchant tailors', 30; Hill, *From patriots to unionists*, p. 133.

and be free from licentiousness, and that the friends of the marquis of Kildare would be 'ever blessed with the Taylor's Thimble'.

Turning a reproachful eye to their opponents, they wished 'A hot needle and a burning thread to all sowers of sedition, and particularly to the by-stander, the misrepresenter' of the presentation of the freedom of the city to the duke of Leinster and his son. They then expressed the hope that 'the needle of distress be ever pointed at the Mock Patriot, whose oratory consists of sophistry, and abuse of superior characters, and who would see his country for interest or discount.' They wished that 'the Corporation of Taylors [may] always be able to disrobe the borrowed plumes of copperplate, from the Faction, which would ever cajole them out of their Liberties.' Their penultimate toast was that the voters of Dublin might be 'as remarkable hereafter in the annals of fame, as the Americans are at this day' and they concluded with a simple salute to 'Kildare and Liberty.'[129]

The politico-economic theme of the tailors' toasts typified those of artisan and merchants guilds in general during the less politically turbulent years between 1756 and 1767.[130] This guild dinner and the presentation of the freedom and gifts to the duke of Leinster and his son may have taken place out of the public eye. Nevertheless, by being publicized in the city's newspapers, such occasions became political events which connected parliament, associational life, the burgeoning newspaper industry and the public, and in the process placed the guilds at the heart of political culture in Dublin.[131] Given that the freemen of the guilds constituted around four-fifths of the votes in the early 1770s, their endorsement of candidates was clearly crucial.[132] By the 1790s the guilds had secured greater powers in their relations with the city corporation, the role of the city commons was enhanced, and although the freemen had lost exclusive trading privileges, 'they had carved out a political role for themselves independent of the aldermen and of the Castle, especially in respect of parliamentary representation'.[133]

CONCLUSION

From the 1750s the guilds were losing their principal function as regulators of trade. With the breakdown of guild control over trade, by the 1780s a class of retailers without a manufacturing base had arisen. By the end of the century, four of the five representatives of the weavers and dyers' guild on the common council were merchants, clothiers, or drapers rather than weavers and dyers, although Hill has shown that several guilds were buoyant and that the connection with

---

129 Dixon, 'Tailors', 150–1.   130 See Martyn J. Powell, 'Political toasting in eighteenth-century Ireland', *Historical Geography*, 91:304 (2006), 514.   131 Ibid.   132 Hill, *From patriots to unionists*, pp 162–3.   133 Ibid., p. 193.

trade, while declining, remained important in the early 1800s.[134] Following the
failed quarterage campaign in the 1760s, the guilds were also ceding their prized
control of access to the franchise. It had been the custom that when applying for
admittance to any guild, an individual was required to present a petition to the
common council for admission to the civic franchise. The petition, which was
based on a certificate of qualification issued by the guild officers, had to pass
both houses of the common council (the board of aldermen and the commons
which claimed the right to admit or reject at their pleasure applicants for the
city franchise). However, as infiltration of the guilds by individuals who were
not qualified by their occupation to be active and interested members of those
bodies increased steadily during the eighteenth century, adherence to that
procedure diminished significantly. As admission to the guild merchant and
to the craft guilds was regarded as a stepping stone to the civic franchise –
the possession of which entitled the holder to the parliamentary franchise – a
growing number of individuals, unconnected with a craft, sought admittance
to a guild by right of birth, marriage, servitude or 'grace especial' purely to
obtain the higher franchise.[135] In the eyes of many such brethren, the Riding of
the Franchises was an expensive pageant whose purpose they increasingly called
into question in the late eighteenth and early nineteenth centuries.

The last traditional Riding of the Franchises in which the full civic hierarchy
was displayed to public view took place in 1782, when 'in addition to the circuit
made by the lord mayor and city regalia, journeymen from several guilds
paraded through the city "according to triennial custom"'. By then, however,
the triennial parade's days were numbered. The guilds had been challenging
the aldermanic oligarchy for over thirty years: such ceremonial shows of unity
were becoming meaningless. Furthermore, although Jonah Barrington would
have us believe that, 'so proud was the Dublin mob of what they called their
fringes [Riding the Franchises], that on these peculiar occasions, they managed
to behave with great decorum and propriety',[136] this was not entirely true. In
the 1730s, for example, when Dublin experienced a severe economic downturn,
the sight of the lavish parade served as a provocation to some poorer elements
among the city's population, as there were reports of 'many idle persons
throwing squibs and stones at the procession'.[137] By the 1780s, the journeymen
had inveigled their way into participating in the Riding of the Franchises,
provoking a hostile response from the opposition press who criticized them
for encouraging idleness and excess.[138] Well ahead of the triennial parade in
August 1785, at a time when the corporation was increasingly critical of 'the
mob' engaged in street disorders, both houses agreed to post notices warning
that participation by journeymen was likely to interrupt work and cause 'a
general dissipation among the lower class of people'. According to Hill, despite

134 Ibid., pp 199, 206–8.   135 Webb, *Guilds*, pp 276–83.   136 Barrington, *Personal sketches*,
i, 160.   137 *CARD*, viii, 150.   138 *Dublin Evening Post*, 17, 20 Aug. 1782.

or because of these precautions, the normally festive occasion ended in tragedy in 1785. When the lord mayor and his entourage arrived at the Coombe, 'where by custom a ritual attempt to take the civil sword was staged, disturbances arose, troops were called, and three people were killed.'[139]

Writing in 1827, Sir Jonah Barrington lamented the abandonment of the Riding of the Franchises by the city authorities which

> began at length to think venison and claret would be better things for the same expense. ... And a wretched substitute for the old ceremony was arranged. The lord mayor and sheriffs, with some dozen dirty constables, now perambulate these bounds in privacy and silence; – thus defeating, in my mind, the very intention of their charter, and taking away a triennial prospective object of great attraction and pride in the inhabitants of the metropolis of Ireland, for the sole purpose of gratifying the sensual appetites of a city aristocracy, who court satiety and indigestion at the expense of their humbler brethren.[140]

Notwithstanding his sentimentality and nostalgia, Barrington grasped the importance of traditional civic culture in providing sites and contexts for the political involvement and awareness of the ordinary people of Dublin. The Riding of the Franchises, along with the many other public pageants, ceremonies, rituals and celebrations through which the guilds expressed their political values and status, embodied their ancient, privileged place in the political structures and culture of the city in the late seventeenth and eighteenth centuries. In the 1830s nostalgia for the principle of guild control remained strong among artisans employed in the building and decorating trades. Indeed, the 1840s saw a concerted though unsuccessful attempt to revive the guilds.[141] By then, however, the political landscape had changed: when the Municipal Corporations (Ireland) Act came into force in 1840, guild representation on the city council ceased.[142] Although not abolished, new priorities and new tensions ensured that the glory days of the city's guilds and their most spectacular street ceremonies were consigned to the past. The Goldsmiths' Company alone would survive and although the Riding of the Franchises persisted into the late nineteenth century, it was a shadow of what it once was.

139 *CARD*, xiii, 422; *Dublin Evening Post*, 13 Aug. 1785; Hill, *From patriots to unionists*, pp 194–5, 195 n. 6. 140 Barrington, *Personal sketches*, i, 160–1. 141 Hill, *From patriots to unionists*, p. 210; *idem*, 'Artisans, sectarianism and politics in Dublin, 1829–49', *Saothar*, 7 (1981), 12–27. 142 Fergus D'Arcy, 'The trade unions of Dublin and the attempted revival of the guilds', *RSAI Jn.*, 101 (1971), 113–27, 116.

Civic unity and the problem of urban poverty: a case study of St Audoen's parish, Dublin, 1655–1700

COLM LENNON

Recent comparative studies of the position of Catholic communities in countries where Protestantism was the state religion have stressed the general amicability of quotidian relations between the confessional groups, a phenomenon characterized by William Sheils as a process of 'getting along' with neighbours.[1] Scholarship devoted to confraternities has, moreover, pointed to salient continuities in the formation of a new social order throughout early modern Europe, as late medieval corporate institutions proved to be adaptable to the task of community-building after the Reformation, especially in the area of poor relief.[2] Notwithstanding some instances of exclusion from the welfare system of all except the doctrinally committed, in practice an eclectic approach prevailed, as in the case of Ireland, where the traditional parish structure with its inherited institutions and lay officials came to bear the weight of civil as well as ecclesiastical administration.[3] After 1560, when the ownership of the parishes fell to the Anglican state religion in Ireland, the small minority of Protestants from long-established families thus enfranchised displayed a visceral opposition to many of the rigorous confessionalizing tendencies on the part of some newcomers from England, who represented the colonial elite under the Tudor and Stuart regimes. By contrast, perhaps due to a strong sense of shared brotherhood and sisterhood, these native Protestants retained their ties with their Catholic fellow urban-dwellers, sometimes joining with them in defence of corporate liberties and civic institutions, including hospitals and almshouses, in the face of state-sponsored political and social innovation.[4]

The history of the intra-mural parish of St Audoen on High Street, Dublin, in the later seventeenth century constitutes an apposite case study of inter-confessional relations in an urban milieu. This is not only because of its central role in the social and religious life of the capital, but also because of the

1 William Sheils, '"Getting on" and "getting along" in parish and town: Catholics and their neighbours in England' in Benjamin Kaplan, Bob Moore, Henk van Nierop and Judith Pollmann (eds), *Catholic communities in Protestant states: Britain and the Netherlands, c.1570–1720* (Manchester, 2009), pp 67–83. 2 For a recent sampling, see Konrad Eisenbichler (ed.), *A companion to medieval and early modern confraternities* (Leiden, 2019). 3 See, for example, Raymond Gillespie, 'Urban parishes in early seventeenth-century Ireland: the case of Dublin' in Elizabeth FitzPatrick and Raymond Gillespie (eds), *The parish in medieval and early modern Ireland: community, territory and building* (Dublin, 2006), pp 228–41. 4 For a discussion of urban solidarity in early seventeenth-century Dublin, see Colm Lennon, *The lords of Dublin the age of Reformation* (Dublin, 1989), pp 190–200.

availability of fairly rich documentation of parish affairs. The recent publication
of the vestry records from 1636 to 1702 brings together most usefully hitherto
scattered sources from a number of archival collections and publications.[5]
There is also a large collection of documents relating to what could be termed
a parallel socio-religious corporation in St Audoen's – the fraternity of St Anne
– that includes minute books, accounts, property deeds from the thirteenth
to the eighteenth centuries and a volume of petitions for charitable donations
from 1655 to the 1720s.[6] A major archaeological and architectural survey of St
Audoen's provides a wealth of topographical information about the church and
its precincts.[7] By examining the records of vestry and fraternity meetings, I wish
to explore in particular how approaches to the relief of the poor and destitute as
administered by the Protestant and Catholic members may reflect the process
of community-building at parish level and the preservation of old bonds across
the religious divide. Furthermore it may be possible to assess how the effects of
the sundering of civic and parochial unity were mitigated, in spite of increasing
sectarian tensions and rivalry between traditional and innovative models of
social solidarity.

Before going on to identify the main demographic, social and religious
contours of St Audoen's parish in the mid- to later seventeenth century, it may
be germane to place it in its municipal context, especially in respect of the civic
oversight of problems such as poverty and vagrancy. By the 1660s the burden
of local administration on Dublin parishes was increasing significantly, with
many day-to-day responsibilities, including fire-fighting and street lighting,
for example, as well as poor relief falling on parish officials.[8] In the sphere of
welfare, the municipality of Dublin had taken over the running of city-wide
institutions for the 'deserving' poor and sick, such as St Stephen's leper-hospital
and the civic almshouse at St John's, Newgate, from the monastic orders, but
tax collecting for their maintenance eventually fell to the lot of the parishes. The
city council did take on the task of corralling and punishing 'strange beggars'
and the badging of licensed ones through its beadles of beggars, but the
parochial authorities ultimately were duty-bound to enforce these measures.[9]
An organized and compulsory parish-based poor law for Ireland to supplement
an act of 1542 failed to emerge before the eighteenth century, as did any new

5 Maighréad Ní Mhurchadha (ed.), *The vestry records of the parish of St Audoen, Dublin,
1636–1702* (Dublin, 2012).   6 RIA, MS 12 D 1 (Account book, 1584–1817); MSS 12 S
22–33 (GSA, Deeds and leases, 13th–17th centuries); MS 12 O 13 ('White book', 1655–
87).   7 Mary McMahon, *St Audoen's church, Cornmarket, Dublin: archaeology and architecture*
(Dublin, 2006).   8 For the expansion of the administrative role of Dublin parishes, see
Rowena Dudley, 'The Dublin parish, 1660–1730' in FitzPatrick and Gillespie (eds), *Parish
in medieval and early modern Ireland*, pp 277–96, and for her study of the development of a
parochial welfare system, see *eadem*, 'The Dublin parishes and the poor, 1660–1740', *Arch.
Hib.*, 53 (1999), 80–94.   9 For early attempts to regulate 'local' beggars in the parishes, see
Dudley, 'Dublin parishes and the poor', 89–90.

centralized institutions such as bridewells or workhouses. As a consequence, for several decades from the 1660s onwards, parishes such as St Audoen's were obliged to be self-reliant, providing indoor and outdoor relief for the poor through a series of *ad hoc* measures, such as cesses, collections, bequests and local almshouses and schools.[10]

In the 1570s, St Audoen's parish had been described as 'the best in Dublin, for that the greater number of the aldermen and the worships of the city are demurrant' therein.[11] Yet, while many families of the civic elite lived on streets such as High Street and Merchant's Quay, the seventeenth-century parish had a mixed social make-up, with many tradespeople living on Bridge Street and Pipe Street, for example.[12] St Audoen's parish also contained at least two almshouses and the municipal free school, as well as the jail at Newgate. A recent estimate has put the population of the parish at about 2,500 in 1636, rising to about 3,500 in 1702 with intermittent fluctuations due to political upheaval.[13] In terms of its denominational composition, the report drawn up by Archbishop Bulkeley of Dublin in 1630 stated that three-quarters of the households in St Audoen's were Catholic. That majority was diminished somewhat by the end of the century, especially due to the influx of Protestant families from England and the Continent, attracted by its centrality in the commercial and cultural life of the city. During the period under examination, the parish vestry, on which were represented some leading families in the Irish Reformation such as Ball and Ussher, as well as newly settled ones such as Wybrants, Percivall and Desminiere, oversaw the maintenance and furnishing of the parish church, the payment of the minister's stipend and the care of the poor and needy, among other responsibilities. Despite their numerically disadvantaged position, for most of the century the older-established Protestants successfully negotiated the changing religious and social currents with minimal communal disruption, through their largely effective management of relations with the large Catholic community in the parish.

While the houses of the Protestant and Catholic families of St Audoen's were intermixed throughout its streets, the communities had long gone their separate ways in terms of centres of worship. By 1618, there were at least three Catholic Mass-houses, two located in private residences and one in the meeting-hall of the fraternity of St Anne, contiguous to St Audoen's.[14] The parish church itself was divided between the southern nave, occupied by the chapel of St

---

10 For the background to the early modern poor law regime in Ireland, see Colm Lennon, '*Dives* and Lazarus in sixteenth-century Ireland' in J.R. Hill and Colm Lennon (eds), *Luxury and austerity: Historical Studies XXI* (Dublin, 1999), pp 46–65.   11 Richard Stanihurst, 'The description of Ireland' in Liam Miller and Eileen Power (eds), *Holinshed's Irish Chronicle* (Dublin, 1979), p. 44.   12 See the cess lists drawn up for the vestry and for the support of the army in the late 1640s: Ní Mhurchadha (ed.), *Vestry records of St Audoen's parish*, pp 144–8.   13 Ibid., p. 13.   14 Colm Lennon (ed.), *Dublin, part II, 1610 to 1756* (Irish Historic Towns Atlas, no. 19, Dublin, 2008), p. 23.

Anne's aisle and a private chantry, and the northern, older nave and sanctuary where Anglican worship was conducted. St Anne's chapel was kept in repair throughout most of the seventeenth century, and there are records of Catholic burials there during that period. The vestry records contain much information on the reconfiguring of church space, including the dismantling of the roof loft in 1639, and the repair of the church in general.[15] The latter was a major concern after the collapse of the church spire in 1668. Records of the parish cess show how the funds collected from households were distributed for these projects, as well as for payment of the clergy's stipend and the relief of the poor. Despite the fact that the parochial incumbent, a prebendary of St Patrick's cathedral, was technically in receipt of a reasonable income of 100 marks (£66 13s. 4d.), there were perennial complaints about the minister being starved of funds. In this connection and others, vestry affairs became regularly entangled with those of a separate, shadow body, the fraternity of St Anne. That institution had come in for criticism in the archbishop's visitation of 1630 for its having 'swallowed up all the church means, which should be for the minister and reparation of the church'.[16]

Changes in the role of this wealthy devotional and charitable association in St Audoen's parish have been used before as a barometer of the religious climate in late medieval and early modern Dublin.[17] Founded by royal charter in 1430 as a chantry college of six priests, the fraternity remained in Catholic hands after the Reformation down to the late 1630s, with notable recusants serving as officers, and controlling the leasing of its extensive property portfolio in town and county. Hostile investigators pointed to a copy in the fraternity's muniments of a papal decree of 1569, enjoining all Catholic confraternity members to lease lands to their co-religionists only, and to use the income derived for the provision of Catholic worship.[18] Notwithstanding this injunction, however, the rent-roll of St Anne's fraternity continued to include the names of prominent Protestants, and indeed a Protestant parishioner, Robert Ball, filled the mastership at a time when the fraternity's charter was being challenged in the 1620s. Largely at the initiative of the prebendary and minister of St Audoen's in the early 1630s, a full-scale enquiry into the activities of St Anne's under the aegis of Thomas Wentworth, the chief governor, was followed by an attempted take-over of the institution by the state church. The proposed coup failed, and among the

---

15 Ní Mhurchadha (ed.), *Vestry records of St Audoen's parish*, pp 17, 42–3, 45–7, 57–8, 66, 72, 84–8.   16 M.V. Ronan (ed.), 'Archbishop Bulkeley's visitation of Dublin, 1630', *Arch. Hib.*, 8 (1941), 59.   17 See Henry F. Berry (ed.), 'History of the religious guild of St Anne in St Audoen's church, Dublin, 1430–1740, taken from its records in the Haliday collection, R.I.A.', *RIA Proc.*, 25C (1904–5), 21–106; Colm Lennon, 'The chantries in the Irish Reformation: the case of St Anne's guild, Dublin, 1550–1630' in R.V. Comerford, Mary Cullen, J.R. Hill and Colm Lennon (eds), *Religion, conflict and coexistence in Ireland: essays presented to Monsignor Patrick J. Corish* (Dublin, 1990), pp 6–25.   18 Robert Ware, *The hunting of the Romish fox* (Dublin, 1683), pp 121–4.

reasons posited at the time for Wentworth's downfall was his interference in the affairs of St Anne's fraternity.[19] Meanwhile, the fraternity continued on as a parish institution for many decades after the early 1640s with a mixed Protestant–Catholic membership. It was principally through their continuing participation in the fraternity of St Anne that the Catholic community retained a corporate presence in parish and municipality, in spite of the ecclesio-political imbroglio of the mid- to later seventeenth century.[20]

Despite the periodic conflicts between them over the funding of parish buildings and personnel, and indeed the more substantial issue of the charter of St Anne's, the two bodies, vestry and fraternity, offered channels for Protestant parishioners and Catholic residents to co-operate in attempting to assure the social welfare of all. Insofar as the religious affiliation of individuals may be identified from their place in the network of civic associationalism, the membership records of the two institutions bear this out.[21] Catholic members of the vestry of St Audoen's became scarce after the 1630s, with only two being elected as churchwardens down to 1700: Lucas Forrestal in 1677–8, and Michael Chamberlain in 1689–90. Forrestal was forced to resign by the archbishop of Dublin and was replaced, but he donated a large bible and common prayer book to the parish.[22] Chamberlain, an alderman and master of St Anne's fraternity, served during the Jacobite restoration of Catholic worship in the parish.[23] At the level of the lesser parish officers, a Catholic was very frequently chosen down to the 1690s as one of the sidesmen, or assistants to the churchwardens, who served mainly as ushers and collectors in church.[24] This reflects the pattern, though in reverse, in the municipality of Dublin in the earlier seventeenth century of electing a Protestant as mayor or one of the two sheriffs in order to present a unified face to the state authorities in defence of corporate privileges.[25]

As a large proportion of Catholic households in the parish represented a substantial corps of contributors to cesses for the poor and other expenditure, their co-religionists were frequently appointed alongside Protestants as assessors, collectors and auditors, no doubt to encourage the payment of the levies. Although parish overseers of the poor were given statutory recognition in the 1665 St Andrew's Act, evidence for their appointment in St Audoen's

19 Ibid., pp 125–6.   20 See a selection of documents from the account book of St Anne's fraternity, 1584–1817 in Ní Mhurchadha (ed.), *Vestry records of St Audoen's parish*, pp 149–54, which counterpoint the records of the vestry.   21 See the methodology employed for an earlier period in the category 'Religion; attitude to the Reformation' in the prosopography of the aldermen of Dublin in Lennon, *Lords of Dublin*, pp 223–76.   22 Ní Mhurchadha (ed.), *Vestry records of St Audoen's parish*, pp 100–1.   23 Ibid., pp 129, 154.   24 Ibid., p. 28; for the phenomenon of Catholics holding officerships in Anglican parishes, see Gillespie, 'Urban parishes in early seventeenth-century Ireland', pp 237–9.   25 For the practice of electing members of the Protestant minority to serve the corporations of seventeenth-century Irish boroughs, see Colm Lennon, 'Bridging division or bonding faction? Civic confraternity and religious sodality in seventeenth-century Ireland' in Stefania Pastore, Adriano Prosperi and Nicholas Terpstra (eds), *Brotherhood and boundaries* (Pisa, 2011), p. 517.

parish relates to the period before 1660 only, when their functions were probably carried out by some of the other parish officers. It may be significant that complaints about Catholic non-compliance occur in the early 1690s when the vestry began to appoint exclusively Protestant assessors and collectors. As non-attenders at divine service, Catholics were evading church collections for the support of the poor, despite enjoying all the benefits of living and trading in the parish.[26] Meanwhile, members of notable Catholic families, such as such as Archbold, Ashe, Barnewall, Caddell, Dowdall, Dowde and Taylor feature among the appointees to office at vestry meetings in the decades from the 1630s. Among the individuals of Catholic affiliation or background who were members of the vestry or were elected to serve were John Dowde the elder and the younger, the former, an alderman, being a member in the 1630s, and the latter an assessor in 1685; Alderman William Purcell, a member in the 1630s, and Simon Purcell who was churchwarden in 1642–3; Richard Caddell, a sidesman in 1680–1; and the aforementioned Alderman Michael Chamberlain who served as churchwarden.[27] Most of these parishioners also had strong connections to St Anne's fraternity.

From the late 1630s to the early 1700s (with the exception of the later 1680s), the masters and two wardens of the fraternity of St Anne were Protestant, usually prominent aldermen or merchants, such as Christopher White, William Smith, Sir William Dixon, John Borr and Peter Wybrants.[28] Borr, Dixon, Wybrants and White had experience of serving as churchwardens or sidesmen of St Audoen's parish, while Smith, a long-serving city councillor, was a churchwarden of his parish of St John the Evangelist. He was thrice mayor of Dublin, and was noted for, among other deeds, presiding over the building of the new Tholsel or city hall.[29] These substantial merchants were evidently well qualified to manage the considerable financial resources of the fraternity, which arose from its extensive rent-roll, but they also played a full part in supervising the fraternity's charitable role and, when necessary, defending its chartered privileges in the face of parochial claims. The long-serving prebendary of St Audoen's, William Lightburne, also sat in on meetings of the fraternity between 1655 and 1677. Among the membership were men and women from long-established civic families who traditionally had ties to the fraternity, including William and Ignatius Purcell, Robert, Christopher and Walter Kennedy, Robert

26 For an act of the vestry of 1693 ordering that Roman Catholics and Dissenters be levied with the parish cess, see Ní Mhurchadha (ed.), *Vestry records of St Audoen's parish*, p. 132: note that sidesmen were to be collectors, assisted by the constables.   27 Ibid., pp 162–73.   28 Between them, they held the mastership or wardenship in 1641–3 (White), 1655–7 and 1663–72 (Smith), 1657–66 (Dixon), 1666–72 and 1677–81 (Borr), 1655–7, 1657–8 and 1672–7 (Wybrants): Berry, 'Religious guild of St Anne', 95.   29 See Raymond Gillespie, 'Mayor William Smith (1642–7, 1663–5, 1675–6) and the building of the Tholsel' in Ruth McManus and Lisa-Marie Griffith (eds), *Leaders of the city: Dublin's first citizens, 1500–1950* (Dublin, 2013), pp 35–43.

Plunkett, Michael Chamberlain, Cecily and Matthew Barnewall and Margaret Jans, almost all of whom were certainly Catholics. The women members were also probably in this category, Anne Ball, Catherine Clarke, Margaret Cooper and Clare Taylor were related to former brothers or sisters, and some of them were petitioners to the fraternity for charitable relief. This pattern of mixed membership obtained down to the early eighteenth century and beyond, but during the mid-to-late 1680s, it appears that Catholic members briefly regained a majority position.[30]

Relief of poverty was a responsibility undertaken by both vestry and fraternity in St Audoen's in the early modern period, though the operation of both regimes, each based on specific grounds of nativity and deservingness, spoke very clearly to differing conceptions of parochial and civic community. In the absence of a national poor law in the seventeenth century, the vestry of St Audoen's undertook the collection of very regular cesses, sometimes referred to as 'the poor cess', but it was also dispersed for other charges, such as officers' salaries. The amount of the cess and individual contributions, 'applotted' by assessors and overseers, was based on the value of houses on the streets of the parish. Thus, in the only full cess lists that survive for St Audoen's (for 1636 and 1644), the contributors' assessed payments range from £1 or £1 10s. in the case of substantial householders, including aldermen, wealthy merchants and state officials to a modest 1s. or 2s. for tradespeople such as a mason, cook, smith and shoemaker. Catholics and Protestants are listed without distinction,[31] and up to 10 per cent of the assessed contributors were widows. Total receipts from the parish cess fluctuated from £59 (in 1644) to £100 (in 1685), though an exceptionally large cess of £180 was raised in 1668 in response to a campaign for repairing the church roof and rebuilding the spire.[32] Of the full amount of cess collected, up to 50 per cent might be expended on alleviation of poverty and neediness in the parish.

The apportioning of funds raised for the poor encompassed the relief of inmates of the parish poorhouses on Skipper's and Keysar's Lanes. The bulk of the fund went for pensions for up to twenty-six members of the parish poor list, as approved by the vestry, each of whom received 26s. per annum. Although the criteria for inclusion are not specified in the case of St Audoen's, other Dublin parishes insisted on denizenship within the parish and belonging to the category of 'deserving poor', that is, either chronically sick or destitute due to ill fortune.[33] Only a small cohort of the deserving parish poor is named in the records, but of these a significant majority were women, some of whom such as Margery

30 See the list of officers and members who attended the meeting of the fraternity on 1 February 1687 that reinstated the six chantry priests of St Anne's: RIA, MS 12 D 1 ('Account book'), f. 283r.   31 Included among the cessed inhabitants was the name of Lavallin Nugent (1569–1635), the founder of a Capuchin friary in Bridge Street.   32 See Ní Mhurchadha (ed.), *Vestry records of St Audoen's parish*, pp 21, 35–41, 59–62, 124.   33 Dudley, 'Dublin parishes and the poor', p. 88.

Conner and Mawde Lenagh may have been of Gaelic background. Others, including Amy Duff, Bele Gerrott and Joane Plunkett, probably belonged to old-established civic families. Some of these poor women and men may have been Catholics, there being no recorded discrimination on the grounds of non-conformity to the state religion, but the parochial framework within which aid was dispensed implied at least a show of confessional loyalty.

Another tranche of the poor cess went towards the support of abandoned infants, who were left 'on the parish'. At any given time there were a number of orphans being maintained in St Audoen's at a cost of £4 each per annum, entrusted to the care of nurses for whose expenses the parish paid up to £5. There was no mention of registration or badging of beggars, or the expulsion of the undeserving poor, as happened in other parishes, but 'importunate' begging was referred to in a vestry meeting in 1672 as presenting a problem.[34] From 1662 appointments to the office of parish beadle took place, though any duties of his in respect of controlling vagrancy are not referred to, except perhaps the 'watching of a poor man found under St Audoen's arch' in 1667.[35] Charity, then, in the parish context, embracing the local and respectable poor, was a facet of vestry administration, drawing upon springs of communal and probably confessional solidarity, and laying the foundations of more streamlined systems of relief in the eighteenth century.

While the parish of St Audoen may have operated a semi-formal regime of poor relief mainly through the vestry, the fraternity of St Anne dealt on an individual, face-to-face basis with petitions from the distressed and infirm members of respectable families with confraternal ties, which had fallen on hard times, especially from the 1650s onwards.[36] These grants, which were drawn from the accumulated rental income of St Anne's, arose out of a broader interpretation of the fraternity's patent as developed by those antipathetic to the purely spiritual role defined for it in the charter of 1430. The serious questions about the fraternity raised by church and state authorities may have failed to secure its dissolution in the 1630s, but under its new Protestant leadership the principle was established of regular financial transfers from St Anne's funds to parochial charges including an annual contribution of £10 to the minister's stipend.[37] There were also donations made to the maintenance of the physical fabric of the church buildings, such as the gift of £100 from the fraternity for the rebuilding of the church and spire in 1668 after they were damaged in a severe storm.[38] The broader mission of 'pious uses' for St Anne's, cited by both petitioners and respondents, for example, in the appeals for alms in the later

---

34 Ní Mhurchadha (ed.), *Vestry records of St Audoen's parish*, p. 93.   35 Ibid., p. 80.   36 The petitions are to be found in RIA, MS 12 O 13 ('White book').   37 RIA, MS 12 O 13 ('White book'), p. 11.   38 Ní Mhurchadha (ed.), *Vestry records of St Audoen's parish*, p. 24. For an earlier donation of £21 7s. 6d. for the repair of the steeple in 1655 and another in 1680, see RIA, MS 12 O 13 ('White book'), pp 12–13, 71.

seventeenth century,[39] reflects the adaptation of traditional confraternal ideals to changing communal relations in Dublin.

Personal requests for welfare payments and benefits came before the meetings of St Anne's fraternity with great regularity from the mid-1650s onwards. For the succeeding decade and a half these assemblies, held in the fraternity's hall in St Audoen's arch, took place several times a year, but thereafter a pattern of exclusively annual gatherings on 26 July, the feast of St Anne, became established. The attendance, which included the master and wardens, varied from six or seven to fourteen, with a female presence of up to a third. The typical petition included a brief reference to the family background of the importunate one, the circumstances of penury or ill-health that had occasioned the dependence on charity and the nature of the relief requested. Most of the petitions for alleviation of poverty, which elicited a positive response from the members of the fraternity, were from women, many of them widows with children and some, such as Mary Cooper, a regular petitioner, who had three young children, and Anne Ball, were members of the fraternity. The former alluded to herself as being a native of Dublin, and a granddaughter of two aldermen and mayors, Nicholas Weston and Matthew Handcock.[40] Anne Ball, who identified herself as formerly Anne Gough, was probably descended from the marital nexus of Ball and Forster with Gough.[41] Service not only of the municipality but also of the state by her father, Patrick Segrave, was cited by his daughter, Ellinor, as grounds for favourable consideration of her request for charity. Protestantism may have been the predominant confessional influence upon these particular Old English families of which the women were members, but there were significant Catholic strands also interwoven through the pattern of marriages of the Goughs and Handcocks.

Although all of the importunate may have had links to St Audoen's parish, the nub of their appeals was their descent from formerly ascendant civic or gentry families, including those of Duffe, Segrave, Luttrell, Weston, Handcock, Gough, Jans, Luttrell or Plunkett. Many such as Mary Duffe, a 'poor widow of sad and low condition',[42] and Mary Bourke, a 'distressed widow', were also connected to former office-holders in St Anne's fraternity.[43] The petitions of two members of the family of Jans, Mary (Werferk) and Edward, made specific mention of the status of their grandfather, Alderman Edward, as a former brother of the fraternity.[44] In the cases of the Jans siblings, and of eighty-year-old Mary Luttrell (alias Goulding), their plight was compounded by the destitution of their families after the 1641 rebellion. Mary, once in a 'plentiful

39 See, for example, RIA, MS 12 O 13 ('White book'), p. 43 (petition of Mary Luttrell, alias Goldinge, 1677).   40 RIA, MS 12 O 13 ('White book'), pp 24, 25; Lennon, *Lords of Dublin*, pp 257, 275.   41 RIA, MS 12 O 13 ('White book', 1655), p. 28; Lennon, *Lords of Dublin*, pp 256–7.   42 RIA, MS 12 O 13 ('White book'), p. 29.   43 Ibid., p. 25.   44 Ibid., pp 45, 58.

condition', was daughter of 'old Thomas Luttrell of Luttrellstown whose fidelitie to the crown, generosity and public spirit were known to the best of the kingdom'.[45] Unable to make a living at home, Edward Jans junior was forced to go to sea. Sailing between Malaga and Algiers, he was captured by pirates, who demanded a ransom of 400 crowns. In his plea for rescue, he cited the example of his grandfather who, as master and brother of the fraternity, had contributed to the protection of others 'in their day of calamity'.[46]

A particularly painful case of scions of a once proud and affluent family brought low was that of the brothers Robert and Walter Plunkett of Rathmore. The Plunketts had played a leading role in both civic and fraternity affairs, Thomas having served as alderman for twenty-four years down to his death in 1627, and as master of the fraternity of St Anne from 1618 to 1621. A noted recusant, he had been a major benefactor of the Catholic mission of revival, having bequeathed £1,000 to the seminary at Douai.[47] His elder son, Robert Plunkett, who was a brother of St Anne's of forty years' standing in 1658, had had his estate of Rathmore, County Meath, sequestered and suffered the loss of a house in Cook Street as a result of the rebellion of the 1640s. Imprisoned for debt in the Marshalsea jail in Dublin for thirteen months in 'a miserable condition', he petitioned the fraternity for a donation towards his costs.[48] His younger brother, Walter Plunkett, who cited his parentage and qualification, stated that he had been deprived of his father's 'plentiful estate' by the 'iniquity of the times' and begged for relief of his indigency in 1667. Later, at the age of eighty-three in 1678, Walter, who was 'weak of body' and whose aged wife was 'sickly', was desperate for help and again threw himself on the charity of the fraternity.[49]

That body responded favourably to the petitions presented, not all of which were from the poverty-stricken. Some were related to rents and maintenance of fraternity property. Although it appears to have retained a Protestant majority at meetings for the thirty years down to the mid-1680s, there is no doubt that there were many Catholic petitioners, including those from the Dublin families of Plunkett, Jans, Luttrell and Chamberlain. And the membership lists reflect the continuity of participation, with at least twelve families that had members in 1636–7 being represented from the 1650s. There is no evidence of discrimination as to religious creed or parish residency in the treatment of the requests, but rather a receptivity to the familial and fraternal claims on its resources. Sums ranging from £10 to 19 shillings were granted as charitable offerings, as well as gifts of coal, and forgiveness of rent arrears. The decisions of the brothers and sisters at meetings in 1678 and 1679, for instance, reflect the response. Among the charitable grants made were £3 for Mary Cooper, 19s. and 40s. for Ellinor Segrave, 50s. for Mary Jans and £10 for Edward Jans, 20s.,

---

45 Ibid., p. 43.   46 Ibid., p. 58.   47 Lennon, *Lords of Dublin*, p. 263.   48 RIA, MS 12 O 13 ('White book'), pp 9, 30.   49 Ibid., pp 39, 41, 50, 54.

40s. and 50s. for Mary Luttrell, and £5 for Walter Plunkett.[50] In thus alleviating the plight of the familiar or 'shame-faced' poor,[51] and maintaining the dignity and pride of former elite families, the fraternity acted as a traditional bridging agency, in these instances across confessional and geographical lines.

For a period in the late 1680s, the religious diversity manifested in both vestry and fraternity meetings was threatened, as political upheavals served as a catalyst for an insistence on confessional orthodoxy. In 1679, the new prebendary of St Audoen's, John Finglas, initiated legal proceedings against St Anne's fraternity, calling for its abolition on the basis of its chartered status as chantry college, and the vexed question of the applicability of its resources to parish purposes. Finglas was particularly exercised by the fraternity's decision to end the payment of the annual supplement to his minister's stipend.[52] The campaign of the prebendary, churchwardens and vestry, elicited the publication of pamphlets on both sides.[53] Efforts to discover documents of the fraternity relating to the rights of the parish were initiated by the vestry, and the case was transferred by the lord chancellor from the court of chancery to be heard by him in his private capacity.[54] Although no determination of the costly suit is recorded and the fraternity continued in existence, it undoubtedly destabilized relations between vestry and fraternity, and internally between members of both bodies. Some were no doubt conflicted, as in the cases of Aldermen William Mottley and William Gibbons, who in 1688 were exempted by the vestry, possibly as dual members, from any concern in the suit, whether it were won or lost.[55] The vestry records provide no hint of contemporaneous national events, though the sundering of bonds is reflected in the exclusion of Catholics after 1690, even from the lesser officerships that they were accustomed to occupy from time to time.

By contrast, a Catholic majority briefly held sway in St Anne's fraternity from 1687 to 1690, under the leadership of the master, Michael Chamberlain, and wardens, Christopher Mapas and Christopher Cruise.[56] They presided over the restoration in February 1687 of the funding arrangements supposedly intended by the founders in 1430, that is, the maintenance of six chantry priests who would say mass every day.[57] In the following year the six nominated priests, Bartholomew St Lawrence, newly designated parish priest of St Audoen's, and five other Catholic clergy, including Michael Moore, the new provost of Trinity

---

50 Ibid., pp 45–52. 51 For the context of poor relief and the categories of the indigent, including the 'shame-faced poor' across a long duration, see Katherine A. Lynch, *Individuals, families and communities in Europe, 1200–1800: the urban foundations of western society* (Cambridge, 2003), pp 103–35. 52 Ní Mhurchadha (ed.), *Vestry records of St Audoen's parish*, pp 113, 117, 121, 122. 53 *The state of the case of St Anne's guild within the church of Audoen's Dublin* (Dublin, 1693); *A further consideration of the case of St Anne's guild* (Dublin, c.1695). 54 Ní Mhurchadha (ed.), *Vestry records of St Audoen's parish*, p. 122. 55 Ibid., p. 128. 56 RIA, MS 12 D 1 (Account book, 1584–1817), p. 559. 57 Ibid., p. 563.

College, were appointed to the six chantry chaplaincies, and were to be paid an annual stipend of £6 sterling by the fraternity. They were to celebrate in St Anne's chapel in St Audoen's until such time as altars in the main church were established.[58] Meanwhile, Father St Lawrence appealed to the duke of Tyrconnell for a top-up of his parochial stipend from the funds of the fraternity and was granted permission to apply to the receiver of the fraternity's revenues.[59] By 26 July 1690 a Protestant leadership had been restored, and in 1692, a meeting of the fraternity, attended by six Protestants, including the new master, Peter Wybrants, 'vacated, disannulled and made void' the reversion to a purely devotional role for St Anne's in 1687.[60]

Despite the sectarian divisions of the 1680s, however, caused by the prebendary of St Audoen's campaign for its closure, and the brief flaunting of its Catholic past, the fraternity of St Anne continued to exist as an association down to the early nineteenth century. It was stripped of its quasi-devotional role by a parliamentary act of 1695 that dissolved Irish chantries (150 years after such a measure was taken in England), but under its renewed Protestant leadership, a coterie of Catholic men and women remained among its membership in the early eighteenth century. St Anne's resumed its regular business of managing properties and rentals, and also granting suits for the alleviation of distress. Among those accommodated on several occasions down to 1700 were Elizabeth Cooper, daughter of Mary, a long-lived sister of the fraternity, whose ancestors included Aldermen Nicholas Weston and Matthew Handcock,[61] and Michael Chamberlain, whose namesake was master of the fraternity 100 years previously. He was helped with regular donations of up to £20 as a brother of the fraternity who 'by the misfortunes of the late times is much reduced to great poverty'.[62] Christopher Mapas, who had been warden of the fraternity from 1687 to 1689, was granted an abatement of rent as he had been kept out of his estate after the surrender of Limerick in 1691.[63] Thus, confraternal bonds, based on shared brotherhood and sisterhood over several generations, continued to hold fast into the early eighteenth century in respect of the relief of the familiar poor.

The alternative models of poor relief as reflected in parish and fraternity approaches ensured that a range of members of the parish and its former ascendant families could gain access to benevolence. With the advancement of public forms of welfare through a legal framework of poor relief, the flexibility that fostered co-operation across denominational boundaries on the ground in St Audoen's was more difficult to maintain. The parish vestry in 1693 had adumbrated the conditionality of the privileges and immunities that extended to Catholics and Dissenters as inhabitants.[64] Moreover, the establishment of

58 Ibid., p. 564.   59 Ibid., p. 562; RIA, MS 12 O 13 ('White book'), p. 68.   60 RIA, MS 12 D 1 (Account book, 1584–1817), pp 563, 567.   61 Ibid., pp 572, 579, 580, 581, 583, 585, 587.   62 Ibid., pp 573, 579, 583, 587.   63 Ibid., p. 585.   64 Ní Mhurchadha (ed.), *Vestry records of St Audoen's parish*, p. 132.

state and municipal institutions such as the bridewell and city workhouse (to which the parish was expected to contribute) for confining mainly those seen as the undeserving poor represented a rigorous regime at odds with the earlier parochial forms of welfare. For its part, the fraternity of St Anne became more integrated within parochial administration. Functioning as a charitable club rather than a religious fraternity for most of the eighteenth century, it devoted much of its funding directly to the maintenance of the church of St Audoen, and it made a standing contribution of £30 or £40 annually to the Blue Coat School in Dublin for poor Protestant scholars. For the Catholic population of St Audoen's, on the other hand, internal confessional solidarity was reflected in the building of an impressive new chapel on Cook Street[65] under an ecclesiastical revival that also came to incorporate sodalities and religious orders of men and women caring for the physical and educational needs of the Catholic poor.

65 Lennon (ed.), *Dublin, part II, 1610 to 1756*, p. 23.

The death of Mark Quin: identity, culture and politics in late seventeenth-century Dublin

RAYMOND GILLESPIE

The dramatic expansion of Dublin in the late seventeenth century produced both challenges and casualties. As the Irish lord lieutenant, the earl of Essex, commented to the king in 1673 'as cities grow more populous, so commonly they become more untractable'.[1] What may have been on Essex's mind was the political turmoil in Dublin over the previous year concerning the introduction of the 'New Rules' for urban government. Others who resided in or passed through the city also commented in a more general way that it had become an unruly and unpleasant place. In the 1660s Richard Head, who had lived in Dublin, expressed his dislike of the city in dramatic form. His play *Hic et ubique* depicted a place full of unsavoury migrants and unsettled charlatans who were prepared to resort to almost any subterfuge to part citizens from their money. John Yarner, Church of Ireland minster of St Bride's parish, likewise worried about drunkenness and unbelief among the inhabitants of Dublin, fearing that it might bring God's judgment on the city.[2] Others were concerned about another potential source of disturbance: the poor. The city authorities, the central government and local parishes responded by beginning to systematize their approach to the relief of the poor and regulate the administration of poor relief in the hope of exercising greater control over this potentially unruly group.[3] A growing and unstable population that was riven by petty feuds was scarcely the stuff of the dutiful and hierarchical city idealized by Mayor William Smith in his image of late seventeenth-century Dublin and celebrated in Robert Ware's history of the city in 1678.[4] Rather it smacked, as Essex realized, of the potential for riot and insurgency.[5] There were also the stories of individual victims of Dublin's social transformation. In a rapidly changing world with few protections the poor could easily fall off the edge of the social cliff to destitution or even death, either at their own hands or as a result of grinding poverty. The rich were not immune from danger with the possibilities of social isolation, political alienation and financial insecurity never far away from their daily lives.

1 Osmond Airy (ed.), *Essex papers* (London, 1890), p. 109.   2 Raymond Gillespie (ed.), 'Rev Dr John Yarner's notebook: religion in Restoration Dublin', *Arch. Hib.*, 52 (1998), 30–41.   3 Rowena Dudley, 'The Dublin parishes and the poor, 1660–1740', *Arch. Hib.*, 53 (1999), 80–94.   4 On Smith see Raymond Gillespie, 'Mayor William Smith and the building of the Tholsel' in Ruth McManus and Lisa-Marie Griffith (eds), *Leaders of the city: Dublin's first citizens, 1500–1950* (Dublin, 2013), pp 53–62.   5 *Letters written by his excellency Arthur Capel, earl of Essex, lord lieutenant of Ireland, in the year 1675* (London, 1770), pp 68–9.

This essay focuses on one casualty of the political and social challenges posed by living in the late seventeenth-century city – the apothecary Mark Quin – and by doing so reveals much about its political worlds and the price they could exact on the residents of Dublin.

I

Nothing was so dramatic in the life of Mark Quin as his leaving of it. According to the coroner's jury that met some days after his suicide, Quin had taken his own life in a very public way on 10 November 1674.[6] Rumour of the events spread and on Saturday 14 November, Revd Dr John Yarner, incumbent of St Bride's parish, scribbled into a blank space in his copy of Ambrose White's *Almanac* for 1665 the memorandum: 'then Mr Mark Quin, alderman of Dublin, having been lord mayor thereof but a few years before and one of good repute and credit between the hours of 9 and 10 in the morning in Christ Church in or near the chapel of St Mary desperately with a new bought razor cut his own throat. God give more grace to us and avert the omen from his church'.[7] The cathedral church was immediately closed, since it needed to be reconsecrated after the shedding of blood, and the proctor of Christ Church included in his accounts for the year the sum of 6s. 'to a guard on Ald[erman] Quin's body per order'.[8] The cathedral was still shut almost a fortnight later when, on 23 November, one of Robert Southwell's Dublin correspondents wrote to him 'for ever since that frenzy committed by Alderman Quin, Christchurch has been shut up till Friday last [20 November] when it was purified or new consecrated'.[9] The form of the ritual was determined in the 1666 liturgy for reconsecrating a church after blood had been spilt 'or any sort of prophanation', possibly composed by Jeremy Taylor, bishop of Down and Connor. This required a formal liturgical procession with the archbishop reciting a number of psalms and one long prayer requesting purification of the church. This was followed by the normal celebration of morning prayer.[10] The urgency of the rite was more than liturgical, the first Sunday of Advent being imminent on 29 November. The shops in the thriving commercial centre around the cathedral had to close as a result of the suicide, resulting in the loss of trade and even some bankruptcies.[11] Despite its reconsecration, the reputation of St Mary's chapel in Christ Church never really recovered from the impact of the suicide. While Dubliners continued to be interred in the chapel into the eighteenth century, Thomas Dineley, visiting the cathedral in 1681, was aware of one tomb 'upon

6 RCBL, C6/1/26/14 no. 33.   7 Gillespie (ed.), 'Rev Dr John Yarner's notebook', p. 35. 8 RCBL, C6/1/15/1, account 1674–5.   9 HMC, *Report on the manuscripts of the earl of Egmont* (2 vols, London, 1905–9), ii, 35.   10 *A form of consecration or dedication of churches and chapels* (Dublin, 1666), pp 33–5.   11 HMC, *Report on the manuscripts of the earl of Egmont*, ii, 35.

which a sad accident happened six years ago, viz. one Quin an alderman of the city cut his own throat, since which time this chapel is neglected and gone to decay'.[12]

What made these events so shocking was that they seemed to be inexplicable. On 6 November, four days before his suicide, Mark Quin had attended the aldermanic board, meeting some of those in the city who knew him best; yet, no one recorded anything unusual about his behaviour or demeanour.[13] Explaining why Quin had taken this dramatic action fell to the coroner's jury that was summoned in Christ Church on 11 November and for which the proctor paid 13s. 4d. in expenses.[14] Summoning a coroner's jury in Christ Church was potentially controversial since it raised the question of jurisdiction over the area around the cathedral. Christ Church was the smallest of the four large liberties in Dublin, comprising the half-acre made up of the cathedral precincts. As a liberty it was exempt from the jurisdiction of the city and under the control of the dean of the cathedral as lord of the liberty. As Matthew Dutton's 1721 handbook for the use of coroners noted of franchises and liberties, 'the coroner of a county can't intermeddle with the death of a man within such liberties' and special arrangements had to be made to investigate these.[15]

The existence of such liberties in Dublin was a continual source of friction between those who held them and the city that claimed jurisdiction over them. In 1672, for instance, the corporation thought it necessary to prosecute the earl of Drogheda for committing to the stocks a constable of St Michael's parish while 'attending the mayor in discharge of his office in the pretended liberty of St Mary's Abbey' on the north side of the Liffey. The episode was regarded as so serious that the council demanded £100 in damages for the constable.[16] This was not an isolated incident. Through the 1660s there had been disputes over the right of both city and state to tax the inhabitants of the Dublin liberties and quarter soldiers there. In 1670 the verger of Christ Church had been assaulted for reading a mayoral proclamation in the liberty that seemed to recognize the authority of the mayor there. However, the most dramatic confrontation between the city and cathedral came in 1684–5 when the city sheriff attempted to seize a resident of the liberty by force, an action that resulted in a riot.[17] Holding a coroner's jury within the liberty was both an important statement of the rights of the cathedral against those of the city and a potential source of conflict with the city. In 1694 twenty-three inhabitants of the liberty protested that the city coroner had executed a writ there and imprisoned one resident.

12 F. Elrington Ball (ed.), 'Extracts from the journal of Thomas Dineley', *RSAI Jn.*, 42 (1913), 290–3.   13 DCA, MR 118, f. 77.   14 RCBL, C6/1/15/1, account 1674–5.   15 Matthew Dutton, *The office and authority of sheriffs, under-sheriffs, deputies, county clerks and coroners in Ireland* (Dublin, 1721), p. 119.   16 DCA MR/36, f. 339v.; *Cal. S.P. dom., 1671–2*, p. 196. 17 DCA, MR/18, p 54b, 77a. Most of the papers on the disputes over the liberty are in RCBL, C6/126/14; Kenneth Milne, 'Restoration and reorganization, 1660–1830' in Kenneth Milne (ed.), *Christ Church cathedral, Dublin: a history* (Dublin, 2000), pp 280–1.

This, they held, was illegal.[18] It is no accident that the verdict of the jury on Quin's suicide survives among papers about the preservation of the rights of the liberty since the document proved that the holding of such legal proceedings demonstrated Christ Church's independence from the city.[19]

The coroner, who would direct proceedings at the inquest, was normally chosen by the city or the county but within the Christ Church liberty this appointment fell to the lord of the liberty, the dean. The coroner selected for the liberty was a safe pair of hands, Sir George Gilbert, an active member of the vestry of St Audoen's parish, churchwarden in 1653–4, an alderman of the city and former sheriff and lord mayor. He probably knew the deceased through their common membership of the board of aldermen in Dublin Corporation. His role was to view the body and take note of the 'length, breadth and deepness' of any wounds. He operated with a jury, which Dutton stipulated in the case of suspected suicide must be a minimum of twelve men. A jury of fifteen men was selected for Quin's inquest drawn mostly from among the residents of the liberty. They came from a wide range of backgrounds. John Bishop was deemed a 'gentleman' in a later deed. Wills reveal that William May was a merchant, Roger Thrupp a victualler, Edward Williamson a tailor, Nicholas Quaytrod a 'gentleman' and John Dickson a goldsmith. Some had lived in the city for a long time. Thomas Finglas was admitted to freedom in 1640 while Edward Stretton, a cook, had only recently arrived, becoming free in 1671 under the act to encourage Protestant strangers to settle in Dublin.[20] The role of this eclectic jury was to hear the evidence of those summoned 'to testify their knowledge touching the death'. It was, as set out in the sample charge provided by Dutton, to determine if the death was murder, suicide or an accident. In reality, the inquest was a ritual of interpretation in which the jury met to consider explanations for the actions of the dead person and anyone who could shed light on these was summoned to give evidence. A good deal was at stake since suicide was a felony and such a finding would render Quin's goods liable to confiscation by the crown.

The coroner's jury took a lenient attitude, as was increasingly the case with coroners' juries in England in the late seventeenth century.[21] They found that between 9 and 10 o'clock on the morning of 10 November, Mark Quin had taken his life but tempered the harsh finding by declaring that the balance of his mind was disturbed and that he was not *compos mentis* when the act was committed.[22] Quin's wife was doubtless relieved at the verdict since it meant that her husband's property would not be forfeit to the crown. The coroner was,

18 RCBL, C6/126/14/34. 19 RCBL, C6/126/14/33. 20 RCBL, C6/126/14/33; M.J. McEnery and Raymond Refaussé (eds), *Christ Church deeds* (Dublin, 2001), nos 1709 1722, 1750; wills are indexed in *Appendix to the 26th report of the deputy keeper of the public records in Ireland* (Dublin, 1895). 21 Michael McDonald and Terence Murphy, *Sleepless souls: suicide in early modern England* (Oxford, 1990), pp 109–43. 22 RCBL, C6/1/26/14 no. 33.

presumably, less happy since if the finding of the jury did not involve a felony, he received no fee for the inquest. The finding of the jury meant that the body could be disposed of. As Dutton explained, 'immediately upon the things [the inquest] being enquired, the bodies of such persons being dead or slain shall be buried'.[23] Since Quin had not been found to be a suicide, his body could be buried in consecrated ground and he was presumably interred in his home parish of St Michael, beside Christ Church cathedral. However, not all suicides were precluded by their actions from burial in a churchyard. In London, the vicar general could issue licences to allow suicides a Christian burial and a similar practice appears to have occurred in Dublin. Certainly the parish register for St Michan's included entries in 1674 for the burial in consecrated ground of Robert Burton, 'beadle of the parish who hanged himself' and in 1686 for Margaret Clark, 'virgin who shot herself'.[24] The practice may have been more widespread than it seems. Were it not for the entry in the parish accounts of St John's parish for the burial of Henry Fletcher 'that stabbed himself' in 1676, the entry in the burial register would reveal nothing more than an ordinary interment.[25] There was a wide range of reactions in the city to Mark Quin's suicide. Some, like the conservative churchman John Yarner, abhorred his actions while others were less sure. The Irish lord lieutenant, the earl of Essex, who himself would commit suicide in 1683 while imprisoned in the Tower of London, was later remembered as saying 'when Alderman Quin cut his throat with a razor ... he [Essex] thought it was an easy kind of death'.[26]

II

Explaining Mark Quin's taking of his own life is not a simple matter. Suicide was rare in seventeenth-century Dublin. Apart from the entries in parish registers there are a few passing references to suicides. The bills of mortality for 1683–4 provide a larger, but still far from complete, sample of suicides. These record five suicides for that year; two by hanging and one each by poisoning, choking and drowning. Fewer people died by their own hand than died on the gallows or of 'the stone' or rickets.[27] What drew attention to Quin's actions was his social standing. Mark Quin was part of the civic political and economic elite of the city. He first appeared in Dublin in early May 1644, described as a merchant, when he was admitted free of the city after having served an apprenticeship there.[28] Nothing is known with certainty of his background. Although there

23 Dutton, *Coroners*, p. 107.   24 Paul S. Seaver, 'Suicide and the vicar general in London: a mystery solved?' in Jeffrey Watt (ed.), *From sin to insanity: suicide in early modern Europe* (New York, 2004), pp 25–47; H.F. Berry (ed.), *The registers of the parish of St Michan* (2 vols, Dublin, 1907–9), ii, 262, 360.   25 James Mills (ed.), *The register of the parish of St John the Evangelist, Dublin, 1619–99* (Dublin, 1905; repr. 2000), pp 161, 271.   26 *Cal. S.P. dom.*, *1683*, p. 202.   27 Gilbert (ed.), *CARD*, v, 611.   28 Ibid., iii, 423.

were a number of Quin families in the city Mark cannot be securely linked
to any of them. There are, however, hints of his background. In 1654 Dennis
Quinne, a Dublin merchant, issued a token stamped with the symbol of a
winged horse, indicating the place where he traded. The same symbol was
shown on a token of Mark Quin, apothecary, issued in the same year.[29] It seems
likely that Mark and Dennis, living in the same house, were closely related; they
were probably brothers. However, little is known about Dennis. In 1655–6 he
was churchwarden in St Audoen's parish, suggesting he was still in the High
Street area, and he died in 1656.[30] One other piece of information about Dennis
is known. In 1652 he married Ann Pinmore in St John's church, Dublin.[31] This
is the first, and last, mention of the Pinmore family in the register, suggesting
that they were recent arrivals in the parish whereas Dennis was probably
already living there. It is, therefore, possible to identify who Mark Quin's father
was since there was only one Quin family residing in the parish in the early
seventeenth century, albeit briefly. Thomas Quin first appears on the parish
cess lists in 1634, suggesting that he had recently moved to the parish, living
in a middling-size house in Fishamble Street. Thomas died and was buried in
St John's parish in May 1639 although his widow continued to live there, at
least up to 1643.[32] Only two Thomas Quins appear in the lists of freemen of the
city and the more likely to be Mark's father is a tailor admitted to freedom by
apprenticeship at Easter 1593.[33] Thomas played little part in the political life of
the city nor did he rise to any prominence in the guild of tailors. These hints
locate Mark Quin as part of the comfortable but not rich middling sort, one of
the Dublin craft-workers with an understanding of the structures of the guild
system and of the workings of the city that would characterize him later in life.

After his admission to freedom, Mark settled into the life of Dublin and in
November 1645 he married Mary Roche of St Werburgh's parish. According
to the marriage licence he was then living in the parish of St Nicholas Without
and was described as an apothecary.[34] The Roche family do not appear in
the surviving parochial material for St Werburgh's. There are two possible
candidates for Mary's father from the freemen's list, John Roche a tailor
admitted to freedom in 1592 and James a merchant admitted in the same year.
Neither of these people became active in civic or guild life. Mark and his wife,

29 R.A.S. Macalister, 'Irish traders' tokens in the collection of the Royal Irish Academy',
RIA Proc., 40 (1931–2), 71.   30 Maighréad Ní Mhurchadha (ed.), *The vestry records of the
parish of St Audoen, Dublin* (Dublin, 2012), p. 164; Arthur Vicars, *Index to the prerogative
wills of Ireland* (Dublin, 1897), p. 389.   31 Mills (ed.), *The register of the parish of St John
the Evangelist*, p. 79 where the name appears as Dennis Qwein.   32 Mills (ed.), *The register
of the parish of St John*, p. 32; Raymond Gillespie (ed.), *The vestry records of the parish of St
John the Evangelist, Dublin, 1595–1658* (Dublin, 2002), pp 89, 128, 134, 137, 152. A John
Quin, merchant, was also associated with the parish, renting property from it, but did not live
there.   33 *CARD*, ii, 264.   34 Royal College of Physicians of Ireland, MS/16; *Appendix to
the 26th report of the deputy keeper of the public records in Ireland.*

therefore, came from similar backgrounds of modest Dublin craft-working stock with little political engagement.

Mark Quin was certainly ambitious. It may have been his drive for advancement that led him into the merchants' guild, though other apothecaries (such as Thomas Smith, Gerard Colley and Sankey Sullyard) had found a home there earlier. Being a member of the guild had both advantages and problems. It placed restrictions on the technical knowledge of Mark Quin as apothecary at a time when medicine was being increasingly influenced by Paraclesian 'chemical' medicine, in which the apothecary had a larger part to play. Some apothecaries in Dublin practised these ideas by manufacturing distillates and other chemical remedies but it required specialist training. The excavations among the detritus of an early seventeenth-century apothecary's shop in Kevin Street has revealed equipment, such as alembics, for the preparation of such 'chemical' remedies.[35] How much Quin would have known of the technicalities of drugs, as opposed to simply importing and retailing remedies as a merchant, is uncertain. However, the advantage of belonging to the merchants' or Trinity guild was that it was the premier guild in the city and had control over the most senior offices, including the mayoralty, and hence could be a route to rapid social advancement. That may have been its attraction for Mark Quin.

One sign of his ambition, and his prospering business, is that by 1648 he had moved to St Michael's parish, where he acquired a house on High Street.[36] In 1652 his eldest son, Thomas, was born there.[37] Socially, this was a considerable step upwards. The parish of St Nicholas Without was on the edge of the city, comprising Francis Street and St Patrick Street wards that were mainly occupied by modest artisans, especially cloth workers. According to the 1664 hearth tax returns roughly half of the houses in this parish were single hearth structures. Almost all of the Francis Street area comprised such houses while St Patrick's Street, closer to St Patrick's cathedral, generally had a larger proportion of three and four hearth houses. St Michael's, while not the richest area of the city, was certainly more prosperous. Here only a sixth of the houses were one hearth buildings while the most common house had three hearths.[38] As Thomas Denton visiting the city in 1687 described High Street it was located west of Castle Street which 'is the most considerable street in the town where the richest merchants, goldsmiths, mercers and other tradesmen of eminent dealing dwell and also the most taverns, in respect of the lord deputy's court and the courts of justice not far from here'. To the east of High Street was industrial Dublin located in the earl of Meath's liberty where the cloth trade was located around Francis Street.[39] This intermediate area between the high-status world to the

35 Alan Hayden, 'Pots, phials and potions', *Archaeology Ireland*, 32:2, issue 124 (Summer 2018), 15–18. 36 DCA, MR 116, p. 8. 37 He was said to be sixteen when he entered Trinity College, Dublin, in 1668 (TCD, MUN/V/23/1, p. 59). 38 *57th report of the deputy keeper of the public records in Ireland* (Dublin, 1936), p. 560. 39 Thomas Denton, *A*

east and the more artisan dominated one on the west was a mixture of both groups and this was reflected in the housing along High Street as recorded in the hearth tax of 1665. Quin's house was clearly a substantial one with five hearths but it was set among houses of its immediate neighbours that ranged between one and twelve hearths. Taking ten houses on either side as Quin's immediate neighbours only two had one hearth each and the most common size of house had two or three hearths, which accounted for half the buildings in this street.[40] When Quin's house was rated for the cess in 1648 it was assessed at 13*s*. in a parish where the average cess was 10*s*. 4*d*. suggesting that it was somewhat, but not much, above the average.[41] Measured by the occupations listed in the grants of freedom, Quin's neighbours were a diverse group including two tailors, two masons, a weaver, a merchant, a trunk maker, a plate worker and a cooper. Most, like Mark, were recent arrivals in the parish since most of the grants of freedom date from the late 1650s. None of Mark's immediate neighbours from the 1648 cess book appears among his immediate neighbours in the hearth money roll of 1665, indicating a high turnover of population in the area.[42]

Mark Quin and his family would remain in the parish of St Michael until his death in 1674. According to a note of the aldermen in 1667 he lived in Cornmarket ward rather than High Street ward within the parish but this may have been a recent development since Lewis Desmerin's name was originally assigned to that ward but was crossed out and replaced by Quin's.[43] The explanation may lie in fact that in 1661 Quin had made a deed of gift to the parish of St Michael of a rent of £2 12*s*. charged on a house called the Flying Horse in High Street. In the 1650s this is where Quin resided and the horse was depicted on the trade token issued by him in 1654. It seems likely that in 1661 Quin had leased the house where he was residing and moved, probably to larger premises, reflecting his new status as alderman and likely enhanced financial position, eastwards towards Cornmarket.[44] In the years after 1660 he became increasingly prominent in the world of the parish. He was an auditor of the parish accounts in 1667 while in 1665 the parish had entrusted him with their valuables by leaving the two parish chests in his house where they remained until after his death. In 1670 he was elected one of five trustees to manage the assets of the parish.[45] He was also known to use his position in the corporation to the advantage of the parish, as in 1663 when he pressed the corporation to repair the water conduit at St Michael's church.[46]

perambulation of Cumberland, 1687–8, ed. Angus Winchester and Mary Wane (Woodbridge, 2002), pp 532, 535. **40** Brian Gurrin, 'The hearth tax rolls for Dublin city, 1663', *Anal. Hib.*, 38 (2004), 67–8. **41** DCA, MR/16, p. 8. **42** Ibid. **43** DCA, MR/18, p. 32b. **44** 'The history of the church and parish of St Michael the Archangel, Dublin', *Irish Builder*, 33 (1891), 91, 184; Macalister, 'Irish traders' tokens', 71. RCBL, P118/5/1, list of benefactions. The annual benefaction for the support of six widows was paid until the early nineteenth century. **45** RCBL, P118/5/1, pp 35, 36, 89, vestry orders, 5 Apr. 1670. **46** *CARD*, iv, 262.

During the 1650s and 1660s Mark Quin's economic fortunes increased. The striking of a trade token in 1654 as a substitute for small change suggests that he was operating in the retail market for drugs rather than importing wholesale quantities. If so, he may have profited from the plague in Dublin in the early 1650s. There is no evidence that would allow quantification of his financial position. In 1672 he was among those described as 'the best estated in the city' but what this meant is uncertain. After his suicide there is a guess by Daniel Healy, a discoverer who hoped to obtain part of Quin's estate, that he was worth £700 a year beside his stock and goods.[47] There are indirect indications of an improvement in Quin's finances after 1660. As the profitability of many of the Dublin mercantile elite increased after the Restoration, they looked for an outlet for surplus capital both as a way of keeping it relatively safe, in the absence of banks, and in the hope of making a return. One strategy was to lend money at interest either to other merchants who needed working capital or to landowners needing to finance their estates. A mechanism for doing this was through the Dublin statute staple. Quin did not lend any money on the Dublin staple during the late 1640s and early 1650s suggesting he had little to invest in this way. In 1657, however, he entered two bonds totalling £600 in the staple which, given that bonds were usually entered into for twice the amount borrowed, suggests loans of £300. This was followed by a lull in his lending activities until 1665 when he again entered two bonds totalling £200. However, the following year he entered four bonds for £1,240.[48] This suggests a profitable business with a growing surplus of cash.

Money lending was not the only way that Quin could utilize the growing free balances in his business – land provided an alternative type of investment, with the added advantage that it yielded not only a return on the investment but also conferred social status on its owner. Quin's main interest was in acquiring property within the city. A list of claims lodged in 1663 by those wishing to be regarded as 'innocents' in the Restoration land settlement records Mark Quin as having nine houses in Dublin.[49] His connections with St Patrick's and Christ Church cathedrals certainly provided him with the opportunity to obtain leases of the cathedrals' urban property. He held a lease of land in Golden Lane from the vicars' choral of St Patrick's until 1666.[50] He also held three tenements with a brick house in Back Lane, which must have been near his own house, from Christ Church cathedral in the 1660s for which he paid a rent of £10 18s. 4d.[51] This property he apparently leased to James Uniack of

47 *Cal. S.P. dom., 1673–5*, p. 429; *Cal. S.P. dom., 1672*, p. 130.   48 Jane Ohlmeyer and Éamonn Ó Ciardha (eds), *The Irish statute staple books, 1596–1687* (Dublin, 1998), p. 138. 49 *An abstract of the claims of all persons claiming as innocents in the city, county of the city and county of Dublin* (Dublin, 1663), p. 49.   50 J.B. Leslie, 'Calendar of leases and deeds of St Patrick's cathedral, Dublin, 1660–89', *RSAI Jn.*, 65 (1935) 35.   51 RCBL, C6/1/15/1, proctor's accounts 1666–7, 1667–8, 1671–2.

Youghal for a rent of £30 with a fine of £100, thus making a substantial profit on his investment.[52] In the late 1660s he leased a house (said to be 'lately built') from another significant urban property owner, St Anne's guild, at the corner of Cook Street and Schoolhouse Lane.[53] While he had access to a significant land bank within the city, that of the corporation itself, he showed little interest in exploiting that opportunity. In an attempt to alleviate its financial problems in the years after 1660 the corporation began leasing some of its property holdings at St Stephen's Green and at Oxmantown Green as part of planned developments and a number of members of the corporation acquired property in these allocations. Mark Quin was ambivalent about the project despite the fact that he was on the corporation committee that had organized it. He drew the first plot on the east side of St Stephen's Green in 1665 but disposed of it by 1667.[54] Outside the city Quin's only property investment was a lease of land in the townland of Johnstown in the parish of Kilcoole, County Wicklow, that he held from the local landowner, the earl of Meath, by 1668. On this he had built three houses of more than one hearth.[55] He clearly had contacts in this area since two of his staple loans in 1665 were to a Wicklow resident, Daniel Cullen. His medical connections may also have introduced him to another Dubliner who was a property owner in this parish, the surgeon general of the army, Sir Abraham Yarner.

Quin's urban property holding was relatively modest. In comparison to his fellow alderman and next door neighbour on High Street, George Surdeville, a tailor, Quin signally failed to maximize his opportunities in the property market. Surdeville became free of Dublin in 1647 and by 1654 was building up a property portfolio with grants from the corporation. In 1654 he had leases from the city for lands at Baldoyle and Tagdoe in Kildare. Surdeville would also acquire property in the corporation developments in St Stephen's Green, Dame Street, Oxmantown and St Stephen's Street.[56] Quin's other close friend, William Whitshed, who in his 1664 will referred to Quin and Surdeville as 'my very loving and dear friends', listed significant urban property in his will in Cook Street, High Street, Cockhill, St Stephen's Green and Winetavern Street as well as his own house in St Michael's parish.[57]

In parallel with his growing economic standing Mark Quin became an established figure in the political life of Dublin. Within the Trinity guild he was warden in 1650–1 and master in 1655–7.[58] His earliest appearance in the

52 R.G. Fitzgerald, 'Some old County Cork families. I The Uniackes of Youghal. Part v Uniacke of Mount Uniacke', *JCHAS*, 3 (1894), 233–4.   53 RIA, MS 12 D 1, pp 291, 297, 348, 371, 406, 416, 430, 448, 471, 498.   54 DCA, MR/36, ff 248v., 281v.; *CARD*, iv, 257, 303, 339–40.   55 Liam Price (ed.), 'The hearth money roll for County Wicklow', *JRSAI Jn.*, 61 (1931), 174.   56 *CARD*, iv, 56, 61, 75, 79, 80, 89, 253, 267–8, 302, 331, 371, 407–8, 437; v, 5; DCA, MR/36, ff 290, 307, 323, 332v., 364, 367, 391v.   57 NAI, Prerogative will book, 1644–84, pp 36–8.   58 H.F. Berry, 'The records of the Dublin gild of merchants known as the Gild of the Holy Trinity', *RSAI Jn.*, 30 (1900), 67. He was charged with custody of four silver cups for

corporation records was in 1649, sitting in the commons, when he was one of those appointed to survey Clonturk before a mortgage was made of it. This was a mere five years after completing his apprenticeship and his rapid advancement was probably helped by the political chaos of the late 1640s and early 1650s. Between 1650 and 1652 he appeared only a handful of times in the corporation records. He was nominated by the commons to undertake several of the routine jobs that aspirants to political office needed to master. He was an auditor of the city accounts in 1650, 1651, 1652 and 1653 and assessor of the military cess in 1650 and 1651. He organized the banquet for the Cromwellian governor of Dublin in 1651.[59] By 1654 he was allocated more interesting tasks including the recovery of money owed by the Commonwealth to Dublin, enquiring into foreigners in the city, investigating the collection of fee farm rents and lobbying for the reduction of the hated military cess.[60] In 1658 he became an alderman admitting him to the political elite of the city at a relatively young age. Again, he was probably helped by the political vacuum of the late 1650s or perhaps by a patron within the aldermanic bench. As the military Cromwellian party that had governed the city in the early 1650s became increasingly marginalized this provided an opportunity for others to entry the political fray.[61] According to the signatures in the Monday book that recorded the meetings of the aldermanic board, Mark was also a regular attender at the board after his election in 1658. Between his election and the end of 1661 he missed only five meetings out of seventeen.[62]

What Quin's politics were during the 1650s is difficult to tell. He did not align himself with the radical Cromwellian party that had dominated Dublin Corporation in the early part of the 1650s.[63] He seems to have been a rather conservative moderate, interested in the affairs of the city but with little liking for radical republicanism or the Cromwellian military who dominated civic politics before 1655. He was, by contrast, friendly with the royalist colonel John Hewetson of Kildare, who bequeathed to him and his wife a mourning suit in his will of 1656.[64] He had no qualms about signing the petition of 1655 against the changes in the customs imposed on Ireland from London which suggests more interest in local concerns than wider ideologies.[65]

Nothing is known about Mark's ecclesiastical preferences in the 1650s but if he attended the church in St Michael's parish, which was close to his house, he would have encountered William Pilsworth who ministered there. Pilsworth continued to use the Book of Common Prayer long after its official prohibition

the guild in 1653 (DCA, Gilbert MS 78, vol. 1, p. 127).   59 DCA, MR/35, f. 9.   60 *CARD*, iii, 504, 505, 514; iv, 9, 18, 29, 33, 51, 54, 64, 70, 72, 75, 77, 101.   61 Ibid., v, 140.   62 DCA, MR/18.   63 For the politics see T.C. Barnard, *Cromwellian Ireland: English government and reform in Ireland* (Oxford, 1975), pp 77–90.   64 John Hewetson, 'The Hewetsons of the county of Kildare', *RSAI Jn.*, 39 (1909), 149.   65 *Cal. S.P. Ire., 1647–60*, p. 572.

in 1647 which would certainly have appealed to a conservative parishioner.[66] A moderate royalism linked to a conservative episcopal outlook would certainly explain why Quin was one of those who was appointed to purge the aldermanic bench of potentially disloyal radicals after the Restoration.[67] Whatever his political and ecclesiastical position during the 1650s he was careful after the Restoration to insure himself and his property against allegations that he may have co-operated with the enemies of the crown. He applied for a decree of innocence under the Act of Settlement of 1663, effectively asking for a pardon for any wrongdoing in the 1650s or earlier and this was granted on 30 June 1663.[68]

Quin moved rapidly through the political ranks of the city after the Restoration. His attendances at the aldermanic board were infrequent, with only three in 1662–6, but he did serve on a number of Corporation committees at the same time suggesting that he may have been more active than his attendance at the board suggests.[69] He developed an expertise in the city's complex financial accounting. In 1655 he was nominated to a committee to simplify the keeping of the city rentals and in 1666 he was on another committee to simplify the city accounts. Almost every year after 1654 he was one of those appointed to audit the city accounts and he was omitted from the audit only for the years when his attendance at the aldermanic board was limited suggesting he may not have been in Dublin for long periods.[70] He was also treasurer of the city in 1669–70.[71] Quin also understood the complexities of land management. It was he, for instance, who in 1662 unravelled the complexities of the 1651 mortgage on the property held by the corporation at Clonturk. The fact that he had been one of the surveyors in 1649 at the negotiation of the mortgage may have aided him here.[72] He also became the man who dealt with renewals of city leases and especially in dealing with reversionary leases.[73]

This commitment to the life of the city was rewarded in April 1667 when he was elected as lord mayor for the ensuing year and was sworn in in October.[74] As was commented of him, and a number of other aldermen, in 1672 they were 'the principal of the aldermen and the most constant in their attendance on the city business'.[75] As lord mayor he attempted to improve the administration of the city. He required that the city accounts be audited more promptly. He demanded that documents be set out in proper form and instituted a reorganization of the

66 St John D. Seymour, *The puritans in Ireland, 1647–1661* (Oxford, 1921), pp 115–16, 167–8. 67 *Cal. S.P. Ire., 1663–5*, p. 499. 68 *19th report of the deputy keeper of the public records in Ireland* (Dublin, 1887), p. 63; *15th report of the commissioners appointed to enquire into the public records of Ireland* (Dublin, 1828), pp 426, 535, 690; Geraldine Tallon (ed.), *Court of claims: submissions and evidence 1663* (Dublin, 2006), p. 185. 69 DCA, MR/18. 70 *CARD*, iv, 75, 362; DCA, MR/36, ff 38, 70, 87v., 106, 120v., 139, 190, 222v., 236, 249, 282v. 71 DCA, MR/36, f. 329v.; *CARD*, iv, 449. 72 DCA, MR/36, f. 198v. For the mortgage DCA, EXP/1201, 1202. 73 *CARD*, iv, 218, 220, 225, 227–8, 228–9, 229–30, 230–1, 238–9, 469; DCA, MR/18, p. 16a. 74 *Cal S.P. Ire., 1666–9*, p. 461; *CARD*, iv, 413, 422. 75 *Cal. S.P. dom., 1672*, p. 131.

city archives, then comprising some forty leases scattered in six large chests. He obliged aldermen to attend the aldermanic board, keeping a record of those attendances during his mayoralty and fining those who did not appear.[76] He was also sensitive to more symbolic manifestations of the city's authority. He reinstituted the Riding of the Franchises that had fallen into disuse and Quin himself led the Riding of the Franchises in his mayoral year, which must have been accompanied by considerable conviviality given that he was allowed £7 10s. for the cost of it.[77] Again it was Quin who finally resolved the problem of the ownership of the great mace presented to the corporation in 1666 and required that it should be carried before the mayor.[78] All this cost money and it was in Quin's mayoralty that the provision for the lord mayor was increased to £500 a year to allow him to 'keep such hospitality as might be to the credit of the mayor and dignity of the city'.[79] This awareness of the status of the city and its rituals suggests that Quin understood the importance of the honour of the city and of being able to make the rights and powers of the mayor and corporation visible on appropriate occasions. This sense of corporatism was central to Quin's understanding of himself and his position as a citizen of Dublin who was rising on the social ladder and needed validation of that new position.

In response to his newly found position in the city after 1660 Mark Quin began to behave as might be expected of one at the pinnacle of the urban hierarchy and in line with his new self-perceived social worth. Apart from his obligations in the parish, in 1661 he supported the poor by establishing an endowment that would yield £2 12s. od. a year to support a number of poor widows in the parish. This was a conservative bequest, limited to the 'deserving poor' and requiring the widows to attend the parish church every Sunday.[80] In 1668 he was an early subscriber to the foundation of King's Hospital school, contributing £100 and an annuity of £5 a year, promising a further £100, making a commitment that made him one of the largest benefactors of the project.[81] Mark Quin transformed himself from urban trader of modest proportions to city benefactor concerned with the good of the city as well as with his own profit.

III

In the immediate aftermath of Quin's sudden death in 1674 the search for explanations began. The most obvious explanation for the suicide was financial difficulties. That seems to have been in the mind of some of the vestry of St

---

76 *CARD*, iv, 433, 441–2; DCA, MR/18, p 31b, 32a. The reorganization of the archives by the clerk of the Tholsel, Sir William Davies, produced the parchment book of leases: see Mary Clark, *Serving the city: the Dublin city managers and town clerks, 1230–2006* (2nd ed., Dublin, 2006), p. 24. 77 DCA, MR/36, f. 289; *CARD*, iv, 442–3. 78 DCA, MR/18, p. 31b; *CARD*, iv, pp 424, 440–1. 79 *CARD*, iv, 430. 80 'History of the church and parish of St Michael', pp 91, 184. 81 *CARD*, iv, 492; Frederick L. Falkiner, *The foundation of the hospital*

Michael's parish. When the parish chest, which had been left in Quin's house for safe keeping in 1665, was recovered in December 1674, in the wake of the suicide, the entire vestry gathered to record that they had

> received the church chest which was in Alderm[a]n Mark Quines into the parish church and upon view unto the chest being publically opened do find that ye money therein to be according to ye books of the churchwardens accounts and ye writings therein to the books according to the church books called the Book of Evidences.

Clearly some were worried that money may have been missing and to prevent this in the future it was resolved that no one would have control over the chest for such a prolonged period again that might permit fraud. It was to be kept on a yearly basis by one of the churchwardens.[82] There are good reasons to believe that money was not the motivation for Quin's actions. After his death the estate attracted the attention of Daniel Healy. Healy was a discoverer who sought out property concealed from the crown and then as a reward asked for a grant of some or all of it. The coroner's jury had found Mark Quin's mind to be unbalanced at the time of the death, but if Healy could convince the authorities that he had committed suicide while sane then his goods would be forfeited to the crown, suicide being a crime. Healy hoped that by engineering a change in the verdict he would be in line to share the profits and he was conspiring at a high level in the London administration to this end, writing to Secretary of State Williamson in December 1674: 'I desire your honour will take care of Alderman Mark Quin and his estate'.[83] If the estate had been encumbered by debt, it would not have been worth Healy's efforts but Healy believed that it was worth £700 a year beside his stock and goods.[84] One final indicator that money was not Quin's problem is that his widow, Mary, was left well provided for by his will and she certainly had cash on hand after the suicide. In 1675, for instance, she made two loans to her son, and Mark's heir, Thomas, who would inherit the business and trade as apothecary. The size of these loans is not known but the bonds entered in the Dublin staple for them totalled £2,000. Given that bonds were usually for double the sum lent the loans were probably for £1,000, a very considerable sum for a widow to find unless it was recently inherited.[85] All this suggests that money was not Mark Quin's problem, and that he had died comfortably off.

If money was not Quin's problem then some form of disgrace, possibly with a sexual tinge to add spice, might have been. The Quins had their fair share of sexual indiscretions in the years after Mark's death. His daughter, Mary,

and free school of King Charles II, Oxmantown, Dublin (Dublin, 1906), pp 59–60. 82 RCBL, P118/5/1, vestry order, 21 Dec. 1674. 83 *Cal. S.P. dom., 1673–5*, p. 442. 84 Ibid., p. 429. 85 Ohlmeyer and Ó Ciardha (eds), *Irish statute staple books*, p. 138.

married Thomas Whitshed and their son, William, continued the Whitshed
family connection with the law and politics. His position as a judge led to
a conflict with Jonathan Swift in 1720 giving rise to a number of scurrilous
squibs written by Swift against Whitshed.[86] As Swift put it in a verse placed in
Whitshed's mouth

> I'm not the grandson of that Ass Quin;
> Nor can you prove it, Mr Pasquin,
> My Grand-dame had Gallants by the Twenties,
> And bore my mother by a Prentice
> This, when my Grandsire knew; they tell us he
> In Christ-Church cut his throat for jealousy
> And, since the Alderman was mad you say,
> Then, I must be so too, *ex traduce*.[87]

Where Swift obtained this story is not known. There is no contemporary
evidence of its accuracy but there is enough circumstantial detail to suggest
that he did not invent it. Swift may have picked it up as gossip and later used
it to good effect. It is possible that what Swift heard was a corrupt version of a
slightly different story not about Mark but about his son, James. In a generally
unreliable account of Mark's grandson (also called James) it was claimed that
the younger James 'was the illegitimate issue of a criminal correspondence', his
father having unknowingly contracted a bigamous marriage with his mother.[88]
This illegitimacy had been alleged in the context of the contested will of the
elder James Quin who had left his property to his son, the younger James.
The basis for these allegations was never established since the case never came
to trial but the allegations may certainly have fed later stories about sexual
misbehaviour within the Quin family and have been transferred through gossip
to Mark Quin.[89]

A third possibility was aired by the discoverer Daniel Healy some ten days
after Mark Quin's suicide. According to Healy, the coroner's jury had found
incorrectly and 'Quin was never distracted nor ever seen distracted in his life'.
Two days before the event Quin was

> dining in this city with several gentlemen, he propounded to them all
> the question that he had read in scripture, Blessed is the man that made
> himself a sacrifice to the Lord, and the holy fathers sacrificed their children
> to the Lord and so he thought it better a man himself should sacrifice his

86 For the complexities of this see Rosemary Raughter, 'The Whitsheds of Dublin: family
ambition, scandal and the dean's revenge', *Local History Journal* (2015), 45–53.   87 Harold
Williams (ed.), *The poems of Jonathan Swift* (2nd ed., 3 vols, Oxford, 1958), i, 350.   88 *The
life of Mr James Quin, comedian* (London, 1766), p. 3.   89 T.P.C. Kirkpatrick, *Henry Quin*

own body also. Besides he went to several in the city in as good sense and reason as any man could be and took them by the hands and said, God be with you for this is the last time you will see me.[90]

Unfortunately, Quin has left nothing that would provide an insight into his religious life but a religious motivation for the suicide might help to explain why the alderman chose Christ Church cathedral as the place to kill himself. John Yarner may have known something when he referred to Quin acting 'desperately' since despair was in the seventeenth century used as a theological description associated with self-harm but it also had secular meanings.[91] If religious belief was a factor in suggesting suicide to Quin, then presumably something must have triggered that bout of religious melancholy. Religious introspection was not unusual in late seventeenth-century Dublin. James Barry, for instance, a youth of fifteen in the Dublin of the mid-1660s, discovered religion as a result of reading the Bible. Daily he retreated into seclusion to meditate on pious books, in particular on Richard Baxter's *Call to the unconverted*, and comparing his own experience with the new spiritual reading. His experience was so transformative that he converted from the established church to Independency.[92] Another Dublin Protestant in 1683, also in search for salvation, made an index to his copy of Samuel Mather's *The figures or types of the Old Testament* that would allow him rapid answers to important spiritual questions such as 'whether thou art under the first or second Adam'.[93] Thus religious introspection was not unusual but in Quin's case it is difficult to see what might have triggered it. Such introspection was usually characteristic of the godly end of the religious spectrum yet what is known about Quin suggests that he was more at home in the middle of that spectrum. There does not seem to have been any change in the incumbent of St Michael's that might have awakened Quin's religious sensibilities through a more evangelical preaching style though it is possible that he attended another church where he encountered such preaching. Religious introspection alone is not a convincing explanation for Quin's actions though it may have been a contributory factor.

What may have triggered a crisis in Quin's mind was not religion but local political events. On 3 April 1672, at a thinly attended meeting of the city corporation (only four aldermen being in attendance), Mark Quin together with six other aldermen and the recorder, Sir William Davies, were expelled from the city council on the strength of a petition of the commons. They were replaced by five new aldermen who were selected by the lord mayor, Sir John Totty, and

M.D. (Dublin, 1919), p. 10.   **90** *Cal. S.P. dom., 1673–5*, p. 428. I have not found an exact scriptural parallel for this.   **91** For example, the discussion of despair in Robert Burton, *The anatomy of melancholy*, ed. Holbrook Jackson (3 vols, London, 1932), iii, 393–4; McDonald and Murphy, *Sleepless souls*, pp 35–40, 43–4.   **92** James Barry, *A reviving cordial for a sin-sick despairing soul in the time of temptation* (2nd ed., Edinburgh, 1722), p. 23.   **93** The copy

hastily sworn in. There were various explanations of this sudden coup. The appointment of a Catholic, the lord lieutenant's secretary, Ellis Leighton, as recorder to replace William Davies led some later commentators to characterize Quin and his comrades as martyrs for the Protestant cause but this was largely a figment of their fevered imaginations.[94] In reality, it seems to have been a factional dispute within the corporation. Its origins lay in November 1671 when the lord lieutenant, Lord Berkeley, tried to increase the authority of the royal administration over Dublin Corporation by imposing a set of rules under the terms of the Act of Explanation of 1665. These reduced the powers of the commons in making appointments to city offices and increased the role of the state, the mayor and the aldermen in this process. It required the aldermen take a series of oaths, including an oath that it was not lawful to take up arms against the king. Most of the Dublin aldermen had no difficulty in taking these oaths but some may have been cautious about the implications of doing so as to swear the oaths was to accept new controls on the city's authority.[95] Quin may have had more serious reservations about taking the oath, seeing it as an infringement of the power and status of the city, which could reflect on him. While most took the required oaths on 6 December, Quin and some of those who would later be involved in the controversy prevaricated until 18 December but finally did agree.[96] Others had reservations and the rules proved particularly unpopular with the guilds. The rules did not prove workable and were withdrawn on 24 March 1671, although they would eventually be replaced by the 'New rules' devised by the earl of Essex in September 1672.

What Berkeley's attempts to control the corporation had done was to stir up a debate about the relationship between central government and the corporation and to scrutinize the extent to which traditional civic rights had been infringed by Berkeley's actions. The petitions and counter petitions that flew between the excluded aldermen and the privy council in the wake of the dismissals all dwelt on this aspect of the case. The defence of the actions of the new aldermanic board against Quin and his colleagues was based on their 'constant loyalty', implying that the actions of Quin and others were questionable. They were accused of 'desiring to alter the ancient governance of the city and to lodge the same in a few hands, whereof they hoped to be the major part themselves, privately and unknown to the lord mayor ... framed several rules and orders for the better regulating, as they pretend, of the city and the same were delivered to the lord lieutenant by the said Sir William [Davies]' and many of these rules

is now in NLI, Dix collection.   **94** [Robert Ware], *The second part of foxes and firebrands* (Dublin, 1682), pp 110–17. Ware clearly knew Quin since he had dealings with him in 1670 about renewing a city lease, DCA MR/18, p. 53a. *A full and impartial account of all the secret consults, negotiations, stratagems and intrigues of the Romish party in Ireland* (London, 1689), pp 13–14.   **95** *CARD*, v, 548–54. This is discussed by J.R. Hill, *From patriots to unionists: Dublin civic politics and Irish Protestant patriotism, 1660–1840* (Oxford, 1997), pp 49–56.   **96** DCA, MR/18, p. 68A; *CARD*, v, 555.

were deemed 'destructive to the ancient constitution of the government'.[97] By contrast Davies, Quin and others defended themselves, complaining that Totty's actions were 'contrary to justice and the ancient usages of the city', a breach of the ancient constitution as they understood it. Others saw Totty as the problem, describing him as 'a person of as much disloyalty as any about this city'.[98] For Quin, whose career as civic official rested on his loyalty to the city, this was a dangerous debate.

Some alleged that in this dispute other, more personal, elements were involved. An account of the politics of the corporation written four days before the dismissals claimed that the debate focused not on abstract ideas but on an attempt by the commons to have Sir William Davies dismissed as recorder and on the resistance of the aldermen to this move.[99] Davies was a long-standing civic servant both as recorder and clerk of the Tholsel and he was a figure of some power within Dublin.[100] It was certainly rumoured that the lord mayor, Sir John Totty, wanted the office of clerk of the Tholsel for himself so as to pursue his 'secret designs of profit and advantage', which led him to 'assume a power never before exercised' with 'subversion of the good government of city' and that this lay at the root of the dismissal of Davies and the aldermen.[101] Others alleged that Davies, keen to ingratiate himself with the lord lieutenant, in the hope of some reward, had engineered the passage of rules.[102] He may have had other motives as it was claimed that the alterations to city government would facilitate the grant to Davies of a long lease of the water revenues of the city.[103]

The matter rumbled on over the summer of 1671 and all meetings of the city council were deferred until matters were resolved. The aldermen took out a writ of mandamus against the corporation and began legal proceedings in King's Bench against their expulsion while Davies travelled to London to plead his case before the privy council.[104] By royal command the case was heard before the privy council in September. After a three-day hearing, it was ordered that the dismissed aldermen and Davies should be restored to office and that all references to the dismissal should be deleted from the corporation's records. However, this was far from an end of the matter. The corporation refused to delete the record of the incident until they were forced to do so two years later, by which time Quin was dead.[105] In August 1672 the earl of Essex observed 'both sides much exasperated against each other and unwilling to come to an amicable end'. The matter flared up again in 1672 when the 'new rules' introduced by the earl of Essex to replace Berkeley's withdrawn rules proved equally unpopular and protests resulted. As Essex commented in October 1673

---

97 *Cal. S.P. dom., 1672*, p. 153. 98 Airy (ed.), *Essex papers*, p. 51. 99 *Cal. S.P. dom., 1671–2*, p. 257. 100 Clark, *Serving the city*, pp 24, 34–5. 101 *Cal. S.P. dom., 1672*, p. 130; *CARD*, v, 12–13. 102 *Cal. S.P. dom., 1672*, pp 127–31. 103 Airy (ed.), *Essex papers*, pp 103–4. 104 DCA, MR/18, p. 82b; *Cal. S.P. dom., 1671–2*, p. 363; *Cal. S.P. dom., 1672*, p. 154. 105 DCA, MR/18, p. 64; *Cal. S.P. dom., 1671–2*, pp 644–5; *CARD*, v, 73.

'many jealousies have lately arise among the citizens' with the city revenues being compromised. This phase of the dispute culminated in the imprisonment of Dr Dudley Loftus, a judge of the prerogative court and a master in chancery, and a welter of petitions and counter petitions about the rules flowed again. Into 1673 things did not improve with Essex noting that the divisions 'rather increase than abate' and the following year he remarked that 'several of their fractious and troublesome men ... begin to stir again' in 'little cabals'. The ring leaders of the dispute frequented not their shops but the coffee houses to stir up trouble.[106] Indeed, even in 1675 Essex thought he could detect further stirrings of trouble in the city.[107] For Quin, the matter must have been a source of continual annoyance in his last years.

This long drawn out civic political crisis clearly had a profound effect on Mark Quin. At its simplest it fractured personal relations. Totty and Quin could not be said to have been intimate friends but they were of similar backgrounds and had common ambitions. Totty, the son of a yeoman from Upton in Cheshire, had become free of Dublin as a glover in 1647 following his brother, Thomas, who was apprenticed to the Dublin merchant Henry Bennet in the late 1620s.[108] Like Quin, ambition had taken him not into the glovers' guild as would have been normal but into the merchants' or Trinity guild, which opened political office to him. Quin and Totty had both been masters of the Trinity guild and were active on the aldermanic board. In 1651 they co-operated on the assessment of the military cess for Dublin and in 1664 both had been sent by the corporation to thank the city's agent for his work in London and to present him with a piece of plate. Clearly they had, at least, been able to co-operate with each other in some areas of life. They both lived in the parish of St Michael and in 1670 became two of five trustees of the parish. In 1671 they were the churchwardens of the parish.[109] After the expulsion of Quin by Totty, it is difficult to see how they could have remained friendly. In the longer term the crisis also affected Quin's relationship with the other aldermen. In the immediate aftermath of his reinstatement to the aldermanic board in September 1672, he resumed his usual pattern of attendance at the board, missing only one meeting but after February 1673 his enthusiasm waned and he attended only three meetings out of ten over the following eighteenth months.[110] He did serve on three committees in the years after 1671 but, in comparison to his earlier years, this was a modest contribution and most of those committees were tidying up of matters he had been involved with earlier such as the King's Hospital, debts due to the city and the maintenance of watercourses.[111] As time passed, his engagement with

106 Airy (ed.), *Essex papers*, pp 14, 101, 186, 192; *CARD*, v, 20.   107 *Letters written by Arthur Capel, earl of Essex, lord lieutenant of Ireland, in the year 1675*, pp 101–7, 113–15.   108 *CARD*, iii, 447; Cheshire Archives, Chester, ZM/AB/1, f. 29.   109 *CARD*, iv, 18, 320; RCBL, P118/5/1, vestry orders, 5 Apr. 1670; 'History of the church and parish of St Michael', p. 184.   110 DCA, MR/18.   111 *CARD*, v, 23, 26, 51.

city became less enthusiastic and as the dispute over the rules continued, his disillusionment grew.

The long drawn-out crisis did more damage than this. As John Yarner had commented of Quin, he was 'one of good repute and credit', the same phrase used of him during the 1672 dispute. His social worth or honour was intimately bound with his position within the city as loyal citizen, civic official, city administrator and successful trader. Honour, or estimations of social worth, served to smooth the workings of everyday life. As one commentator said to Quin and the excluded aldermen in 1672 'most of them being merchants it is feared their credit may be blasted in foreign parts'.[112] It was not simply a matter of personal finances. Mark Quin was not part of a stable inherited social world. He, and his family, had benefited from the economic growth of late seventeenth-century Dublin. He had certainly acquired the trappings of wealth but demonstrating that he had acquired the values of honour was more difficult. Yet this sense of self-worth was vital since it regulated the tensions and risks of schism in the city by setting common assumptions for the world of the elite. Mark did this by aligning himself with the institutions of the city that could allow him to demonstrate his loyalty and provide a sense of his historical worth that would compensate for the absence of a significant genealogy that marked out men of honour and credit whose families were well-known and trusted. His participation in urban government further validated his sense of self-worth marking him out as a man with the social skills and status, as well as wealth, needed for this role. When his relationship with the city institutions was questioned over a prolonged period between 1671 and 1674 it had a profound impact on his own self-worth and self-understanding. It may well have triggered the religious crisis that Healy noted, prompting a crisis of self-worth and giving rise to thoughts of sacrifice as a way of compensating for the schism in the city that Quin may well have thought of as a judgment of God that required a response. Ultimately, the loss of faith in the public man by Quin's private self may well have led to his suicide.

IV

At their meeting on the fourth Friday after 25 December 1674 Dublin Corporation noted the death of Alderman Mark Quin and nominated a successor.[113] Quin was both created and destroyed by civic politics. Over his lifetime he had ensured that his family was placed on an upward social trajectory. If his father's origins have been correctly identified, he moved his family from the artisan group into that of trade and finally into the world of the gentry. Certainly, the eighteenth-century life of James Quin, Mark's grandson,

112 *Cal. S.P. dom., 1672*, p. 131.   113 *CARD*, v, 100.

recorded that his 'education was such as suited the station which seemed allotted to him, that of a gentleman'.[114] His sons were all provided with the trappings of social position. Mark's eldest son, Thomas, who inherited the business and was admitted free of the city as a merchant at Christmas 1674, after this father's death, had been educated in Trinity College, Dublin.[115] He lived in his father's house in High Street and died in 1685. His brother, James, was sent to Lincoln's Inn in London where he practised law, dying, after a turbulent career, in 1710.[116] Their sister, Mary, married Thomas Whitshed, the son of Mark's friend from St Michael's parish, who was a lawyer, educated at Trinity College, Dublin, who would be MP for Carysfort in the parliament of 1692–3.[117] The family's elevation had come at a price. Dublin certainly allowed Mark Quin to move up in the social order so that he could reinvent himself as a city father, displaying the virtues of loyalty to the city and reliever of the poor. However, this self-understanding was fragile and the vagaries of civic politics were capable of undermining Quin's self-image as effectively as it had constructed it.

114 *Life of Mr James Quin*, p. 4.   115 TCD, MUN/V/23/1, p. 59.   116 *The records of the honourable society of Lincoln's Inn* (2 vols, London, 1896), i, 316.   117 *HIP*, vi, 538.

Dublin in an 'era of improvement': the public and the growth of the eighteenth-century city

JAMES KELLY

In September 1764 the *Caledonian Mercury* carried a report from Dublin in which readers of the newspaper were provided with an account of 'the improvements carrying on in this metropolis'.[1] Prepared by a resident, who highlighted the 'splendid palace' recently erected at the bottom of Grafton Street to accommodate the provost of Trinity College, the writer was so enthused by the 'works which are carrying on in abundance', he confidently forecast that Dublin must, 'in a few years, … be the most magnificent city in Europe'.[2] He did not specifically anticipate the impressive architectural undertakings completed during the decades that followed, John (Fiott) Lee observed in 1807, equipped the city with 'fine beautiful streets' and, in James Gandon's Custom House, one of 'the finest buildings in Europe', but his remarks indicate that the growth of the city was a source of considerable local excitement.[3] In keeping with this, the volume and tone of architectural and allied comment published in Ireland appreciated in tandem with the expansion of the city from a position during the middle decades of the century when it was intermittent and, attitudinally ambivalent at best, to a point spanning the late 1780s and early 1790s when, coinciding with the unprecedented pace of expansion, it was commonplace. Furthermore, it was overwhelmingly optimistic in its assessment of the implications for the city of the growth that was then underway. Mood is inherently mutable, of course, and it altered perceptively, beginning in 1793, as the less desirable consequences of rapid urban growth – land price inflation, high rents, over supply and allegations of corruption – assumed greater visibility, with the result that the lustre of improvement lost some of its previous sheen though the 'general appearance of the city' continued to improve; Dublin was, one well informed observer pointed out in 1797, 'extremely beautiful'.[4] The utility of such commentary as a source of information on the expansion of the eighteenth-century city does not require elaboration.[5] It is valuable, particularly,

1 *Caledonian Mercury*, 12 Sept. 1764. The *Caledonian Mercury* was published in Edinburgh. The title quotation is from, *Freeman's Journal*, 18 Aug. 1787. 2 *Caledonian Mercury*, 12 Sept. 1764. 3 Quotation taken from the notes of John (Fiott) Lee, who visited Ireland in 1806: Angela Byrne (ed.), *A scientific, antiquarian and picturesque tour: John (Fiott) Lee in Ireland, England and Wales, 1806–1807* (Hakluyt Society: Abingdon, 2018), pp 100, 101. 4 Rolf Loeber and Magda Stouthamer-Loeber (eds), 'Dublin and its vicinity in 1797', *Ir. Geog.*, 35, 2 (2002), 146. 5 For which see, inter alia, Jacqueline Hill, *From patriots to unionists: Dublin civic politics and Irish Protestant patriotism, 1660–1840* (Oxford, 1997);

for what it reveals of how the residents of the city, vested interests with a stake in the outcome, and the contemporary commentariat (which embraces visitors and travellers as well as those writing in the press) responded to the transformative impact of vigorous urban growth.

It can come as no surprise that Dublin's demographic, physical and economic expansion excited increasing interest as the city grew rapidly in the second half of the eighteenth century. According to a contemporary estimate, the population doubled (from 69,000 to 140,000) between 1678 and 1778, and the ensuing 'prodigious increase' prompted another to observe, a decade later, that 'it is the general opinion there are nearly 200,000' in the city, which secured it a place among the most populous cities in Europe.[6] Though a large proportion of the published commentary on the condition of the city was prompted, then as earlier, by quotidian concerns – among which the state of the streets featured prominently – the implications of the deterioration of critical parts of the city's infrastructure such as the ('old') Custom House, the Tholsel and Essex Bridge, and calls for the re-location of the Custom House or for the construction of a new Exchange or King's Inns were replete with long-term consequences for the look and shape of the city. This was accented by the increasing scale of privately sponsored residential initiatives, for though these excited less controversy, and thus less comment than public building initiatives, the order of the Fitzwilliam estate's ambitious scheme for Merrion Square and the Gardiner family's plans for the lands they owned on the north side of the river were not just too grand to be passed over, they dovetailed with an increasing interest in the way in which the city was expanding to ensure that these (and other) welcome developments were embraced within the narrative devoted to the city's growth and improvement. This complemented and was complemented by the augmenting preoccupation of the city's population with the demeanour of the urban space in which they lived, worked and recreated.

The respectable, whose preferences and priorities were crucial in determining what constituted an agreeable urban space, were to the fore for this reason in urging the exclusion of demotic sports such as throwing at cocks,

Edward McParland, 'Strategy in the planning of Dublin, 1750–1800' in Paul Butel and L.M. Cullen (eds), *Cities and merchants: French and Irish perspectives on urban development, 1500–1900* (Dublin, 1986), pp 97–107; Edward McParland, *James Gandon: Vitruvius Hibernicus* (London, 1987), pp 35–7, 42–4; David Dickson, *Dublin: the making of a capital* (London, 2014), chs 4 and 5. 6 The population figures are from *Exshaw's Gentleman's and London Magazine*, December 1778, p. 70; 'Population of Dublin', *Times*, 24 Jan. 1788. For a reliable modern assessment, which confirms the trend but offers a more informed perspective, see David Dickson, 'The demographic implications of the growth of Dublin, 1650–1850' in Richard Lawton and Robert Lee (eds), *Urban population development in western Europe from the late eighteenth to the early twentieth century* (Liverpool, 1989), pp 178–89. According to the figures published in 1778, Dublin was the fourth most populous city in Europe, smaller than London (900,000), Paris (600,000) and Amsterdam (250,000), but larger than Rome (130,000), Venice (100,000) and Bordeaux (100,000).

bull running and ball playing from the streets.[7] They expressed comparable unease with ill-maintained road surfaces, unpaved pathways, malodorous aggregations of refuse, poor lighting and the absence of a reliable water supply. They manifested less interest in the living and working environments of the artisanal and plebeian, but they were neither unaware of the implications of urban overcrowding nor uncritical of the unsightly ribbon developments of cabins on the roads leading to the city.[8] Their response to social problems as diverse as infanticide, child kidnapping, child stripping, faction fighting and other examples of what they conceived of as criminal and anti-social behaviour indicates that they prioritized sanction over rehabilitation and remediation and allowed for no connection, still less a direct link, between living conditions and behaviour.[9] If, as this suggests, public commentary on the subject of Dublin's expansion did not prioritize presenting solutions to the city's ills, they did not ignore such matters entirely. The perception that urban expansion was an unequivocal social good was never shared by all, of course. But its embrace within the concept of progress, which was identified as an unambiguous public good, and the utilization of the term 'improvement' to define the process as the city set about replacing its old medieval streetscape and tired public buildings with modern (neo-classical) exemplars offers an opportunity to explore how contemporaries viewed the topographically formative programme of urban growth pursued in Dublin during the second half of the eighteenth century.

RAISING AWARENESS: THE 1750S, 1760S AND 1770S

The paucity of comment in print suggests that municipal urban development was not a subject of active public discourse in Dublin during the first half of the eighteenth century though a number of signature buildings were constructed during that time.[10] This may have something to do with the fact that pertinent

7 In this respect, Ireland echoed the response of 'civic leaders' in England: Emma Griffin, *England's revelry: a history of popular sports and pastimes* (Oxford, 2005), p. 108; James Kelly, *Sport in Ireland, 1600–1840* (Dublin, 2015), pp 24–6, 208–36.   8 *Volunteer Evening Post*, 5 May 1787; Philip Luckombe, *A tour through Ireland* (London, 1780), p. 19. Luckombe commented: 'In general the outskirts of Dublin consist chiefly of huts, or cabins, constructed of mud dried, and mostly without either chimney or window.'   9 See James Kelly, 'Responding to infanticide in Ireland, 1680–1820' in Elaine Farrell (ed.), *'She said she was in the family way': pregnancy and infancy in modern Ireland* (London, 2012), pp 189–204 (Open access: http://humanities–digital–library.org/index.php/hdl/catalog/book/pregnancyandinfancy); *idem*, '"This iniquitous traffic": the kidnapping of children for the American colonies in eighteenth-century Ireland', *The Journal of the History of Childhood and Youth*, 9:2 (2016), 233–46: DOI: 10.1353/hcy.2016.0048; *idem*, '"Horrid" and "infamous" practices: the kidnapping and stripping of children, c.1730–c.1840', *IHS*, 42:162 (2018), 265–92; *idem*, *The Liberty and Ormond Boys: faction fighting in eighteenth-century Dublin* (Dublin, 2005).   10 See Edward McParland, *Public architecture in Ireland, 1680–1760* (London, 2001).

decisions, such as that taken in 1711/2 to purchase properties to permit the 'enlargement of the street or passage ... on Cork Hill' in order to enhance the environs of Dublin Castle, were made behind closed doors, which minimized the opportunities for public participation.[11] But the fact remains that the fledgling press showed little interest in such matters.[12] Moreover, this remained the case for some time, for when in 1728 the lords justices directed that a number of 'old houses' on College Green were 'pulled down' to facilitate the construction of the elegant Palladian Parliament House that set a high architectural bar for public buildings in the city thereafter, it elicited little comment in the public sphere though this was the first part of a decade-long project to which £40,000 (Irish) had been assigned by 1732.[13] It was not that there was no interest in the improvement of the city then, or proposals for its enhancement,[14] but it was confined within a narrow circle and, apart from its limited utilization as a medium to advertise the availability of houses to rent, the continued lack of engagement with the subject in the public sphere is notable.[15] Matters were certainly not assisted by the faltering performance of the economy. The interruption of building reported in 1742 to Viscount Fitzwilliam (whose ownership of the Fitzwilliam estate on the southern edge of the city ensured he was a key figure in shaping its growth) was temporary, but his agent's perception that 'the town is overbuilt' indicated that urban development awaited an improvement in the economic environment.[16]

If so, it was not long in coming. The susceptibility of the country to climatic and environmental crisis in the years spanning 1720 to 1745 was not conducive to urban development, but the improvement in the kingdom's fortunes, once it put behind it the disruptive economic and costly demographic effects of famine (in the late 1720s, 1740–1 and 1744–5), encouraged a more expansive attitude.[17] This had many dimensions, among which the recognition in the capital that

---

11 Dawson to Jacob Peppard, 8 Mar., Dawson to Lucas, 22 Mar., Dawson to Vice-treasurer, 22 Mar. 1711/2 (NAI, Military entry book, 1711–13, MS 2553 ff 64, 74).   12 See Robert Munter, *The history of the newspaper in Ireland, 1685–1760* (Cambridge, 1966).   13 Lords justices to lord lieutenant, 20 Nov. 1728, Estimates for preparing the Blue Coat Hospital, 24 June 1729, Lawson to lords justices, 8 June 1738 (NAI, Calendar of miscellaneous letters and papers prior to 1760, ff 187, 191, 227); 'Description of Dublin in 1732' in *CARD*, x, 523; McParland, *Public architecture in Ireland, 1680–1760*, ch. 7.   14 In 1735, Gabriel Stokes, a mathematical instrument-maker, who prepared a response to the architect Richard Castle (*Observations on a later essay of Mr Richard Castle* ... (Dublin, 1735), published *A scheme for effectually supplying every part of the city of Dublin with pipe-water, without any charge of water-engines, or any water-forcers, by a close adherence to the natural laws of gravitation* ... (Dublin, 1735).   15 *Dublin Gazette*, 30 Oct. 1732, 5 Aug. 1757.   16 Mathew to Fitzwilliam, 18 Dec. 1742 (NAI, Pembroke Estate papers, 97/46/1/2/4/32).   17 See L.M. Cullen, 'Economic development, 1750–1800' in W.E. Vaughan and T.W. Moody (eds), *A new history of Ireland*; iv, *Eighteenth-century Ireland* (Oxford, 1986), pp 159–95; David Dickson, 'Society and economy in the long eighteenth century' in James Kelly (ed.), *The Cambridge history of Ireland*, iii: *1730–1880* (Cambridge, 2017), pp 153–78.

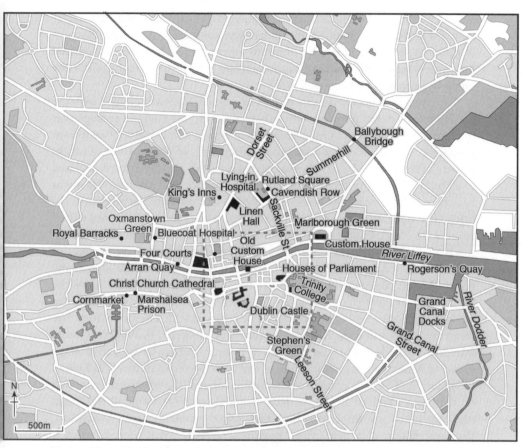

Map 1. (*above*) Dublin, 1750–1800: places mentioned in the text.

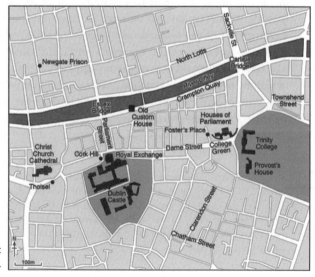

Map 1a. Dublin, 1750–1800:
places mentioned in the text.

important aspects of its infrastructure required urgent attention was particularly salient. The likelihood of this being undertaken was increased by the willingness of those who embraced the ethic of improvement, which assumed an increased influence on economic thinking, to contemplate how the topography of the city might be purposefully re-modelled.[18]

The 1750s was notable in this respect as economic growth chimed with the need to refurbish key features of the urban fabric and the mounting recognition that the city was in need of modernization to elicit a number of well-conceived proposals. The most urgent was the replacement of Essex Bridge, which, readers of the *Dublin Weekly Journal* were alerted on 25 May 1751, was closed to all but pedestrian traffic because one of the 'arches' had given way. It might have been still worse as, the newspaper advised its readers in the next issue, the bridge had not functioned properly since 1704 when 'one of the arches fell in' because 'the stones and rubbish of the said arch were never moved'.[19] While it was undeniable that the 'overflowing [of] the cellars and quays in times of floods' attributed to the faulty bridge provided ample grounds for its ongoing refurbishment (along the lines undertaken in 1751), the recommendation of the 'committee' of merchants, which was convened to identify what was 'proper to be done', that the existing bridge should be replaced with a new one 'forty five feet wide, which will make room for six carriages' answered to a different, more interested, agenda.[20] This did not equate in every particular with that of the Guild of Merchants, which was one of the most powerful interests in Dublin Corporation. The well-publicized 'battles' involving 'the workmen' employed on the project and an alliance of local 'fellows' (possibly Ormond Boys) and 'the watchmen of three parishes' and other problems, notwithstanding, the construction of a new bridge was pursued with 'great success' when it commenced in 1753.[21] Encouraged by the Committee of Merchants, which had made the public aware of its preference by advertising its readiness 'to receive proposals with a plan and estimate ... to rebuild ... the bridge', the newspaper reading part of the population was kept informed of progress in the expanding public sphere. As a result, George Semple, the talented local architect, to whom the task was entrusted, was warmly applauded for the 'care and diligence' with which he oversaw construction. Moreover, the 'noble fabrick' of the bridge was in a state of sufficient readiness for the lord mayor to traverse 'in his coach' on 7 April 1755, though it was not until the summer that the public was alerted to the fact that workmen had embarked on demolishing houses 'on the west-

18 Toby Barnard, *Improving Ireland? Projectors, prophets and profiteers, 1641–1786* (Dublin, 2008); Gordon Rees, 'Pamphlets, legislators and the Irish economy, 1727–49', *Ir. Econ. & Soc. Hist.*, 41 (2014), 20–35; James Kelly, 'Jonathan Swift and Irish economic crisis in the 1720s', *ECI*, 6 (1991), 7–36.   19 *Dublin Weekly Journal*, 25 May, 1 June 1751.   20 *Dublin Courant*, 27 July 1751; *Dublin Weekly Journal*, 8 June, 27 July 1751.   21 *Universal Advertiser*, 20 Jan., 17, 24, 27 Feb., 3, 29 May 1753, 6 Aug. 1754; *Pue's Occurrences*, 30 Dec. 1752, 6 Aug. 1754.

side of Essex Bridge ... in order to widen and make the passage uniform to the bridge'. Significantly, since this further development, newspaper readers were advised, 'add[ed] greatly to the beauty of that spacious building' (the bridge), it emboldened those, possessed of a larger vision for the improvement of the city, who conceived of the new bridge as merely a first step.[22]

Schemes for additional works did not take the merchants and traders of the city by surprise. But whereas the replacement of a bridge that was 'in a decaying and ruinous condition' with a new wider structure was welcomed by them, they regarded the suggestion that it was time 'to build a new Custom House on the north side of the Liffey at an undetermined location westwards of Bachelor's Lane' with disquiet. Contrary to its champions, who maintained that it would prevent delays and reduce costs by permitting 'the greatest dispatch' in loading and unloading vessels, mercantile interests were convinced that the relocation of the Custom House would complicate their ability to conduct business, which must inevitably injure their livelihood.[23] There was more than a hint of special pleading in the manner in which their apprehensions on this score were articulated, but their sentiments were genuinely felt, and they guided the way in which merchants and allied interests contrived to frustrate attempts in 1750, 1751, 1752 and 1753 to progress a scheme to build a 'new bridge over the River Anna Liffey, to the eastward of Essex Bridge'.[24] The details of the means by which the merchants ensured this outcome were not admitted to the public sphere, but the triumph with which, according to reports, 'the merchants, traders, and other inhabitants of the city' celebrated the outcome in 1751 and 1753 demonstrated that they possessed a sizeable reservoir of support in the city.[25] Indeed, it seemed then that the mercantile interest could determine the fate of any major scheme of public works since their resolve, in 1755, 'to prevent the inconveniences that are apprehended from the removal of the General Post Office' from College Green to a new location thwarted another analogous improving initiative for which a good argument could be made.[26]

---

22 James Kelly, 'Political publishing, 1700–1800' in Raymond Gillespie and Andrew Hadfield (eds), *The Oxford history of the Irish book*, iii: *The Irish book in English, 1550–1800* (Oxford, 2005), pp 215–33; *Pue's Occurrences*, 30 Dec. 1752, 6 Aug. 1754, 12 Apr. 1755, 12, 29 June 1756; *Universal Advertiser*, 26 June, 3 July, 11 Sept., 16, 30 Oct., 3, 6 Nov. 1753, 13, 16 Apr., 25 June, 6, 24 Aug. 1754, 4 Jan., 11 Feb. 1755; *Public Gazetteer*, 13 Nov. 1759.   23 Address to George II from captains, masters and owners of vessels trading to Dublin, 17 Aug. 1751 (TNA, SP63/317 f. 24); *CARD*, ix, 389–90; James Kelly, 'Representations of the Revenue Commissioners with respect to a "New Custom House" in Dublin, 1771–1781', *Irish Architectural and Decorative Studies*, 21 (2018), 137–8.   24 *Munster Journal*, 16 Apr. 1750; *Dublin Courant*, 29 Oct. 1751, 29 Feb. 1752; *Pue's Occurrences*, 2 Nov. 1751; *Universal Advertiser*, 24 Feb., 10, 13, 24 Nov. 1753; William Smyth to Ralph Smyth, 29 Oct. 1751 (NLI, Smythe of Barbavilla papers, MS 41591/1); William Fitzwilliam to Viscount Fitzwilliam, 8 Nov. 1753 (NAI, Pembroke Estate papers, 97/46/1/2/7/28); *CARD*, ix, 337, 400–1; x, 10–11, 24, 106–8.   25 *Universal Advertiser*, 8 Dec. 1753.   26 *Pue's Occurrences*. 1 July 1755.

If it was apparent by then that the metropolitan mercantile interests, and the nexus of administrators, developers, property owners and others eager to get on with developing the city possessed incompatible visions, the situation was complicated further by the fact that the latter did not speak with one voice. Viscount Fitzwilliam, in particular, had little reason to look positively upon such schemes as were being proposed. The Fitzwilliam estate, and others who had invested in Ringsend (and Irishtown) when it was as close as large ships could get to the city, had lost out when, following its establishment in 1708, the Ballast Office dredged the bay and river and 'made the same navigable up to the Custom House' (then on what is now Wellington Quay).[27] Fitzwilliam adopted a studiously neutral position on the question of a 'new bridge' as a result when it was actively agitated in the early 1750s, and declined to act when he was urged (by William Fitzwilliam, his agent) to seek the inclusion of a 'savings clause' in legislation which assigned money for the rebuilding of Essex Bridge and the completion of the South (harbour) Wall.[28] Fitzwilliam's priority was the development of Merrion fields on the city's southern suburb, and as he set about giving expression to his plan for what an admirer described as 'the grandest and greatest square in Europe', it was already evident by 1764, as 'building on the north side of Merrion Square [proceeded] briskly', that the public's interest was piqued by the accelerating pace of development.[29] Though some of the problems Fitzwilliam encountered might have been of interest to the wider population as speculators (among them George Faulkner, the newspaper editor) responded to the acceleration in construction by purchasing 'lots of ground', which they conveyed to 'undertakers' to develop, a majority of the space assigned in the press to issues appertaining to the city at this time engaged not with the nature and implications of development but with more ordinary matters.[30] Thus though readers in the 1750s were regularly alerted to the recreational possibilities of 'the New Gardens in Great Britain street' (which were developed by Bartholomew Mosse with the same fundraising purpose as the nearby 'long room' where 'concerts of music' were held at noon every Monday and Thursday to fund the Lying-in Hospital); and made aware of the fact that 'the walks' round Stephen's Green had been 'put in good order', these reports competed for attention with the more numerous and less uplifting accounts of urban problems.[31] These included vandalism; perennial difficulties

27 Mathew to Viscount Fitzwilliam, 19 Apr. 1744, William Fitzwilliam to Viscount Fitzwilliam, 8 Nov. 1753 (NAI, Pembroke Estate papers, 97/46/1/2/5/14, 97/46/1/2/7/28); H.A. Gilligan, *History of the port of Dublin* (Dublin, 1988), pp 14–16.   28 William Fitzwilliam to Viscount Fitzwilliam, 23 Oct., 6, 22 Nov., 22 Dec. 1753, 12 Feb. 1754 (NAI, Pembroke Estate papers, 97/46/1/2/7/25, 27, 29, 31, 34).   29 Bull to Fitzwilliam, 20 Sept. 1762, Vallancey to [Fitzwilliam], 134 Nov. 1764, Wilson to Fitzwilliam, 26 Jan. 1765 (NAI, Pembroke Estate papers, 97/46/1/2/6/62, 70, 71).   30 *Dublin Courant*, 28 Aug. 1762. For other examples see *Public Gazetteer*, 2 Oct. 1759.   31 *Dublin Courant*, 26 Feb. 1751; *Public Gazetteer*, 9 Oct. 1759.

with the city's pavements, of which it was observed in 1761, 'many part whereof, this long time, have been in a dangerous condition'; street lighting, which was uneven and unreliable; the encroachment upon and obstruction of bridges and passage ways by street sellers and alms seekers; and continuing problems with the disposal of refuse and animal waste as a result of which large dunghills and 'heaps' of putrefying 'ordure and offal' added olfactory assault to the other problems, notably flooding, that were a recurring feature of life in the capital.[32] They also exacerbated, and were exacerbated by the ongoing challenge of service provision and street maintenance. There were instances of good practice, exemplified by the manner in which the commissioners who were responsible pursued the paving of Dame Street in 1774.[33] But the inability of the municipal authorities to prevent the construction of offensive and substandard buildings, such as the slaughterhouse erected without permission 'against the wall of his majesty's Iron Yard in Lower Abbey Street' or the 'front of twenty feet creeping up by the side of the Tholsel', allied to the fact that it was left to 'residents' to pursue these matters, was indicative of a seriously deficient regulatory environment.[34] This did not pass unnoticed, but the suggestion presented to readers of *Faulkner's Dublin Journal* in 1750 that Dublin should follow the example of 'London, and other great cities abroad', and stipulate that 'new buildings, foundations, holes etc. are enclosed by wooden rails and boards' fell on deaf ears.[35] It did not mean that health and safety was entirely taken for granted. The generous public response to the collection that that was instituted in 1766 to assist the widows and children of the six men who died on Merrion Square when 'the rear of two new-built houses suddenly gave way and fell to the ground' pointed to the capacity to mobilize public opinion, but it did not result in a shift in the assignment of responsibility, which remained with workmen.[36]

In the context of this incident, and ongoing reports of lucky escapes when buildings collapsed, there was plenty to engage the corporation.[37] They did not give these, or allied matters, priority but they did not ignore them either. Readers of the *Public Gazetteer* were informed in 1761 that 'the most expedient method for enlightening the city' was discussed at a 'post assembly' in the summer of 1760.[38] Street lighting was of modest consequence, however, when set beside the implications of the plans that were being hatched for future development.

---

32 *Pue's Occurrences*, 28 Jan. 1758; *Public Gazetteer*, 24 June, 30 Aug. 1760, 14 Feb., 1 Sept. 1761, 13 June 1761, 28 July 1764; *Freeman's Journal*, 14 Feb. 1767; *Hoey's Public Journal*, 10 Jan., 6 Apr. 1772, 23 Oct. 1773; *Hibernian Journal*, 2, 21 June 1773, 6 Sept., 4 Nov. 1776; James Kelly, 'Climate, weather and society in Ireland in the long eighteenth century: the experience of later phases of the Little Ice Age', *RIA Proc.*, 120C (2020), 273–324. 33 *Saunders's News Letter*, 8 Aug. 1774. 34 Minutes of the revenue commissioners, Apr. 1773 (TNA, CUST1/123 f. 49v.). 35 *Faulkner's Dublin Journal*, 24 Nov. 1750. 36 *Dublin Courier*, 21 Feb. 1766; *Public Gazetteer*, 22 Feb., 15 Apr. 1766; *Hoey's Public Journal*, 18 Oct. 1771. 37 *Public Gazetteer*, 4 July 1761; *Hibernian Chronicle* (Cork), 4 Oct. 1770; *Hoey's Publick Journal*, 10 Sept. 1773. 38 *Public Gazetteer*, 24 June 1760.

The key issue at that moment was whether those who were enthused by 'the elegant manner' in which the new Essex Bridge was finished would realize their aspiration to open up a broad avenue, and, the *Public Gazetteer* reported, extend 'the passage from Essex Bridge to Cork Hill, and thence ... to be continued to ... [Dublin] Castle, either in a direct line or by opening a square where Lucas's Coffee House now stands'.[39] As George Semple, whose reputation as an 'undertaker' stood high at this moment, let it be known that he favoured the scheme, and the Wide Streets Commission had been established by act of parliament in 1757 to bring it about, it seemed that the outcome was already determined.[40] But this was to underestimate the challenges the commissioners encountered as they set about the task.[41] Specifically, it underestimated the determination of the city's merchants who, having successfully countered every attempt to advance the plan to build a new bridge closer to the sea, were now focused, readers of the *Public Gazetteer* were advised in 1764, on advancing their scheme to establish a 'new exchange' in place of the Tholsel, where they currently conducted this business, in the heart of the old city.[42]

Though the public was alerted to the fact that the matter was under active discussion when it was reported in 1764 that 'the merchants and traders' had met with the lord mayor on 31 July to discuss the issue, when news leaked out a year later that a king's letter for £8,000 had been issued for a 'new square' instead of an Exchange, it seemed as if the merchants had been rebuffed.[43] But this was to misjudge their resolve; the significance of the fact that the duke of Northumberland had, during the course of his short Irish vice-royalty (April 1763–June 1765), agreed to the construction of a 'merchants Exchange building'; and the attraction of the 'reserved ground upon Cork Hill, opposite Parliament Street' as a location.[44] The tone of the report relaying this news to the public, along with the additional information that 'the merchants and traders of the city of Dublin' were sufficiently encouraged by events, specifically the allocation of money to pay for the compulsory acquisition of property in the area, in 1766 to 'come to a resolution to graft a scheme on the state lottery now depending in England, to raise a fund, in order to facilitate the erecting an

39 Ibid., 13 Nov. 1759, 18 Sept. 1762; *Universal Advertiser*, 3 Jan. 1758.   40 *Universal Advertiser*, 3 Jan. 1758; *Public Gazetteer*, 13 Nov. 1759; Edward McParland, 'The Wide Streets Commissioners: their importance for Dublin architecture in the late 18th–early 19th century', *Quarterly Bull. IGS*, 15:1 (1972), 2–3, 6; Murray Fraser, 'Public building and colonial policy in Dublin, 1760–1800', *Architectural History*, 28 (1985), 103–4; George II, chap. 19: *An act for making a wide and convenient way, street and passage from Essex Bridge to the Castle of Dublin, and for other purposes...*   41 *Universal Advertiser*, 2, 20 Jan. 1759; *Dublin Gazette*, 15 July 1760; *CARD*, x, 19.   42 For contemporary perspectives on the state of the Tholsel see *Pue's Occurrences*, 27 Jan. 1756; *Freeman's Journal*, 6 Apr. 1765, 18 Aug. 1787, and continuing opposition to 'a new bridge eastwards of Essex Bridge' see *Universal Advertiser*, 21 Oct. 1755; *CARD*, xi, 44–5.   43 *Public Gazetteer*, 31 July 1764; *Oxford Journal*, 10 Aug. 1765.   44 Ponsonby to Wilmot, 24 Aug. 1765 (PRONI, Wilmot papers, T3019/5089); *Public Gazetteer*, 17 Mar. 1766; Fraser, 'Public building and colonial policy in Dublin', 104–6.

Exchange', was certainly positive. It would, it was observed laconically, benefit both 'the trade of the kingdom' and the metropolis. This anodyne response provided little indication of the behind the scenes manoeuvring that had led to this, though it may be that some readers were sufficiently *au fait* with proceedings to interpret the inclusion in the news report of an appeal that no other 'like' scheme was 'attempted' as an indication of the depth of unease lest another plan was pursued.[45]

No rival initiative emerged to complicate further this particular drama, though the competition launched by the trustees to identify 'the most elegant and commodious plan' for the new Exchange served to keep the issue in the public eye. More significantly, in so far as public awareness of the issue and its relevance for the city was concerned, it prompted a public exchange – the first of its kind – on the merits of what was being proposed, between those who might be characterized as idealists, for whom this represented an opportunity to demonstrate the capacity of good architecture to shape the way people lived, and those who adopted a more pragmatic approach to what was possible.[46] Prompted by the impending deadline (1 January 1769) for the receipt by the committee tasked with identifying 'the most elegant and commodious plan' for an Exchange, the debate commenced with the publication on 31 December 1768 of the first of five essays or 'observations on the architecture' in which, their author, Andrew Caldwell (1733–1808), a young man of 'independent property', outlined at some length the principles and considerations that should guide any programme of architecturally inspired urban development.[47] Part architectural critique, and part manifesto, Caldwell was convinced that that 'the scheme for embellishing the city [of Dublin] with a magnificent Exchange' represented the opportunity to embark on a programme of works that must, over time, effect a profound transformation on what it meant to live, work in and experience the city.[48] He did not believe that this would be assisted by the location of the Exchange on Cork Hill, however, and having demonstrated that he was more than usually well informed on matters architectural, by providing a penetrating critique of Dublin's major buildings (Parliament House, most notably), he went on to suggest a number of possible quayside alternatives in the fifth, and final, essay in the series.[49] Since neither these, nor College Green, which was his own preference on aesthetic grounds, were practical possibilities, the primary value of his commentary by this point lay not in his discussion of the limitations of Cork Hill as a site (which were revealing) but in his general

45 *Dublin Gazetteer*, 10 May 1766; *Public Gazetteer*, 29 Nov. 1765, 17 May 1766; *Freeman's Journal*, 26 Jan., 25 June 1768; Kelly, 'Representations of the Revenue Commissioners', 138–9.   **46** *Freeman's Journal*, 30 July, 3 Sept., 29 Oct., 10 Dec. 1768; Edward McParland, 'James Gandon and the Royal Exchange competition', *RSAI Jn.*, 102 (1972), 58–72.   **47** See James Kelly (ed.), 'Andrew Caldwell's "Observations on Architecture", 1768–9: context and text', *ECT*, 36 (2021), 93–155.   **48** [Essay 1], *Freeman's Journal*, 31 Dec. 1768.   **49** The essayist's assessment of Parliament House extended over two 'essays': *Freeman's Journal*,

counsel that 'all improvements and alterations' should, following the example of
'great and opulent cities', be pursued in the knowledge that it was 'impossible to
complete a scheme of magnificence at once'. Convinced that those responsible
had not given the matter sufficient thought, he pointed to the 'prodigious
advantages' that must have accrued to the city, and to College Green specifically,
if Parliament House had been 'placed at right angles with the College Green',
and 'a magnificent church, or some other public building' was built opposite.
Instead, he pointed out, the city had passed up on an opportunity to create 'the
most superb spectacle that could be boasted of in Europe'.[50] He had a more
modest vision for Cork Hill if the decision to locate the Exchange there was
reversed, but his surmise that government would in time 'give a magnificent
front to that part of the Castle' if the Guild of Merchants could be persuaded
to 'leav[e] Cork Hill open' was consistent with his overall vision for the city.
It also demonstrated that he had not just pondered the matter deeply but
sought to identify possible solutions. This was the implication, certainly, of his
further suggestion that 'a wide street might be opened between the College
and Parliament House down to the river' Liffey, and of his invocation of the
improved vista and access that would ensue if 'Sackville Street ... [was also]
continued down to the river'. Indeed, he concluded provocatively, since it
echoed 'the strong tendency that the city discovers to enlarge itself eastward
and to push down to the sea', the 'necessity' of a new bridge complemented the
arguments favouring the relocation of the Custom House.[51]

Though the extended critique that Andrew Caldwell presented readers of
the *Freeman's Journal* of a number of Dublin's most admired buildings may
not always have sat easily with his earnest recommendations as to how the city
might best be developed, the combination of knowledge and opinion he brought
to bear meant his intervention constituted something of a new departure in
the public engagement with architectural matters. It must have left a deeper
impression had it caught the public mood, but it was so obviously contrary to
what the mercantile interest sought that it was dismissed, somewhat cruelly, as
nothing more than the 'reverie' of a man who, on the evidence of his writing,
was disposed to 'build castles in the air'.[52] It took insufficient cognizance of the
complex and costly preparations that had been undertaken to prepare the site
for construction. Moreover, Caldwell's timing was not opportune, for no sooner
had the deadline for the receipt of 'plans' passed than the Trustees put them on
public display, which ensured that the building's form, and not the location, was
the primary focus of attention. Caldwell's 'observations' were not ignored but
as a majority of those who commented publicly were prompted by pragmatic

3, 10 Jan. 1769. **50** 'Observations on Architecture, Essay the fifth, [parts 1 and 2]',
Freeman's Journal, 21, 24 Jan. 1769. **51** 'Observations on Architecture, Essay the fifth,
[part 1–4]', *Freeman's Journal*, 21, 24, 31 Jan., 7 Feb. 1769; McParland, 'The Wide Streets
Commissioners', 9. **52** *Freeman's Journal*, 14, 18 Feb. 1769.

considerations – the most urgent of which was the construction of the long-contemplated building – contrary to their author's purpose, the 'observations' assisted the public to buy into the process.[53] In any event, the exchanges were not long sustained, with the result that when the exhibition closed 'public discussion' of architectural matters was all but 'laid aside'.[54]

It did not cease entirely. Ongoing comment in parliament dovetailed with reports on current building projects – a military hospital in the Phoenix Park, for example, and attempts to provide for 'the paving, cleansing and enlightening the streets' – to ensure that these matters enjoyed an increased profile in the press.[55] It is less clear if this mirrored the mood of the public at large, as, based on what was reported, public interest in the 1770s was intermittent, and contingent on the popular perception of the matter at issue. One such moment occurred in 1772–3 when The Committee for Conducting a Free Press provided a platform for some lively exchanges on the merits of the plans of Thomas Cooley and others for a new Blue Coat Hospital.[56] The re-location of the deteriorating Custom House inevitably aroused stronger emotions, and, reflecting this, they were manifest on the pages of the *Freeman's Journal* once more in 1774 and during the winter of 1775–6.[57] Prompted by an attempt by the Revenue Commissioners to secure the funding and powers required to give effect to what was described in 1773 as 'a scheme ... to build a new custom-house to the east of the present, and on the north side of the Liffey', the press soon teemed with reports on the issue.[58] Most of the information relayed to the public took the form of summations of proceedings in parliament, but the coalition of 'merchants, traders and manufacturers' that was committed to resist the scheme did not want for advocates.[59] It maybe that they could not, on their own, have withstood the determined effort of John Beresford, who took the lead on behalf of the Revenue Commission in the House of Commons in 1774 and 1775–6, to take the plan forward, but the fact that their voice resounded loudest in the public sphere was an important factor in ensuring that no material progress was made.[60]

This notwithstanding, the decade spanning the late 1760s to the late 1770s witnessed an identifiable appreciation in interest in the changing topography of the city's landscape and of the import of the acceleration in building that was underway. The increased readiness with which architectural improvement

53 Ibid., 20 Jan., 11, 14, 21, 24 Feb., 7, 21 Mar. 1769. 54 Ibid., 16 May 1769. 55 *Public Gazetteer*, 11 Feb., 1 May, 1 Nov. 1766; *Freeman's Journal*, 1 Apr. 1766; *Public Advertiser*, 1, 12 Mar. 1768; *Hibernian Chronicle*, 9 Nov. 1769; *Hoey's Public Journal*, 25 May 1770, 4 Mar., 13 Sept. 1771. 56 *Freeman's Journal*, 12, 15 Dec. 1772; *Hoey's Publick Journal*, 8 Mar., 2 Apr., 18, 21 June 1773. 57 Kelly, 'Representations of the Revenue Commissioners', 139–41; *Freeman's Journal*, 27 Aug., 1 Sept. 1774. 58 *Hoey's Publick Journal*, 11 June 1773. 59 *Freeman's Journal*, 5 Feb., 8, 10, 12, 15 Mar. 1774, 19 Jan., 12 Dec. 1775. 60 Ibid., 10 Mar., 15 Sept. 1774, 20 Feb. 1776.

was seen as contributing 'to the honour and grandeur' of the city represents a useful index. This sentiment was proffered in 1768 in a, for then, isolated commentary on the merits of undertakings then in contemplation to replace the rundown Newgate prison with a new building on Little Green, and to re-locate the 'market-house in Thomas Street' to Oxmantown Green in order, the report averred, 'to widen the great passages into the city'.[61] The report was premature, but it echoed the increased public interest in such matters. It was facilitated by the emergence of new larger circulation newspapers – the *Hibernian Journal* (1772) and *Dublin Morning Post* and its sister title the *Evening Post* (1778) notably.[62] Moreover, it was not as if the citizenry of the city did not have increasing reason to applaud what was taking shape in their midst even when they were not inherently spectacular as was the case with the addition to the Linen hall in 1768 of 'a most beautiful … attic story' and the observation a decade later that the extended 'range of quays on either side of [the] river [Liffey] is at once the boast and ornament of the city'.[63] These were properly lauded achievements, as, the Royal Exchange excepted, a majority of the projects that were commented upon in the press during the late 1760s and the 1770s were of this order. These include the ongoing work to expand the quays eastwards on both sides of the river Liffey, which proceeded disagreeably slowly for those who conceived that continuous quays 'would add so much, as well to the beauty as to the convenience of our metropolis'.[64] The addition of a 'new chapel' to the Magdalen Asylum in Leeson Street in 1769–70 and the Workhouse in 1771; the laying of the foundation stone of a new lighthouse 'at the east end of the piles' in Dublin Bay in 1771; the completion of the ongoing programme of 'repairs' to St Werburgh church in 1771; the laying of the foundation stone of the Grand Canal in 1773; the opening of a new market house at the Coombe in 1774; the erection of a new Marshalsea Prison off Thomas Street in 1777; new building in Parliament Square, Trinity College, in 1778, even the opening up of access 'from Summerhill to Ballybough Bridge', were all endorsed as examples of what the lord lieutenant, George, Lord Townshend, described as instances 'of opening and beautifying the city'.[65] But, no more than the 'repairs' that were made to Parliament House and the Four Courts, which were lauded as being 'completed to the utmost perfection' in 1771; the enclosure in 1773 of ground, once part of Oxmantown Green, to permit construction to commence on a new

61 *Public Gazetteer*, 2 Feb. 1768; *Hoey's Publick Journal*, 24 June 1771. The foundation stone of the new gaol at Newgate was laid in October 1773 (clearing of the ground have commenced a month earlier): *Hoey's Publick Journal*, 10 Sept., 29 Oct. 1773. 62 Kelly, 'Political publishing, 1700–1800', pp 215–33. 63 *Public Gazetteer*, 9 Apr. 1768; *Dublin Evening Journal*, 18 Apr. 1778. 64 *Public Gazetteer*, 4 Apr. 1761, 16 July 1768. 65 *Hibernian Chronicle* (Cork), 15 Jan. 1770; *Public Gazetteer*, 9 June 1771; *Hoey's Publick Journal*, 10, 26 Apr., 6 Sept. 1771, 16 Apr. 1773; *Saunders's News Letter*, 9 Dec. 1774; *Freeman's Journal*, 5 June 1777; *Dublin Evening Journal*, 14 Feb. 1778; Townshend to Rochford, 11 Sept. 1772 (NAI, Irish correspondence, MS 2446).

Blue Coat Hospital in place of the existing 'ruinous and wretched' building; and the repairs required to keep St Werburgh's church open, they were not transformative.[66] They were certainly not of the order or ambition of the plan, emanating with the Wide Streets Commissioners, of 'opening one grand street from the Castle down to College Green', which Lord Townshend declined to recommend in 1771 on the grounds of cost.[67] This was a setback to those who thought on a grand scale, but it did not spell the end for a scheme that many conceived 'the greatest and most crowded thoroughfare' (Cork Hill and Dame Street) in the city required. It would be 'to the eternal disgrace of taste and public spirit' if the street 'ornamented with three of the most superb buildings Dublin has to boast of, the College, Parliament House and Royal Exchange, [was] left in its present narrow and incommodious state', it was observed in the *Dublin Evening Journal* in 1778. But the lack of recent progress was a reminder to the public that urban improvement was, as Andrew Caldwell had pointed out in 1769, frequently achieved over a long time span.[68]

The increased space devoted to reporting the development of the city was paralleled by a greater readiness to look favourably on the changes that were being brought to the city's topography and the city's building stock as a consequence of urban expansion. It did not mean that the public now trusted the combination of planners, developers and officials who were the primary architects, and advocates, of change. The applause showered on the judges of the Court of King's Bench and the recorder of the city (Samuel Bradstreet) when they successful resisted the attempt by the chief secretary, John Blaquiere, to enclose part of the Phoenix Park that had previously been a public road, demonstrated clearly that the suspicion of the motives of those who were in the vanguard promoting development (which informed much of the popular unease with the proposal to relocate the Custom House) remained strong.[69] It was in evidence once more in 1778 in the vocal resistance to the plan to vest responsibility for the management of the city's streets in a paving board,[70] and in the enduring negative reaction to the suggestion, which can be traced back to the 1680s, that the Four Courts should move from their current cramped situation in the shadow of Christ Church cathedral to a more becoming location such as College Green or a more spacious site north of the river. 'The removal of the Four Courts would unhinge the property of ten thousand persons, who it is computed, must actually suffer thereby no less than one hundred thousand

66 *Hoey's Publick Journal*, 6, 13 Sept. 1771, 2, 29 Apr., 13 May 1772, 8 Mar., 2, 12 Apr., 18, 21 June 1773. 67 *Hoey's Publick Journal*, 30 Dec. 1771, 10 Aug. 1772; *Freeman's Journal*, 8 Aug. 1772; Townshend to Rochford, 11 Sept. 1772 (NAI, Irish correspondence, MS 2446). 68 *Dublin Evening Journal*, 24 Mar., 7, 24 May 1778. 69 *Hibernian Chronicle* (Cork), 26, 30 Jan., 13 Feb. 1775. 70 *Dublin Evening Journal*, 31 Mar., 2, 4,7, 9, 11, 16 Apr. 1778; *Exshaw's Gentleman's and London magazine*, Apr. 1778, pp 244–5; Finnian Ó Cionnaith, *Exercise of authority: surveyor Thomas Owen and the paving, cleansing and lighting of Georgian Dublin* (Dublin, 2016), ch. 2.

pounds; besides the inevitable ruin of more than five thousand tradesmen and their dependent families', commented *Hoey's Publick Journal* in 1772.[71] The successful completion of the Royal Exchange diminished the certitude with which such sentiments were advanced as the 1770s moved toward a close and commentators united with merchants, officials and others in 1778–9 in publicly celebrating 'the grandeur of design [and] excellence of workmanship' that were identifiable in a building that 'is an unrivalled pattern of modern architecture, and scarcely exceeded by antiquity'.[72] There was more than a hint of hubris in these observations. But they echoed the increasing pride that Dubliners were taking in their city, and mirrored the warmer welcome now accorded the announcement of new projects. These included the Palladian style plans of Provost John Hely-Hutchinson for Trinity College, which had the potential, it was observed optimistically in 1778, to turn Parliament Square into one of 'the most finished … courts in the British dominions'.[73]

Hely-Hutchinson's scheme for Trinity included the placement of a statue of the University's 'foundress, Queen Elizabeth, in the Library Square'.[74] This feature of his plan was not realized, but the endorsement afforded the suggestion echoed the broader welcome in the city for statues and memorials. Though the ideological import of the statues that were added to the Dublin urban landscape in the eighteenth century has elicited more notice than their aesthetic impact, the interest in commissioning new statues mirrored the desire to beautify the city that was one of the consequences of its growth and the growing interest taken in its improvement.[75] None of the statues that were erected in the late 1750s and 1760s emulated those previously put in place to William III or George I as statements of Irish Protestant attachment to the Protestant succession. The most ambitious attempt was the 'elegant and magnificent' equestrian statue of George II by John Van Nost, which was 'exhibited to publick view' in 1758. The location, a year later, of a statue to General William Blakeney on Sackville Street Mall and of an 'an elegant metal bust' of Frederick the Great on Prussia Street in 1760 demonstrated that it was not necessary to plan on a grand scale, and it spurred a sequence of private and public commissions as others sought to avail of Van Nost's skill and ingenuity. They were not all completed, but their very suggestion echoed the increased eagerness to create a city that 'gave pleasure' to its residents.[76] Indicatively, one of the earliest actions of the trustees of the Royal

71 *Hoey's Publick Journal*, 30 Dec. 1771, 10 Aug. 1772; *CARD*, v, 346, 608–10.   72 *Dublin Evening Journal*, 9 Apr. 1778; *Freeman's Journal*, 11 Apr., 15 Oct. 1778, 1 Jan., 29 May 1779.   73 *Dublin Evening Journal*, 18 Apr. 1778; *Exshaw's Gentleman's and London magazine*, Feb. 1778, p. 127.   74 This idea was previously floated in 1774: *Saunders's News Letter*, 2 Nov. 1774; *Exshaw's Gentleman's and London magazine*, Feb. 1778, p. 127.   75 See Robin Usher, *Protestant Dublin, 1660–1760: architecture and iconography* (Houndsmill, 2012), ch. 3; *Dublin Evening Journal*, 14 Apr. 1778.   76 *Public Gazetteer*, 29 Mar. 1760, 5 July 1763, 31 Mar., 24 Apr. 1764, 23 Feb. 1768; *Saunders's News Letter*, 9 Dec. 1774; *Universal Advertiser*, 21 July 1754, 3 Jan. 1758; *CARD*, x, 82–4, 210–13.

Exchange was to approve the erection in 1779 of a statue in Parian marble to Charles Lucas, the dominant municipal politician of his generation, in 'a niche on the west staircase'.[77]

It was clear to the residents of the city by that point that Dublin was, in the words of Philip Luckombe, a travel writer whose informative tour of Ireland was published in 1780, 'no contemptible city'. Luckombe did not glide over the problems caused by the 'general badness of the streets' or the condign poverty.[78] He followed Thomas Campbell (1733–95) in this respect. Writing from Dublin in 1775, Campbell compared the situation of 'the bulk of this city' to 'the worst part of St Giles' in London, but he also acknowledged that 'the new streets are just as good as ours'. He singled out Merrion Square, which was still far from complete, as 'very elegant' and the quays as the city's 'principal beauty', but he was otherwise largely matter of fact, because, he commented, 'there are but few buildings here of any note'.[79] Campbell was not consciously reserving judgment. He sought to describe accurately what he observed, and the fact that his description was reprinted in the *Dublin Evening Journal* suggests he did so with some success.[80] This is not to imply either that the public did not take such matter seriously. The comment in a later issue of a sister newspaper that 'so desirable an object as that of widening and ornamenting … the principal streets of this great city, cannot fail of giving pleasure to the public in general' may have overstated the consensus in the city on this point, but it was an apt summary of the situation then, and it was sufficient to ensure that the major improvements that were made to the city in the 1780s did so against a backdrop of overwhelming public endorsement.[81]

'THE SPIRIT OF IMPROVEMENT'[82] AT WORK: THE 1780S

Echoing the positive response that greeted the completion of the Royal Exchange in 1778–9, the tone as well as the increased volume of coverage devoted to architectural issues and its implications for the city was increasingly positive in the 1780s. It was as if the fulcrum of public opinion, which had for decades reflected the sentiment of the vested mercantile and municipal interests that highlighted the disruptive implications of proposals to re-locate

77 *Exshaw's Gentleman's and London magazine*, June 1779, p. 374; *Freeman's Journal*, 15 Oct. 1778; *Cumberland Pacquet*, 22 June 1779.   78 Luckombe, *A tour through Ireland*, pp 17–19.   79 *Dublin Evening Journal*, 23 Apr. 1778; Thomas Campbell, *A philosophical survey of the south of Ireland in a series of letters* (London, 1778), letter one, pp 2–16.   80 *Dublin Evening Journal*, 23 Apr. 1778. Campbell's view was echoed by John Conway Potter, who confided his disappointment at what he saw: Potter to Potter, 29 Oct. 1778 (National Library of Wales, Wigfair papers, MS 12433D f. 2).   81 *Dublin Evening Post*, 7 May 1778.   82 For three instances of the usage of this term see *Dublin Evening Post*, 1 July 1783; *Volunteer Evening Post*, 2, 7 June 1787.

the Custom House and the Four Courts north of the river Liffey, had tilted
from apprehending to welcoming development, and to choose now to endorse
it as a manifestation of the broader enthusiasm for national improvement.[83]
This shift was assisted by the parallel reinforcement in the conviction with
which the Protestant nation, represented in parliament by the energized Patriot
interest and externally by the politicized middling sort, pressed for and secured
the reform of the kingdom's commercial and constitutional relationship with
Great Britain.[84] It was not that the development of Dublin was identified as
one of the Patriots' priorities, as George Ogle and Edward Newenham, who
were prominent in their ranks, were to the fore resisting Beresford in the House
of Commons and presenting the corporation's alternative to his efforts to pave
the way to relocate the Custom House.[85] They could count also on the support
of political activists in the city, the Society of Free Citizens most notably, who
echoed the concerns of those who apprehended the consequences if 'the center
of the city' moved eastwards from the 'old city' and Liberties towards the sea.[86]
But the ebullient optimism that characterized public discourse at this moment
encouraged increasingly confident pronouncements as to the city's future
prospects. Moreover, there seemed to be no shortage of undertakings to back
it up. It was evident, for example, in the hope expressed in December 1780 that
work then underway at Stephen's Green 'will be finished to an elegance and
propriety befitting the Irish metropolis'.[87] It was given more general expression
in 1781 when a resident of the city, writing for *Exshaw's Gentleman's and London
Magazine*, opined positively of the 'public buildings' then being constructed
that they were 'an ornament to the city'.[88] It was an assessment others were
happy to echo, though it lent itself to hyperbole and encouraged problematic
comparison. This is readily identifiable in the description of Stephen's
Green in 1781 as 'one of the finest and most spacious squares in Europe';[89]
of Merrion Square in 1788 'as vastly superior to anything of the kind in any
city in Europe'; of the improved Parliament House in 1787 as a contender
for the title of 'the most superb building in Europe'; and in the comparably
hubristic pronouncement uttered in 1785 that once the plans to widen 'Dame

83 See, for example, the report published in 1787 avowing that there was 'coal and iron' in
county Leitrim 'sufficient for many years' domestic consumption' as cause for the development
of these mines: *Saunders's News Letter*, 25 Aug. 1787.   84 See, inter alia, James Kelly, 'Patriot
politics 1750–91' in Alvin Jackson (eds), *Oxford companion to Irish history* (Oxford, 2014), pp
479–96; Vincent Morley, *Irish opinion and the American Revolution, 1760–1783* (Cambridge,
2002); Stephen Small, *Political thought in Ireland, 1776–1798: republicanism, patriotism and
radicalism* (Oxford, 2002), ch 2–3.   85 *Freeman's Journal*, 19 Apr., 24 Nov. 1774, 12 Dec.
1775.   86 *Hibernian Journal*, 30 Oct. 1775; *Freeman's Journal*, 19 Jan. 1775.   87 *Dublin
Evening Post*, 21 Dec. 1780.   88 *Exshaw's Gentleman's and London magazine*, Sept. 1781,
p. 503.   89 This claim was affirmed later the same decade when the suggestion that the
Green was enclosed within an 'iron pallisade' was welcomed as 'an improvement that would
render it not only the finest square in Europe, but a delightful public garden little inferior to
the Tuileries at Paris': *Saunders's New Letter*, 30 July 1789.

Street and some other avenues are completed, we shall have to boast of a trading
quarter superior to any (at least as to its *coup d'oeil* and external appearance) in
the British dominions'.[90] It was a meretricious claim, but it was of a piece with
the perception that 'the spirit of improvement, which has for some time past
been exhibited in Dublin', continued to strengthen, and that if it was sustained
that the city must in time be utterly transformed.[91] According to a commentary
published in the Castle-subsidised *Volunteer Evening Post*:[92]

> Dublin begins, it is said by those who visit the sister kingdom, to rival the
> metropolis of Great Britain in elegance and architecture, and to exceed
> her in paving and lighting of the streets.

The *Dublin Evening Post*, which occupied a different space on the ideological
spectrum, concurred:[93]

> To what degree of magnificence is the city of Dublin improving! At every
> end we view new edifices rising, each vying with the other; at the east end
> a Custom House; at the west a massy range of buildings for Four Courts
> and offices. Add to these the beautiful improvement made at the east side
> of the Parliament House. As the west side is to be made uniform with
> it, it is to be hoped … taste and spirit … will … clear round that noble
> structure, and leave a complete open from the west entrance to Anglesey
> Street. Dame Street being then widened so as to open a view from the
> Royal Exchange, of the College and Parliament House, that great avenue
> would then become truly beautiful.

Though comments of this ilk nourished an exaggerated sense of pride in the
city in some quarters in the 1780s, the scale and number of developments that
were pursued during these years encouraged this response. The key undertaking,
because it had been debated for so long, and because it led inevitably to the
decision to build a new bridge eastwards of Essex Bridge and to address the
ongoing problems posed shipping by the silting of Dublin Bay, was to build
a new Custom House on the north side of the river on ground closer to the
sea.[94] Since the Revenue Commissioners, whose project this was, had learned
from previous controversy that it was in their interest (John Beresford explained
to James Gandon) to keep 'this business a profound secret [for] as long as we

---

90 *Dublin Evening Post*, 21 Dec. 1780; *Exshaw's Gentleman's and London Magazine*, Mar. 1785,
p. 167; *Dublin Evening Post*, 24 July 1787; *Dublin Morning Post*, 23 Sept. 1788.   91 *Exshaw's
Gentleman's and London Magazine*, Mar. 1785, p. 167; see also *Volunteer Evening Post*, 7 June
1787.   92 *Volunteer Evening Post*, 2 June 1787.   93 *Dublin Evening Post*, 24 July 1787.
94 See Kelly, 'Representations of the Revenue Commissioners', 144–5; Fraser, 'Public
building and colonial policy in Dublin', 113–16.

can to prevent clamour', preparations were concealed from the public until workmen began 'laying out the ground for sinking a foundation' in July 1781.[95] The decision, which was taken shortly afterwards, 'to encompass the area in which the building, with all its offices, is to be erected' behind 'a strong pailing of boards' was guided by the same calculation, and while it did not secure the site against assault (in September 1781), it did at least mean that the workmen who were employed on the site were free to concentrate on the task for which they were employed.[96] This was not without complication because 'the rotten and spongy texture of the field allotted for this immense building' presented particular problems, but the difficulties that were encountered would have been still more challenging if the mercantile and other interests who conceived of it as an existential threat had not been caught by surprise.[97] They contrived, unsuccessfully, to regain the initiative by making clear their 'abhorrence' at what was underway. But the efficacy of their effort to extend the dominance of their voice in the public sphere was fatally undermined when, synchronous with its publication as a separate title in August 1781, the *Freeman's Journal* published the complete text of *Considerations on the removal of the Custom House* in which the main arguments against the relocation of the Custom House were forensically examined and rejected.[98] It is not apparent who was the author of this pamphlet, but it was a decisive intervention. It did not silence the voice of the 'injured citizens' who sustained a strong opposition to the project in print through the autumn and winter of 1781–2, but it fatally weakened the credibility of the organized protest the corporation presented to the lord lieutenant, with the result that the building's opponents not just failed to regain the initiative in the public sphere, their arguments reverberated increasingly weakly against a backdrop of frequent news reports, which apprised the public of the progress of the building.[99] This did not deter those critics who insisted on labelling the building a 'national folly', but theirs were increasingly isolated voices and by 1783 readers of the *Freeman's Journal* were not just regaled with positive accounts of what was being achieved, they were encouraged to look forward to its being ready for the 'dispatch of business'.[100] This was premature, but once the 'eastern wing' of the building was visible 'above the ground', it was clear to all but a minority of diehards that the Revenue Commissioners had won the day. As a result, the 'factious and prejudiced people' who persisted in their

95 *Freeman's Journal*, 17 July 1781; Beresford to Gandon, 15 Jan. 1781 in James Mulvany, *The life of James Gandon* (Dublin, 1846), p. 44. Gandon adopted the same approach to the construction of what became Carlisle Bridge; by 'keeping his plans concealed from public inspection', he effectively restricted the opportunity of the press, and public, to comment: *Dublin Morning Post*, 23 Sept. 1788. **96** *Exshaw's Gentleman's and London Magazine*, Sept. 1781, p. 503. **97** *Freeman's Journal*, 17 July 1781. **98** *Considerations on the removal of the Custom House* (Dublin, 1781); *Freeman's Journal*, 2, 4, 7, 9 Aug. 1781. **99** *Freeman's Journal*, 4, 7, 9, 11, 14, 16, 18 Aug., 8, 13, 22, 29 Sept., 2, 4 Oct. 1781, 5 Jan. 1782; *Hibernian Journal*, 10 Aug. 1781. **100** *Freeman's Journal*, 6 May 1783, 1 May 1784.

opposition to the building focused on its cost and on questioning the reason for its construction by characterizing it as 'the [Revenue] Commissioners' palace'.[101]

While the authorities were unable to insulate the Custom House against criticism, the evident practical and aesthetic merits of the building that emerged on the north side of the Liffey impressed the public at large and by 1786 opinion was overwhelmingly positive. 'There never was a building of such magnitude, elegance, and useful importance, expedited in a shorter time', it was reported in the *Freeman's Journal*, and this positive view was frequently affirmed thereafter as the building was brought to completion.[102] It was mirrored by the positive reaction to other 'improvements', as they were now routinely denominated, that were taking place across the city. The press played an important part in enabling this attitudinal change to take hold by providing their readers with an unprecedented flow of information on an unprecedented diversity of projects. Among these, the 'improvements' that were made to Parliament House, which involved adding a portico to the House of Lords, largely internal changes to the House of Commons, the addition of 'a curtain wall' and the demolition of 'old houses' nearby were singled out because they 'served to give the parliamentary pile a grand appearance'.[103] The overall effect was enhanced by additional 'new buildings' (the most high profile of which was Daly's Club House) in the newly configured and newly named Foster Place, which were labelled on completion 'as a great embellishment to our city'.[104] More modest, and less costly, additions to the fabric of the Royal Barracks and the laying of 'the foundation for the erection of a new Four courts in Inns Quay' in 1785; 'improvements' in 1786 to the chief secretary's lodge in the Phoenix Park; the completion in a 'superb manner' in 1788 of the 'new rooms' at the Rotunda, 'which formerly made such a despicable shabby appearance'; the demolition of 'old buildings' (also in 1788) in 'the middle square' in Trinity College and refurbishments to Dublin Castle; and further additions to the Linen Hall in 1789 reinforced this impression.[105] Meanwhile, the removal in 1787 of the Mall, which was one of the defining

101 *Exshaw's Gentleman's and London Magazine*, Apr. 1784, p. 224; Mulvany, *The life of James Gandon*, p. 57; *Hibernian Journal*, 28 June 1786; *Freeman's Journal*, 11, 22 July, 9, 23 Sept. 1786, 7 June, 6 Sept. 1787, 25 Aug., 22 Dec. 1789; *Dublin Morning Post*, 9, 21 Feb., 8 Mar., 1 Apr. 1788, 7, 24 May 1791, 3 Jan. 1792; *Ennis Chronicle*, 7 Jan., 22 June 1790; Loeber and Stouthamer-Loeber, 'Dublin and its vicinity in 1797', 137–8.   102 *Freeman's Journal*, 9 Nov. 1786, 26 Apr. 1788, 30 Apr. 1789; *Hibernian Journal*, 26 Aug., 21 Dec. 1789; *Walker's Hibernian Magazine*, Nov. 1791, p. 479; *Dublin Morning Post*, 17 Apr. 1794.   103 *Saunders's News Letter*, 12 Sept. 1785, 28 Dec. 1787; *Freeman's Journal*, 5, 19 Jan., 5 Dec. 1786; *Volunteer Evening Post*, 2, 23 June 1787; *Ramsey's Waterford Chronicle*, 6 Oct. 1789; *Hibernian Journal*, 2 Oct. 1789; *Dublin Morning Post*, 17 Aug. 1790.   104 *Dublin Morning Post*, 10 May, 16 Sept. 1788; *Freeman's Journal*, 10, 29 Dec. 1789; *Hibernian Journal*, 5 Apr. 1790.   105 *Dublin Evening Post*, 29 Dec. 1785, 24 Mar., 1 Sept. 1787; *Hibernian Chronicle (Cork)*, 27 July 1786; *Volunteer Evening Post*, 2 June 1787; *Freeman's Journal*, 3 Feb., 20 Sept. 1788, 1 Oct 1789; *Dublin Morning Post*, 7 Feb., 5 Apr. 1788, 3 Apr. 1790.

features of Sackville Street, when it existed in its own urban enclave, generated
expectations that it must, once the fountain bedecked with 'the magnificent
colossal statue of Neptune' promised by the lord lieutenant (the duke of
Rutland) was put in place, 'form one of the finest streets in Europe', added to
the perception that the city was being transformed for the better.[106] It certainly
encouraged those with ideas for further improvement to the city, and in its
environs.[107] In the case of Sackville Street, which was conceived of as a priority
by many, attention focused on its relationship with the Lying-in Hospital and
Rutland Square and on its 'continuation ... towards the intended bridge' over
the Liffey. The sale of building lots at the southern end of the street and the
welcome afforded the announcement in 1789 of the 'intention' to take 'down
the two houses in Gardiner's Row that projected across the top of Cavendish
Row in Rutland Square in order to continue the latter in a direct line to Dorset
Street' were both evidence of progress in that respect and an illustration of the
public's endorsement of the major urban remodelling that was taking place.[108]
Meanwhile, south of the river, hopes were high that plans for a 'new street of
70 feet wide' called Great Clarence Street, linking Grand Canal Street and
Rogerson's Quay, would transform the relationship of the quays with south side
suburbs.[109]

   Though developments on this scale were the preserve of major developers
and the Wide Streets Commission, there were other, more numerous, smaller
initiatives that reinforced the prevailing positive mood. One may instance the
warm response afforded the announcement in 1783 by Sir John Allen Johnston,
the MP for Baltinglass, that it was his intention to rebuild Clarendon market
and to transform that quarter of the city by 'opening a handsome street from
Chatham Street to William Street, and another from Clarendon Street to King
Street'.[110] His scheme was dwarfed, to be sure, by the opportunities forecast
for the 'north-eastern quarter' of the city as this area was opened up by a
combination of new 'passages' created by the Gardiner estate and the realization
that the impact of the relocation of the Custom House to the North Lotts must
have a transformative effect upon this area. Indeed, development proceeded at
such a pace there in the late 1780s that some felt justified in claiming that 'a
new town had arisen ... in the north-east vicinity of the city'.[111] This was to

106 *Volunteer Evening Post*, 6 Mar., 24 May, 2 June 1787; *Dublin Evening Post*, 1 Sept. 1787;
Freeman's Journal, 3, 6 Mar., 1 May, 4 Sept. 1787, 5 Jan. 1788.   107 Suggestions and
schemes for the removal of 'inconveniences' on the roads into Dublin, and on the desirability
of initiatives to integrate and link developments such as the Circular Road were advanced: see
Dublin Morning Post, 2 Oct. 1790, 2, 18 June 1791; *Hibernian Journal*, 31 May 1786; *Dublin
Weekly Journal*, 1 May 1790. These and other comparable schemes are beyond the scope of
this essay.   108 *Freeman's Journal*, 3 June 1784, 26 Mar., 7 Apr. 1789; *Exshaw's Gentleman's
and London Magazine*, Apr. 1789, p. 221; *Dublin Morning Post*, 3, 7 Apr. 1790.   109 *Dublin
Morning Post*, 23 June 1791.   110 *Dublin Evening Post*, 1 July 1783; *Hibernian Journal*, 31
May 1786.   111 *Freeman's Journal*, 4 Oct. 1788; *Hibernian Journal*, 25 May, 22 Dec. 1789,

exaggerate the order of what had been achieved by that point, but such was the enthusiasm then for 'forming regular streets' and 'elegant avenues' that no plan seemed unrealizable.[112]

One of the biggest schemes of all, of course, and one that offered clear evidence of the length of time that it could take to bring a major project of urban improvement to realization was the Fitzwilliam estate's plan for Merrion Square, which proceeded at an accelerated pace in the late 1780s.[113] The announcement in September 1788 that 'workmen have commenced enclosing the centre ground ... for the purpose of beautifying it' certainly brought renewed focus to the square, and to the fact that it was identified well in advance of its completion as 'not only ... a very great ornament to this metropolis, but ... vastly superior to any thing of the kind in any city in Europe'. Though not uncharacteristic of the overly confident tone of much domestic architectural commentary by this time, it acquired purchase in this instance from the fact that as development accelerated in the late 1780s the square was described as 'the most desirable situation in town for persons of rank and fortune to reside in', and a 'great ornament to that fashionable quarter of the city'.[114]

In an illustration of the allied eagerness to ensure that the development of Merrion Square was integrated into that of the rest of the expanding city, one commentator concluded his paean to the former with the observation that once the 'new' eastern bridge was in place, residents of the square would enjoy 'easy communication ... with Rutland Square', which was also proceeding apace on the city's northside contiguous to the Lying-in Hospital.[115] This ensured, once the decision to construct a new bridge in line with Sackville Street was 'finally determined' upon in September 1788, that the active speculation that had surrounded the subject since the embarkation on the construction of a new Custom House in 1781 was finally brought to a close. It was not replaced by informed discussion of what type of bridge was most appropriate, however, because of James Gandon's refusal to share his 'design for the bridge'. It was only when building commenced that the public observed the unfamiliar mode of construction that was employed. As a result, it was not until the project was well advanced and the merchants and traders of the capital lobbied to have a drawbridge incorporated into the design that the matter became a source of

16 Aug. 1790; *Dublin Weekly Journal*, 25 Sept. 1790.   112 *Freeman's Journal*, 18 Sept. 1787; *Exshaw's Gentleman's and London Magazine*, 48: Apr. 1788, p. 446; *Hibernian Journal*, 28 July 1790; *Dublin Morning Post*, 25 Sept. 1790.   113 See Nicola Matthews, 'Merrion Square' in *The Georgian squares of Dublin: an architectural history* (Dublin, 2006), pp 57–88.   114 *Volunteer Evening Post*, 7 Aug. 1787; *Freeman's Journal*, 27 Sept., 4 Oct. 1788, 8 Oct. 1791, 18 Feb., 20 Mar., 6 June 1792; *Dublin Morning Post*, 23 Sept., 4, 23 Oct. 1788, 23 Sept. 1790, 2 June 1791; *Hibernian Journal*, 12 Aug. 1789, 6, 22 Sept. 1790, 21 Sept. 1791, 15 Feb. 1792; *Dublin Weekly Journal*, 25 June 1791.   115 *Dublin Morning Post*, 4 Oct. 1788; *Freeman's Journal*, 7 Oct. 1790; Anthony Duggan, 'Parnell Square' in *The Georgian squares of Dublin: an architectural history* (Dublin, 2006), pp 7–32.

lively exchange.[116] The proposition was rejected, with the result that when the bridge was opened to traffic in November 1792, it reflected Gandon's design.[117] The expectation then was that an 'avenue to Carlisle Bridge from College Green' would soon follow, but when it was apparent that this was not to be, and that those who crossed the river using the bridge were obliged 'to make their way ... through dirty alleys', the optimism which greeted its opening was superseded by regret at the lost opportunity.[118] It did not entirely explode the optimism of those who had conceived of it as a transformative event in the history of the city, but it served as a reminder to those who cheer-led development at this time that it was not a story of uninterrupted progress.

This was not a conclusion that can have surprised seasoned observers, or those, who were more aware of the practicalities and, perhaps, of the challenging financial issues encountered by the Wide Streets Commissioners, who entertained fewer illusions about the time that could elapse between conception and completion.[119] There can be little doubt, certainly, but that the tardiness the public associated with the manner that the Wide Streets Commissioners pursued the plan of transforming Dame Street was a cause of keen disappointment.[120] By comparison, the failure to replace the 'tottering' Tholsel on Skinner's Row with a bespoke new building, which was long the presumption, excited less comment, and its fate was sealed in 1791, when a grand jury identified it as a 'nuisance', and it was pulled down with no plans for its replacement.[121] There was disappointment too that 'the old ruinous houses' that obscured the eastern front of Parliament House and 'the nasty brothel houses of Fleet Street' that 'hid' part of the 'new [parliament] building' were still in place.[122] But the issue that excited most negative comment (in the early and mid-1780s particularly) was the failure to proceed urgently with the removal of the 'bar or heap of sand washed down the mountains' that gathered in Dublin Bay at the point that the Dodder entered the sea, as a result of which ships entering the bay routinely ran aground. Persuaded that the problem could be solved by 'turning the Dodder behind the South wall', the expectations with which municipal mercantile and

116 *Dublin Morning Post*, 7 June, 23 Sept. 1788, 13 Apr., 20, 22 May, 19, 24 June, 3, 27, 31 July, 17, 24, 26, 28 Aug., 14, 19 Oct. 1790, 21 July 1791; *Freeman's Journal*, 3, 31 Aug., 11 Sept. 1790; *Hibernian Journal*, 25 Aug. 1790, 27 Aug. 1792; Fraser, 'Public building and colonial policy in Dublin', 114. 117 *Dublin Weekly Journal*, 13 Aug. 1791; *Dublin Morning Post*, 12 May, 9 June, 25 Aug., 18 Oct. 1792; *Hibernian Journal*, 8 June, 22 Aug. 1792. 118 *Dublin Evening Post*, 31 May 1792, 11 Apr. 1793; *Dublin Morning Post*, 9 June, 29 Nov. 1792, 7, 11 Apr., 9 May 1793. 119 This point was well made in 1768–9 by the 'essayist' (Andrew Caldwell) on architecture: *Freeman's Journal*, 31 Dec. 1768. For the financial challenges facing the Commission see Fraser, 'Public building and colonial policy in Dublin', 115–19; McParland, 'The Wide Streets Commissioners', 8, 18, 23–4. 120 *Dublin Morning Post*, 23 Oct. 1781, 24 May 1788, 8 Apr. 1790, 18 June 1791; *Dublin Weekly Journal*, 1 May, 26 June, 2 Oct. 1790. 121 *Freeman's Journal*, 18 Aug. 1787; *Saunders's News Letter*, 16 Jan. 1789, 21 Apr. 1791; *Ennis Chronicle*, 17 June 1790; *Hibernian Journal*, 6 May 1791; *Dublin Morning Post*, 9 July 1791. 122 *Dublin Morning Post*, 1 February 1791.

marine interests looked to parliament to legislate so that work could proceed seemed destined to be soon gratified when on 24 October 1781 the *Hibernian Journal* reported that 'the heads of a bill are again prepared for altering the course of the river Dodder, by making it disembogue to the eastwards of Irishtown'. It was not to be.[123] It was subsequently reported in *Saunders's News Letter* that the much-anticipated bill was deferred in response to a promise by Viscount Fitzwilliam that he would assume the responsibility, but, if so, the lack of action combined with the failure to present a bill during the 1783–4 session, to disappoint those for whom this was, in the pointed words of one commentator, 'more necessary to the kingdom than the vain pageantry of stupendous edifices'. As a result, severe criticism was directed at those, John Beresford and Viscount Fitzwilliam most notably, who were accused of failing to protect 'the navigation to the capital' and of prioritizing the wrong issues.[124] This was hardly fair criticism, but it underlined the gravity with which the matter was regarded. It also had the effect, when in the autumn of 1784 'two more vessels … broke … their backs on the banks which the river Dodder is forming', of spurring parliament into action. The introduction in 1785 of a bill 'for improving the port and harbour of Dublin', and the enactment of an amended measure in 1786 was the signal for the initiation of a programme of works the most notable feature of which was the construction of a 'wall' that both prepared the way for a much needed new bridge that provided the neglected village of Ringsend with a lifeline, and an ambitious scheme of dock development (to accommodate the anticipated increased flow of shipping) that was to be one of the major additions to the city in the 1790s.[125]

In 1790 when the author of a short commentary published in the *Dublin Morning Post* took stock of the 'public buildings of this city, particularly those for the dispensation of justice and commerce', he highlighted five – the new Custom House, the Parliament House, the Royal Exchange, the Royal Barracks and the new Four Courts – that were 'fixed on scites admirably designed to benefit the city at large'.[126] One cannot fault his choice, but he might, equally justifiably, have invoked any of a number of other 'improvements' that also showed the city in a good light, which, the city's many admirers delighted in pointing out, meant that Dublin surpassed Paris, Vienna, Madrid, Berlin and Potsdam in the 'elegant uniformity in the disposition of the buildings'.[127] Moreover, this was not the total of the city's accomplishment:

123 *Hibernian Journal*, 24 Oct. 1791; *Saunders's News Letter*, 24 Aug. 1781; *Dublin Evening Post*, 14 Nov., 20 Dec. 1781.   **124** *Dublin Evening Post*, 14 Dec. 1782, 6 May 1783; *Freeman's Journal*, 18 Oct. 1783; *Hibernian Journal*, 19 Dec. 1783, 8 Feb. 1784; *Saunders's News Letter*, 28 Oct., 15 Dec. 1784.   **125** Gilligan, *History of the port of Dublin*, pp 44–5; 26 George III, chap. 19; *Hibernian Journal*, 27 Oct. 1784; *Saunders's News Letter*, 10 Jan., 5 May, 30 Nov., 28 Dec. 1785, 13 Aug. 1787; *Dublin Evening Post*, 5, 23 Apr. 1785, 13 May 1788; *Dublin Morning Post*, 27 May, 26 June, 21 Aug., 30 Oct. 1788.   **126** *Dublin Morning Post*, 10 June 1790.   **127** *Freeman's Journal*, 26 June 1790.

Add to the ... magnificent public buildings, the widening, paving and
lighting of our streets, the erection of uncommonly handsome public
fountains at the terminus of each, the laying out new squares, the forming
docks near that matchless pile, the new Custom House, the completing
of canals and other improvements ... and let any man who has not been a
resident of this city and its neighbourhood for twelve years, return back,
and say, whether an extraordinary change [has not been] made ...'.[128]

This was not posed as a rhetorical question, but it might well have been. What
it, and other comparable commentaries demonstrate is the pride that the public
had come to express in their capital city. The invocation of the network of water
fountains that had recently been put in place was indicative, for though they
had an obviously utilitarian purpose – that of providing the populace with a
ready supply of clean water – they were also justifiably regarded as a 'beautiful
addition' to the streetscape, which accounts for the many newspaper reports
of their placement on Sackville Street, Mary Street, in the centre court of
the Royal Hospital, opposite the Blue Coat Hospital on Oxmantown Green,
and most notably of all, on the west side of Merrion Square.[129] The fountain
erected on Merrion Square in 1791–2 as a memorial to the duke of Rutland
who died in office in 1787 was twice built and taken down before a location was
identified that showed it to best effect.[130] This might, at this remove, seem like a
classic example of administrative indecision, whereas it can equally reasonably
be seen as a manifestation of the respect those who bought into the 'spirit of
improvement' had for the city and their eagerness to ensure that Dublin was a
pleasing place in which to live.

FALTERING OPTIMISM: THE 1790S

The confidence and optimism that was a feature of commentary on the
expanding city in the 1780s persisted into the early 1790s. It was even suggested
then that it had wrought a fundamental change in attitude as in advance of the
opening of the new Custom House the anticipation that it must prove 'of great
advantage ... to the mercantile body' elicited an acknowledgement that the public
was 'indebted to the Commissioners of the Revenue, under whose immediate
inspection it has been carried out'.[131] Meanwhile, an acceptance that the once-

---

128 Ibid., 3 Aug. 1790. 129 Ibid., 28 Mar. 1789; *Dublin Morning Post*, 1, 3 Apr., 5 June
1790, 15 Sept. 1791; *Saunders's News Letter*, 5 May 1785; *Dublin Morning Post*, 19 July 1787;
Exshaw's Gentleman's and London Magazine, 49 (Apr. 1789), p. 221; *Dublin Weekly Journal*,
3 Apr., 1 May, 12 June 1790; *Hibernian Journal*, 7, 23 June 1790, 4 May 1791. 130 *Walker's
Hibernian Magazine*, Sept. 1791, pp 287–8; *Dublin Morning Post*, 1 Oct. 1791, 14 June
1792. 131 *Dublin Morning Post*, 19 Mar. 1791.

controversial 'tax for paving, cleansing and lighting the metropolis' had not only contributed to the visible enhancement of the city's streets but also provided the funds that permitted 'the lighting and improving of all the great avenues to the city' suggested that the population was also 'reconciled' to this impost.[132] This may have been an exaggeration, but it is clear that the confidence that flowed from what another contemporary identified approvingly as the 'the rapid improvement and bold spirit of speculation, which are manifested in the eastern quarters of this metropolis', encouraged further grand schemes. One example, emanating with 'a spirited individual' eager to take advantage of the fact that once Carlisle Bridge was open to traffic Townshend Street would 'be nearly central to the fashionable world', was to construct 'an extensive range of buildings' devoted to 'exercise and amusement'.[133] Another idea that was given airing was 'to run the South Wall as far as Howth' thereby creating a channel sufficient 'to admit vessels of any depth up the river'.[134] Still another, which emanated with Luke Gardiner, Lord Mountjoy, who was the principal developer on the city's north side, conceived of 'building an oval Circus at the back of Eccles Street' that would be linked by 'a street ... sixty feet wide' extending in different directions to Oxmantown Green and the (North) Circular Road,[135] Meanwhile, not to be outdone, Rogers of Rogerson Quay contemplated an ambitious plan for a 'new town' on the grounds between Sandymount and Ringsend; Viscount Fitzwilliam pondered following Merrion Square with a 'new square ... between Baggot Street and Donnybrook Road'; Dublin Corporation determined on building a new Mansion House; while the commencement of a scheme to replace 'the old cubic lamps' in the Liberties with 'globes with double burners' contradicted 'the general complaint ... that improvement and building towards the sea, must be hurtful to the habitations to the west' of the city.[136]

This was the implication also of the plan of the Wide Streets Commissioners, following the demolition of the Tholsel, to 'take down the whole side of Skinner-row and to extend its breadth as far as Christ Church Yard, separating the precincts of the church from the street by a low parapet wall with an iron pallisade'. The preparedness of the Commissioners to work with the commissioners responsible for 'repairing the walls and quays of the river Liffey' in clearing 'away all the old buildings between Crampton Quay and the old Custom House' illustrated that their horizon was not fixed to the east. This was reinforced by various schemes, plans and suggestions emanating from different quarters for the 'improvement of the present approach[es]' to and the 'embellishment of the avenues' and streets of the metropolis, which manifest

132 Ibid., 17 Apr. 1794.   133 *Dublin Evening Post*, 30 Aug. 1792.   134 *Dublin Morning Post*, 19 Mar. 1791.   135 *Dublin Weekly Journal*, 2, 9 Oct. 1790; *Dublin Morning Post*, 9 Oct. 1790.   136 *Dublin Weekly Journal*, 20 Mar. 1790; *Dublin Morning Post*, 26 Aug. 1790, 18 June, 1 Oct. 1791, 25 Aug. 1792; *Cork Gazette*, 27 July 1791.

no obvious evidence of geographical prioritizing.[137] These suggestions for development bear equal witness to the strength of the 'spirit of improvement' as any of the celebrated grand plans that dominated the news columns. But the fact that there was no signature 'public building'[138] to excite the public meant that the undertaking that now commanded most notice was the ambitious scheme to provide the city with docks commensurate with its commercial ambition and to connect the harbour to the ongoing programme of canal development.[139]

In the late 1780s, as the works on Dublin Bay and the programme of canal development that had been underway for several decades progressed, the maximization of the economic benefit of these major infrastructural undertakings assumed increased prominence in the public sphere. The prospective benefits to the city of linking the Grand and Royal Canals to the river Liffey and the port possessed compelling appeal, and the main newspapers regaled their readers with encouraging reports of the steps that were being taken towards its realization.[140] The lord lieutenant, the earl of Westmorland, contributed by his presence to lay 'the first stone of the first lock on the Royal Canal' in a ceremony at Glasnevin in November 1790. This was the sort of public endorsement the directors of the company responsible for the canal required if they were to realize this ambitious scheme and they had a useful ally in the press, which not only reported the lord lieutenant's warm reception in suitably flattering terms but also described the development that occasioned his presence as 'unparalleled by any public work ever carried on in this kingdom'.[141] This was hyperbole, but it was consistent with the perception of those who unhesitatingly characterized the canal as a 'great national undertaking'.[142] They

---

137 *Freeman's Journal*, 4 June 1789, 19 Sept. 1793; *Dublin Morning Post*, 9 Oct. 1790, 21 May, 21 Sept., 5, 8 Oct., 22 Dec. 1791, 7 July, 16 Aug. 1792, 2, 4 May 1793; *Ennis Chronicle*, 26 May 1791; *Hibernian Journal*, 27 Sept., 8 Oct. 1790; *Dublin Weekly Journal*, 31 July 1790, 8 Oct. 1791. The state of the street continued to be a subject of comment during the 1780s and early 1790s; the fact that it was reduced by comparison with the situation in the 1770s is consistent with the view that the Paving Board had made a difference, though reports of neglect in the early 1790s indicates that those who maintained that the contrast between the main and side streets was correct: see *Dublin Morning Post*, 27 Mar., 26 Aug. 1790, 3 Feb., 7 Apr., 20 Aug. 1791, 1 Nov. 1792; *Hibernian Journal*, 20 Aug. 1790.   138 The city did secure a new House of Industry, which was built near Channel Row 'by order of the administration' in 1791–2, and an undertaking to rebuild the House of Commons which was badly damaged by fire on 27 February 1792, but they did not have the same impact as precious undertakings: *Dublin Morning Post*, 8 Oct. 1791, 12 May 1792; *Ennis Chronicle*, 1 Mar. 1792; *Freeman's Journal*, 1 Mar. 1792; Loeber and Stouthamer-Loeber (eds), 'Dublin and its vicinity in 1797', 137. The roof of the House of Commons 'fell in' as a result of the fire.   139 Ruth Delany, *The Grand Canal of Ireland* (Newton Abbot, 1973); V.T.H. and D.R. Delany, *The canals of the south of Ireland* (Newton Abbot, 1966).   140 *Exshaw's Gentleman's and London Magazine*, 49 (June 1789), p. 334; *Freeman's Journal*, 6 Oct. 1789; *Dublin Morning Post*, 1 Apr., 17, 24 June, 11 Dec. 1790, 7, 14 Apr., 25 Aug., 11, 18 Oct., 17 Nov. 1792; *Dublin Evening Post*, 10 May, 3, 15 Sept., 8 Oct. 1791; *Hibernian Journal*, 22 Aug. 1792.   141 *Dublin Morning Post*, 11, 13 Nov. 1791; *Dublin Evening Post*, 11 Nov. 1791.   142 *Dublin Morning Post*, 21 July 1792.

were encouraged in this attitude by the announcement (after considerable speculation as to the best option)[143] in October 1791 that William Jessop, the engineer, had 'laid out' the 'several parts of the floating and graving docks', and that he had done so in so 'masterly' a fashion that meant the thirty-two acre site 'will be the noblest works of the kind in Europe'.[144] Though the design, which had been 'exhibited' in the 'great coffee room of the Royal Exchange', was 'on a grand scale', it was deemed 'commensurate to the rising prosperity of this country'.[145] It would, it was pointed out, when taken together with the active programme of bridge and road building that was also being pursued, provide the capital with direct and efficient communication with the country, which must, the *Dublin Morning Post* pronounced confidently in 1792, raise it within a decade to the 'first rank' of European cities:

> Before the nineteenth century shall commence, Dublin, will be not only the most convenient, but in first rank of the superb cities of Europe; every entrance from the east, the south and the west will present a magnificent bridge, a beautiful canal, and an elegant avenue ...[146]

While the residents of Dublin in the early 1790s basked in the suggestion that their city could continue to look forward optimistically to the future, there were signs that the speed with which the city had grown had created its own problems, which cast the expansion of the city in a less positive light.[147] The most readily identifiable of these was the increase in land prices and the related 'rage of speculation in building'. Though mention of speculative investment is to be found in a reference dating from 1787 to building land 'at the rere [*sic*] of Merrion Square', it was more pronounced 'in the vicinity of the new Custom House', as ground, once given over to fields and orchards, was either leased or sold at record prices in 1789 to 1790 to those who were eager to profit thereby.[148] There is no contemporary index of the pace at which rents and land values rose. But assertions to the effect that land 'in certain situations in the vicinity' of Dublin had reached 'a monstrous price' by the summer of 1789, and that this was quantified at 150 per cent 'in the vicinity of Sackville Street and Rutland Square' in August 1790 indicates that it was well in train by then. It had further to go, moreover, as the prospect of profits fuelled interest, with the result that, as well as Summerhill, which held a particular attraction for the 'dabblers in building' – 'the merchants, manufacturers, and even clerks in the treasury' who were tempted to speculate – lands once deemed 'unprofitable

143 See, inter alia, ibid., 11 Apr. 1789, 27 May, 7, 14 Aug. 1790.   144 Ibid., 8 Oct. 1792. Others estimated the site at 18 to 21 acres: *Hibernian Journal*, 24 June 1791.   145 *Hibernian Journal*, 13 May 1791.   146 *Dublin Morning Post*, 7 Apr. 1792.   147 *Saunders's News Letter*, 6 Dec. 1786.   148 *Hibernian Journal*, 26 Aug. 1789, 25 June 1790; *Volunteer Evening Post*, 19 May 1787; *Freeman's Journal*, 26 Aug. 1790, 14 May 1793; *Clonmel Gazette*, 10 July 1790.

and unwholesome' made high prices.[149] This constituted a justifiable risk in the case of the 'waste ground' at the lower end of Townshend Street and the 'waste ground of Marlborough Green'. It was more hazardous in the case of the coastal property of Scaldhill, Sandymount, for which a high price was sought in 1790, but in an environment where 'the price of houses' on prized quayside locations had risen by 'near an hundred per cent' by the summer of 1792 speculation seemed warranted.[150] Moreover, it was not confined to the east of the city, and the hinterland of the new Custom House and Carlisle Bridge. It was here, newspaper readers were informed, that speculation was at is most intense during those years spanning the end of the 1780s and early 1790s when what was described as 'the present rage for building' was at its strongest. But the 'enormous' prices paid in the summer of 1791 for 'the lots of ground that are to form the new street leading from Cornmarket to Cook Street' in the city's liberties confirmed what reports from other areas of the city and its hinterland also suggested that the price and building boom impacted, albeit not equally, most parts of the city and its near environs.[151] It was fuelled by underlying demand, moreover, though it is proper to query if this was sufficient to justify the optimistic pronouncement, printed in April 1792, that contracts had recently been agreed to add a further 1,200 houses to the city's stock.[152] More worrying still was the claim in June that both the cost of living and 'house rents are considerably cheaper in every part of London'.[153]

This did not come as a shock to those who had long regarded the accelerated rate of growth in the city nervously. Though much of the ongoing criticism of the pace and nature of urban development appealed for legitimation to the enduring conviction that that city living was inherently corrupting – it 'has always brought on a corruption in the manners of its own inhabitants' – it was intensified in this instance by the perception that Dublin's 'magnificence' was 'attained at the expence of keeping all of the rest of the kingdom poor'. This was mistaken, but it prompted calls, in 1791, for legislative intervention 'to restrain it [the growth of Dublin] within some rational bounds' lest it should 'become a serious grievance to the country'.[154] Since this was a minority view, it is unsurprising that MPs failed to do as requested. Moreover, because the property market was strong, there was no incentive to do so though there were identifiable signs of disquiet, as the perception that development disproportionately advantaged a minority took firmer hold, and critical attention came to focus on the Wide Streets Commissioners.

---

149 *Hibernian Journal*, 16 Aug. 1790; *Dublin Morning Post*, 15 Mar. 1791, 25 May, 11 June 1793; *Freeman's Journal*, 12 Apr., 26 May 1791, 14 May 1793.   150 *Hibernian Journal*, 26 Aug. 1789, 29 Apr. 1793; *Dublin Morning Post*, 26 Oct. 1790, 15 Mar., 30 Aug., 1 Oct. 1791, 7, 31 July, 25 Aug. 1792; *Ennis Chronicle*, 1 Dec. 1791.   151 *Dublin Morning Post*, 21 July 1791, 18 Oct. 1792; *Dublin Weekly Journal*, 23 July 1791; C.J. Woods (ed.), *Charles Abbot's tour through Ireland and North Wales in 1792* (Dublin, 2019), p. 57.   152 *Dublin Morning Post*, 26 Apr. 1792.   153 Ibid., 14 June 1792.   154 *Limerick Chronicle*, 22 Apr. 1771;

Though its largely aristocratic membership was reason enough for some to question their decisions, the Wide Streets Commission evaded sustained critical scrutiny in the 1780s. This did not liberate it from the suspicion that it was an unaccountable cabal whose members pursued a programme of improvement that answered first to their private interests. It was not a criticism that could easily be sustained when it came to explaining the delays to the development of Dame Street, or other changes to the streetscape that the commissioners were urged repeatedly to expedite, but the tone in which criticism of its failings in this respect were couched sharpened once Carlisle Bridge was opened to foot traffic in 1792. Impatient at the delay in providing appropriate access, accusations of 'partiality and jobbing' multiplied.[155] Attention focussed particularly on the powerful figure of the chief commissioner of the revenue, John Beresford, who now operated out of what was portrayed as palatial offices in the new Custom House, though this was less damaging to the reputation of the Commission as a whole than the perception that they sought 'to satisfy no one except themselves'.[156] This was unfair. But it echoed in a metropolis many of whose residents had reached the conclusion that the combination of delays, difficulties in negotiating the city streets, boarded houses, and other obstacles they encountered daily was proof that 'public convenience' was being sacrificed on the altar of the Commission's 'caprice and obstinacy'.[157]

These accusations did not assist the Wide Streets Commission to acquit itself of its responsibility, which was, the *Dublin Morning Post* reminded the public in 1793, 'to superintend the improvement of the city', but, in the absence of firm evidence, they were no more than suspicions.[158] This is what made the claim, advanced in the House of Lords by Barry Maxwell, the second earl of Farnham, in July 1793 that the Commission had not just favoured Henry Ottiwell, who was employed in the 'general office' of the Revenue Commissioners, when he leased seven plots of development land on the North Strand in 1789, but had done so in a manner that was financially disadvantageous to the organization. Convinced that this provided them with the evidence 'of peculation', as it was termed, they had long suspected, and that they could use it to compel the commissioners to be more open and responsive in the way it conducted its business, the commissioners' critics seemed set fair to achieve the reforms they had long believed necessary when the committee of the House of Lords that investigated the allegation determined that the Commission had entered into 'a hasty and improvident bargain with Ottiwell'.[159] The report's findings were strongly contested. But it was not until the 1794 session, when the matter was

Dublin Morning Post, 8 June, 18 Dec. 1790, 30 Aug. 1791; *Freeman's Journal*, 28 May, 30 Aug. 1791. **155** *Dublin Morning Post*, 20 Aug. 1791, 31 May, 13 Sept. 1792, 2 May, 24 Aug. 1793; *Freeman's Journal*, 28 Apr. 1792, 14 May, 22, 24 Aug. 1793; *Hibernian Journal*, 4 Sept. 1793, 19 Sept. 1794. **156** *Dublin Morning Post*, 24 Aug. 1793. **157** Ibid., 21 Aug. 1793; *Hibernian Journal*, 30 Oct. 1795. **158** *Dublin Morning Post*, 2 May 1793. **159** Ibid., 7 July 1793, 27 Mar. 1794. For proceedings in 1794 see James Kelly (ed.), *IHL Proc.*, ii, 450, 463–4,

properly investigated, that the Commission was exonerated. Deemed to have behaved properly, they contrived both to discredit the findings of the Farnham report and to explain the process whereby the original decision was taken.[160] This did not always reflect well on the Wide Streets Commissioners. It reflected still more badly on Farnham and on the Commission's various critics, but this was less consequential in moulding public opinion than the fact that when the matter was finally put to bed in 1796, the public felt still justified in its belief that 'millions are squandered away in prodigality and corruption'.[161] There was no suggestion that this was due to the manner in which key aspects of the city's management and improvement were delegated to bodies such as the Wide Streets Commissioners, the Paving Board, the Grand Canal Company, even the Ballast Board, but the side-lining of Dublin Corporation that was an inevitable consequence of the establishment of these and other bodies had not passed unnoticed, and there were those who concluded that this was imprudent as well as inappropriate.[162]

While the Ottiwell investigation inevitably dulled the sheen of the image the 'improvement' of the city had acquired in the 1780s, the damage was contained by the capacity of the legislature to investigate such matters away from prying eyes, and by the skill with which the Commission's champions employed the press both to justify their procedures and to disprove the allegations levelled at them.[163] There was no evading the reputational fallout however, or its broader implications, for even if the Commission successfully refuted the damaging imputation that they had 'mismanaged a public concern' and countered with the accusation that they had been subjected to 'much vulgar misrepresentation', both the details that were admitted into the public sphere allied to the fact that it was twice investigated by the House of Lords had a negative effect.[164] This can be identified in the assertion, present in the midst of an otherwise ordinary report on the impact of high winds in December 1794, that the standard of 'building has of late years been reduced to a more fraudulent science than even jockeyship'.[165] Moreover, the fact that its publication coincided with the end of the booming housing market reinforced this tendency. There is much about this that remains to be unpicked, but it appears that difficulties were experienced late in 1792. These were not then of sufficient magnitude to interrupt development,

482–3, 512, 515–20, 528–9.   160 Kelly (ed.), *IHL Proc.*, ii, 512, 515–20, 528–9; *Freeman's Journal*, 13, 29 Mar. 1794, 5 June 1795; *Dublin Morning Post*, 27 Mar. 1794.   161 Loeber and Stouthamer-Loeber (eds), 'Dublin and its vicinity in 1797', 139; *Freeman's Journal*, 11, 16 Feb., 16 Mar. 1796.   162 See Beresford's observation in the House of Commons, 8 Mar. 1792, reported in *Dublin Morning Post*, 10 Mar. 1792; *Saunders's News-Letter*, 18 Nov. 1796.   163 For the response in the press see, in particular, the point by point refutation of the Farnham report published in the *Dublin Morning Post*, 27 Mar. 1794, and the still longer summative account of the whole affair: *Dublin Morning Post*, 29 Apr. 1794. Loeber and Stouthamer-Loeber (eds), 'Dublin and its vicinity in 1797', 139.   164 *Dublin Morning Post*, 13 July 1793, 21 Oct. 1794, 19 Apr. 1795.   165 Ibid., 13 Dec. 1794.

but they intensified in 1793 when builders, unable to find credit to enable them to continue, brought construction to a halt and 'above 300 houses [were] left half finished'.[166] To compound matters, when speculators were unable to secure the rents they had anticipated on properties in Summerhill, the residential market declined till a point was reached in the spring of 1794, when there were 'no bidders' for houses offered for auction on Arran Quay, and this continued as houses and lands available to 'lease forever' in the hinterland of Carlisle Bridge and the new Custom House in 1794 and 1795 found no purchasers.[167] Some attributed 'the damp ... upon building speculation' that the country also experienced at that moment to the fact that Britain and France were at war. But it is perhaps better accounted for by reference to the economic downturn that gripped the city at that point and the retrenchment that inevitably followed the unsustainably high speculative investment that was a feature of the boom years of the late 1780s and early 1790s.[168]

This did not herald a return to a moment prior to the building take off when, the state of the streets excepted, the 'improvement' of the city was a subject of intermittent and passing comment. Indicatively, when Sackville Street was opened for carriages in September 1794, the report conveying this news included an encouraging reference to the fact that 'Sackville Street is now the first situation in Dublin for business'.[169] The positive mood was vitiated more than a little by ongoing concern at the absence of 'some opening from College Green to Carlisle Bridge, which might afford the public a tolerable passage, instead of the abominable chain of nuisances which at present ... endanger the limbs and the lungs of every passenger', but this was only one of a veritable litany of 'reproaches to public decency' that the press now routinely associated with the poor state of the city's streets.[170] Moreover, it was not as if there were no positive developments to report. The announcement in October 1795 that £20,000 had been subscribed to pay for the erection of a suite of 'Commercial Buildings' on Dame Street was one, and there were other 'improvements' on the upper quays, 'new streets to the south-east of Carlisle Bridge', that elicited further, but now more rarely articulated assertions that they were of a quality 'inferior to none in the first cities in Europe'.[171]

This was an effective rhetorical device of course. It was also of doubtful pertinence in these instances. The comparison was more legitimately drawn in 1796 when, after several years of sustained endeavour, the Grand Canal Docks

---

166 Newenham to Washington, 11 Feb. 1794 in C.S. Patrick (ed.), *The papers of George Washington*, presidential series, vol. 15 (Charlottesville, 2009), pp 218–22.   **167** *Dublin Chronicle*, 16 Oct. 1792; *Freeman's Journal*, 6 Apr., 7, 14 May, 20 June 1793; *Dublin Morning Post*, 1 Apr., 29 Nov. 1794, 17 Apr., 21 May 1795; *Hibernian Journal*, 23 Nov. 1792, 6 May 1793, 3 Aug. 1795.   **168** *Dublin Morning Post*, 16 Oct. 1794.   **169** Ibid., 11 Sept. 1794.   **170** *Hibernian Journal*, 19 Sept. 1794, 28 Oct. 1795; *Dublin Morning Post*, 27 Sept., 16, 27 Dec. 1794; *Saunders's News Letter*, 17 Mar. 1796.   **171** *Dublin Morning Post*, 25 Sept., 16 Oct. 1794; *Saunders's News Letter*, 28 Mar. 1796.

were completed. Opened by Earl Camden, the lord lieutenant, on St George's day (23 April), the presence of the vicegerent lent a suitably celebratory tone to the occasion, and delighted the crowd, overestimated at 150,000, which revelled in the inauguration of this 'very great undertaking'.[172] By comparison, the completion of the refurbishment of the House of Commons chamber in time for the commencement of the 1796 parliamentary session excited less notice, but the publication of a detailed account of the elegance to which it was restored indicated that it set a high standard. It also provided an opportunity for city residents to affirm its claim to possess a building that was not just equal, but 'in point of elegant simplicity and grandeur of design, the present House of Commons is the first room in Europe'.[173] It was, it might be observed, a pointless claim, but it captured the pride the population now had in the city as a result of the major 'improvements' that had been made over a period of little over a decade-and-a-half. There may well have been a certain weariness in the manner in which it was relayed in the *Dublin Weekly Journal* in February 1797 that 'the much desired and (scandalously) long-delayed opening of the south avenue to Carlisle Bridge' would take place later that month, but it was the realization of a long-anticipated expectation.[174] Moreover, it was genuine, for though the most welcome additions to the cityscape in the years immediately following – the commencement of the building of the King's Inns in 1800 and the completion of the law offices to the east of the Four Courts in 1801 – did not register with the public as strongly as previous major public buildings, they helped to sustain the belief they engendered that, whatever the implications of the Act of Union, the recent pattern of growth bode well for the future of the city.[175]

CONCLUSION

This was not to be, of course. Within a decade, the confidence that expansion had brought the city had all but evaporated, and Dublin was embarked on a prolonged phase characterized by self-doubt rather than confidence.[176] The truth of the matter, as the informed and percipient observations of the city made in 1797 recognized, was that though Dublin aspired to elegance, and was possessed of a variety of 'extremely beautiful' public buildings and attractively 'paved and lighted' principal streets, its side streets were 'filthy and diabolical'.[177] The streetscape would have been much worse to be sure, had the city not

172 *Saunders's News Letter*, 28 Mar., 25 Apr. 1796; see also Loeber and Stouthamer-Loeber, (eds), 'Dublin and its vicinity in 1797', 145.   173 *Saunders's News Letter*, 17 Nov. 1796.   174 *Dublin Weekly Journal*, 18 Feb. 1797.   175 *Cork Advertizer*, 4 Aug. 1801; *Ennis Chronicle*, 8 Aug., 10 Oct. 1800.   176 Hill, *From patriots to unionists*, pp 285–95; Dickson, *Dublin: the making of a capital city*, pp 273–95.   177 Loeber and Stouthamer-Loeber (eds), 'Dublin and its vicinity in 1797', 146.

embraced the 'spirit of improvement' that peaked in the 1780s and early 1790s, and that meant that Dublin then presented a face to the world in which residents and visitors alike found much to admire. This was assisted, doubtlessly, by the fact that it took place during an era of demographic and economic growth; it is improbable it would have occurred in their absence. Be that as it may, it is useful to trace how the citizenry engaged with it, and to explore how the suspicion with which they long regarded plans for expansion yielded in the 1780s to pride, guided by the recognition that they were witnesses to the creation of a large, elegant and in places truly impressive urban space. It might not have achieved the architectural heights that Andrew Caldwell conceived possible in 1768, but it was a palpable advance on what had once characterized the city, and it was properly commented on approvingly by visitors and enjoyed by many of its residents.

'Idle castle building airy schemes': John Black III and the 'improvement' of eighteenth-century Belfast

JONATHAN JEFFREY WRIGHT

By the mid-1760s, the town of Belfast was undergoing a period of sustained and transformative growth. As merchants and ship owners seized on the economic opportunities offered by linen and the North American emigrant and Caribbean provisions' trades, the economic contraction characteristic of the first half of the eighteenth century was reversed and the town's population began to swell.[1] On the whole, the picture was a bright one. But problems could also be discerned. Largely confined within the bounds of its seventeenth-century ramparts, Belfast was cramped and somewhat shabby. Its streets were smelly and dirty, its public buildings – few enough in number – were in want of repair and, more seriously, there were signs that social order was beginning to strain.[2] In 1756–7, harvest failures and grain hoarding led to an outbreak of food rioting and a spike in deaths among those identified as 'poor', highlighting starkly the precariousness of life among the town's lower orders.[3] Faced with these problems, one contemporary, the Belfast-born merchant John Black III, pondered solutions. Writing to his son George, in July 1765, Black III made reference to an earlier letter he had addressed to 'our friend M^r. Biggar' – an agent of Belfast's absentee landlord, Lord Donegall – in which he had included 'an anonymous memorial of what alterations & improvements might be made for his lordships & inhabitants advantage of Belfast'.[4] As outlined in his letter to his son, Black III's proposals for the improvement of Belfast were wide-ranging. He began by recommending the building of 'the soe much wanted a new church' and 'proposed a poor house or hospitall for the Christian & charity relief of the sick & the distressed who are seen in such numbers on your dirty streets'. Next, he suggested the construction of 'a new road from the Malone turn pike in a direct line over a new bridge over the black watter where a sluice & a mill might be erected' – a road that would

---

1 Raymond Gillespie, *Early Belfast: the origins and growth of an Ulster town to 1750* (Belfast, 2007), pp 128–9, 156, 158–9, 167, 171; Norman E. Gamble, 'The business community and trade of Belfast, 1767–1800' (PhD, Trinity College Dublin, 1978), pp 11, 81–93, 266–95, 318–20. 2 Gillespie, *Early Belfast*, pp 161, 167–8; *idem*, 'Making Belfast, 1600–1750' in S.J. Connolly (ed.), *Belfast 400: people, place and history* (Liverpool, 2012), pp 123, 126–7, 130, 134; S.J. Connolly, 'Improving town, 1750–1820' in *idem* (ed.), *Belfast 400*, pp 161, 162–3, 179. 3 Gillespie, 'Making Belfast', pp 139–40; James Kelly, *Food rioting in Ireland in the eighteenth and nineteenth centuries* (Dublin, 2017), pp 98–9. 4 For Bigger as an agent of Donegall see John Black III to Alexander Black, 14 Mar. 1764 (PRONI, D719/72). When quoting from primary sources original spelling has been maintained, but capitalization has been minimized and, in some instances, punctuation has been added for the sake of clarity.

link Belfast to its immediate hinterland and provide a new way of entering the town. Following this, he turned his attention to the town's existing streetscape, detailing a raft of possible improvements. The flattening of 'ruinous buildings', including 'the old guardhouse' and the 'old tottering houses on the church yard side of Church Lane', would facilitate the enlargement of the town's entrance, the expansion of Markethouse Square and the construction of 'a square of green walks to the front of the castle northward'. A 'public walk' could also be laid out in the unpleasant square terminating Broad Street, an exchange could be constructed for the town's merchants and new streets could be developed. More ambitiously, the unused 'strand' that lay adjacent to 'Warren Street' could be put to use as a site of industry and the town's docks and quaysides could be bettered:

> a bridge might be built over the dock att the opening of Queen Street to have the readyer communication from the customhouse quay by an opposite street in a direct line into Warren Street & by which the millstone bank as it was formerly called butt now the strand opposite & north of the customhouse might soon invite moneyed people to wall it in on the channel side & soon make it a thronged built habitation.

This would, he pronounced, be a fit project for 'a joint society of wealthy friends' who would, in developing the area, 'lay there a good foundation for the benefit of themselves & their posterity'.[5]

There was much to digest in all of this, and Black III was well aware that his prescriptions might appear far-fetched. As he drew his letter to a close, he quipped that they were 'idle castle building airy schemes'.[6] But it would be a mistake to dismiss them as mere flights of fancy. For one thing, as the antiquarian Isaac Ward long ago noted, they reflected 'an intimate acquaintance with the wants of his native town'.[7] Moreover, a number of improvements strikingly similar to those recommended by Black III *were* made during the 1770s and 1780s. A new church was erected, albeit a decade after Black recommended it, between 1774 and 1776. Likewise, a poor house and exchange were constructed, and by the mid-1780s spacious new streets had been developed, including Linen Hall Street, which ran due south from the town to another new building, the White Linen Hall. By the early 1810s, this building's surrounding grounds had been railed off and planted, creating a walkway similar to those recommended by Black III.[8] Without conforming in every respect to his suggestions, these

5 John Black III to George Black, 18 July 1765 (PRONI, D4457/214). A transcript of this letter is also available (PRONI, D1401/5) and it is presented in full, with helpful annotations, in Isaac W. Ward, 'The Black family', *UJA*, 2nd ser., 8 (1902), 180–6.   6 John Black III to George Black, 18 July 1765 (PRONI, D4457/214).   7 Ward, 'Black family', 185 n.6.   8 Ibid., p. 182 n.2, 183 n.1 and n.2, 185 n.2; Gillespie, *Early Belfast*, pp 168, 170–2; Connolly, 'Improving town', pp 162–4, 167–70; Jonathan Jeffrey Wright, "'The Donegalls' Backside":

developments demonstrate that Black III's scheme for the improvement of Belfast was far from unrealistic.[9] But whether realistic or not, his detailed proposals merit further attention. As one scholar has recently suggested, eighteenth-century Belfast was not just a 'physical space'. It was, in addition, a mental construct that existed in the imagination of its inhabitants and reflected 'common ideas about what the town was and how it worked'.[10] More than a series of practical recommendations, Black III's proposals for Belfast's improvement offer access to one such set of ideas, and viewing his letter of July 1765 alongside his other surviving writings – in particular the revealing journal he kept from 1751 to 1766 – offers an opportunity to reconstruct the ways in which he conceived of his world and thought about society.[11] But before turning to consider his proposals for the improvement of Belfast more closely, we might first consider the nature of his relationship with the town.

I

On the face of things, it appears surprising that John Black III should have concerned himself with the development of Belfast. His family's connections with the town were long-established – his grandfather, John Black I, having settled there in the mid-seventeenth century – but Black III spent the bulk of his life elsewhere.[12] The son of John Black II, an Atlantic merchant whose career had taken him to France and the Caribbean, Black III was born in Belfast in

Donegall Place, the White Linen Hall and the development of space and place in nineteenth-century Belfast' in Georgina Laragy, Olwen Purdue and Jonathan Jeffrey Wright (eds), *Urban spaces in nineteenth-century Ireland* (Liverpool, 2018), pp 61–83.   9 Ward, 'Black family', 185 n.6.   10 Gillespie, 'Making Belfast', p. 124.   11 A copy of Black's journal, or, more properly, his Laus Deo book, is available in PRONI in four gatherings: T1073/7 (Jan. 1751 to Sept. 1754), 8 (Dec. 1754 to Oct. 1759), 12 (Jan. 1760 to July 1762) and 16 (Aug. 1762 to May 1766). Its pages are not consistently paginated, nor are the individual entries consistently dated. In what follows, the journal is cited by giving a date deriving from the page heading, along with the archival reference in parenthesis, that is, Laus Deo, Sept. 1754 (PRONI, T1073/7). Where two or more successive pages bear the date in the heading, a numeral will be added in parenthesis, that is, Laus Deo, 28 July 1753 (1) (PRONI, T1073/7). For an overview of the journal, see David Kennedy, 'The journal of John Black of Belfast, merchant, 1751–66', *Bulletin of the Irish Committee of Historical Sciences*, 93 (1961), 2–3. A brief extract of the journal, dating to December 1754, can also be found in Ward, 'Black family', 186–7.   12 Jean Agnew, *Belfast merchant families in the seventeenth century* (Dublin, 1996), p. 212. For previous work on the Black family see, inter alia: Agnew, op. cit., *passim*; *The correspondence of Joseph Black*, ed. Robert G.W. Anderson and Jean Jones (2 vols, Farnham, 2012); George Benn, *A history of the town of Belfast from the earliest times to the close of the eighteenth century* (London, 1877; repr. Belfast, 2008), pp 522–4; L.M. Cullen, *Anglo-Irish trade, 1660–1800* (Manchester, 1968), pp 94, 148–9, 163; Gamble, 'Business community', *passim*; James Livesey, *Civil society and empire: Ireland and Scotland in the eighteenth-century Atlantic world* (2009), pp 128–262; Kennedy, 'The journal of John Black'; Joseph McMinn, 'An engraving of Blamont, County

either 1681 or 1682 (sources vary), and was raised for a life in trade.[13] Detailing his early years in a self-penned memorial, jotted in his journal in June 1763, Black III noted that he had received an early education in Belfast '& in Air in Scotland', following which he was 'Sent to Dublin & bound prentice there att about 17 years of age to his <u>Unckle Ald. Eccles</u>'.[14] After this, he was 'sent … by his pious & worthy father & his unckle in 1699 to be a factor with Geo. Boyd a distant relation of the Blacks born att Coleraine'.[15] Although hailing from Coleraine, Boyd was based in Bordeaux – in Louis Cullen's estimation, one of eighteenth-century Europe's 'dominant Atlantic ports' – and it was there that Black III would spend much of his life.[16] By 1713 he had struck out on his own, 'becoming a factor himself with the good will of all acquainted with his good intentions', and three years later he married 'the virtuous gracefull Margaret Gordon', daughter of Robert Gordon, 'a factor from Aberdeen in low circumstances by his attachment to the Jacobite party'.[17] In the years that followed, Black III fathered fifteen children and established himself as a prosperous and well-known figure in Bordeaux society, acquiring both a 'town house cellar &c' and a 'country estate', and establishing what he described as an 'intimate acquaintance' with the sometime president of the Bordeaux parlement, the writer and philosopher Montesquieu.[18]

Armagh', *Seanchas Ard Mhacha*, 17 (1996–7), 89–94; William Ramsay, *The life and letters of Joseph Black* (London, 1918); Henry Riddell, 'The great chemist, Joseph Black, his Belfast friends and family connections', *Proceedings of the Belfast Natural History and Philosophical Society*, 3 (1919–20), 49–88; *Partners in science: letters of James Watt and Joseph Black*, ed. Eric Robinson and Douglas McKie (London, 1970); *The Bordeaux–Dublin letters 1757: correspondence of an Irish community abroad*, ed. L.M. Cullen, John Shovlin and Thomas M. Truxes (Oxford, 2013), pp 54, 67–8, 75, 97–9; Ward, 'Black family'; *An Ulster slave-owner in the revolutionary Atlantic: the life and letters of John Black*, ed. Jonathan Jeffrey Wright (Dublin, 2019). **13** Ward, 'Black family', 177, 186–7; Agnew, *Belfast merchant families*, pp 211–12. A family tree in the Black family's papers gives Black III's year of birth as 1681, but he himself gave it as 1682: 'Black family tree' (PRONI, D4457/363); Laus Deo, Dec. 1756, 2 June 1757 and 22 June 1757 (PRONI, T1073/8). **14** Alderman Eccles was, Sir John Eccles, who served as mayor of Dublin between 1710 and 1711, and whose niece, Jane Eccles, was Black III's mother. Agnew, *Belfast merchant families*, pp 211, 224–5; Riddell, 'The great chemist', 61–2. **15** Laus Deo, 14 June 1763 (PRONI, T1073/16). This June 1763 account is one of a number of short biographical statements penned by Black III. Two years earlier he included a similar account when making power of attorney arrangements for his sons, and a third account dates from 1754, when he sketched a short family history in his journal – see, Laus Deo, Dec. 1754 (PRONI, T1073/8); Riddell, 'The great chemist', 61–2; Ward, 'Black family', 186–7; Livesey, *Civil society and empire*, p. 130. **16** Ward, 'Black family', 185 n.6, 186; *Bordeaux–Dublin letters*, ed. Cullen et al., pp 31 (for quote), 36. **17** Laus Deo, 14 June 1763 (PRONI, T1073/16). 'Low circumstances' should be understood in relative terms. 'The house of Robert Gordon was', Louis Cullen notes, 'the most prominent Scottish house [in Bordeaux] *c*.1700, and remained so for another three decades.' *Bordeaux–Dublin letters*, ed. Cullen et al., p. 34. **18** 'Black family tree' (PRONI, D4457/363); Laus Deo, 10 July 1751 and 29 June 1754 (PRONI, T1037/7); Riddell, 'The great chemist', 63–4; Gamble, 'Business community', p. 254; Agnew, *Belfast merchant families*, p. 189; William Doyle, *Origins*

Black III returned to Belfast in 1725 and 1738, on the first occasion visiting his 'sick & bedrid aged father', and on the second responding to reports of the 'distress' of his widowed sister, Priscilla Arbuckle.[19] But it was not until 1751 that he attempted to return to Ireland on a more permanent basis, attempted being the operative word. Books, family papers and the paraphernalia of life among the middling orders ('copper playtes' and silverware, 'messatintos' and a 'spy glass') were boxed up and shipped to Ireland, while legal documents were acquired authorizing two of Black III's sons – John (that is, John Black IV) and James – to take control of his Bordeaux property and conduct business on his behalf.[20] Such arrangements suggest that Black III was serious about resettling in Ireland. Yet, in July 1753, he made an impromptu return to Bordeaux, greatly surprising his son John, and delighting his 'former friends & acquaintances' in the town's exchange, who offered 'demonstrations of love affection joy & esteem' and expressed the hope that he 'would now settle with them for the future'.[21] Black III's response was non-committal: he would rely on God to guide him, as he had done before.[22] In the event, he remained in Bordeaux for the next four years, weathering a period of 'trouble & anxiety', early in 1756, when an order expelling Britons from France was issued, and the outbreak, later that same year, of the Seven Years War.[23] When granted permission to remain in Bordeaux, Black III attributed it 'to the publick's good opinion & report of my lyfe & inoffensive conduct amongst them these 56 years past'.[24] In reality, most of Bordeaux's British and Irish merchants appear to have been permitted to remain.[25] Nevertheless, the period was a troubled one. In May 1756, Black III endured 'a most impertinent visitt from a neighbour … who inquired about my religion marriage children possessions with envious questions about my property', and the following March he remarked on 'the malicious & inveterate reports in these soe prejudiced troublesome times to all who bear the name of English'.[26] By the end of the month he had 'resolved to return to Ireland', and on 5 April 1757 he left Bordeaux for good.[27]

Upon returning to Ireland, Black III spent several weeks in Dublin, before proceeding to Blamont, a property in County Armagh that the family had acquired several years previously, and that he had used as a home (of sorts) when he sojourned in Ireland during the period 1751 to 1753.[28] With its ornamental

of the French Revolution, (2nd edn., Oxford, 1988), p. 87; Kennedy, 'The journal of John Black', 3. **19** Laus Deo, 14 June 1763 (PRONI, T1073/16); 'Black family tree' (PRONI, D4457/363). **20** 'List of books sent to Belfast, 15 March 1751' (PRONI, D4457/64); Laus Deo, 12 Mar. 1751, 10 July 1751 and 14 Oct. 1751 (PRONI, T1073/7). **21** Laus Deo, 28 July 1753 (1), 28 July 1753 (2) and 4 Aug. 1753 (PRONI, T1073/7). **22** Laus Deo, 4 Aug. 1753 (PRONI, T1073/7). **23** Laus Deo, 1755–1756, Mar. 1756, 10 Mar. 1756, 10 Apr. 1756 and May 1756 (1) (PRONI, T1073/8); *Bordeaux–Dublin letters*, ed. Cullen et al., p. 43. **24** Laus Deo, May 1756 (1) (PRONI, T1073/8). **25** *Bordeaux–Dublin letters*, ed. Cullen et al., pp 43–4. **26** Laus Deo, May 1756 (1) and Dec. 1756 (PRONI, T1073/8). **27** Laus Deo, 31 Mar. 1757 (PRONI, T1073/8). **28** Laus Deo, 14 Oct. 1751 (PRONI, T1078/7); Laus Deo, 14 May 1757 (PRONI, T1073/8); McMinn, 'An engraving of Blamont', 89–94; *An*

gardens, 'majestic grove of ash and elm', 'fish pond' and 'drawing room lined with Morocco leather', Blamont appears to have been an idyllic retreat and many years later Black III's grandson – another John Black – recalled it fondly and urged that it be kept within the family on the grounds that his 'grandfather of sacred memory was much attached to it'.[29] A glance at Black III's journal suggests otherwise. During the period 1751 to 1753 his residence at Blamont had been punctuated by absences as he visited family in Belfast, Dublin and Scotland, and travelled – '159 miles in 10 days' – in counties Monaghan, Enniskillen, Donegal and Londonderry.[30] He was no less peripatetic following his return to Ireland in 1757. As early as 6 June 1757 he travelled from Blamont to Belfast, remaining there for the better part of a month, before returning to Blamont on 2 July.[31] By 8 August he was on the move again, travelling once more to Belfast, where he stayed until the twenty-fifth of the month, and in the years that followed he shuttled regularly between Blamont and Belfast, spent long spells in Dublin and, between September 1760 and June 1761, visited the Isle of Man and undertook a lengthy tour of England.[32] Blamont did have its uses. It offered 'solitude' and 'tranquillity', relief from 'citty busle & noise' and a retreat where Black III could recuperate from the indulgences – 'too much babble cheer & bottle' – of urban sociability.[33] But its charms could pale. Restful solitude could easily become lonely isolation. Having travelled to Belfast, late in August 1760, Black III characterized Blamont as 'this too lonesome abode'.[34] Likewise, in November 1761, he noted that it was 'too moist [and] melancholy an abode for winter', and by January 1766 he was contemplating its sale.[35]

By contrast, during the period 1757 to 1758, Black III made a concerted effort to acquire a property in Belfast. This process had begun prior to his return to Ireland. In February 1754, while still in Bordeaux, he wrote to John Gordon, who had been appointed two years previously as an agent of Lord Donegall, Belfast's landlord, 'reminding [him of] his promise that when the Donegall family renewed the leasehold att Belfast my self & myne should nott be forgott butt favored to some convenient preference'.[36] Three years later, in June 1757, he despatched a similar letter, in which he complained of 'nott having in this place of my nativity 1682 house or covering where to recline my

---

Ulster slave-owner, ed. Wright, p. 69 n.13.   **29** *An Ulster slave-owner*, ed. Wright, pp 69–70, 103.   **30** Laus Deo, 14 May 1752, 14 July 1752, 18 Aug. 1752, 4 Nov. 1752, 16 Jan. 1753 and 10 May 1753 (PRONI, T1073/7).   **31** Laus Deo, 2 June 1757 and 1 July 1757 (PRONI, T1073/8).   **32** Laus Deo, 19 July 1757, 10 Aug. 1757, 1 Sept. 1759 and Oct. 1759 (PRONI, T1073/8); Laus Deo, Jan. 1760, 10 Sept. 1760, 23 Sept. 1760, 16 Nov. 1760, 24 Jan. 1761, 23 Feb. 1761, 7 Apr. 1761, 8 May 1761, 21 May 1761, May and June 1761, Sept. and Oct. 1761, 24 Nov. 1761 and Mar. 1762 (PRONI, T1073/12).   **33** Laus Deo, 1 July 1757 and 10 Aug. 1757 (PRONI, T1073/8); Laus Deo, Mar. 1760 (PRONI, T1073/12).   **34** Laus Deo, 24 Aug. 1760 (PRONI, T1073/12).   **35** Laus Deo, Sept. and Oct. 1761 (PRONI, T1073/12); Laus Deo, 9 Jan. 1766 (PRONI, T1073/16).   **36** Laus Deo, 15 Jan. 1752 and Feb. 1754 (PRONI, T1073/7).

hoary & weary head' and requested that Gordon 'think on assigning me some plott of ground by lease whereon I might build a dwelling to my self & for my posterity with offices gardens &c'.[37] At around the same time, he prepared a 'succinct memorial' for the prominent Belfast merchant Valentine Jones. In this, he outlined his family's 'present dispersed circumstances', explained his desire to 'gather' his children in Belfast and complained that he lacked 'a convenient mansion' in which to do so. Jones offered a possible solution. The 'castle kitchen garden', a plot of land in the grounds of the old Belfast Castle – which had burnt down in 1708 – would be ideal for Black III's purposes. But there was a problem: the lease for the plot was 'possessed during her lyfe by Mad.ᵐ Banks'. Unperturbed, Black III called on Banks and managed to secure her consent to his 'endeavours to obtain a lease' for the land, a development 'which surprized nott a little M.ʳ Jones & others who doubted of her soe easy complyance'.[38] Over the next twelve months, Black III negotiated and corresponded with the agents and trustees of the Donegall estate in a bid to formalize the arrangement, but in July 1758 disaster struck when he was informed of 'poor weak Mad.ᵐ Banks' loss of memory & denyall of her having signed the cession'.[39] With this, the arrangement fell through.

Several months later, in November 1758, Black III explored a second option, contacting Daniel Mussenden – yet another of the town's more prominent merchants – with a 'proposall for buying the remaining lease of 2 old houses &c att the foot of Pottinger's Entry the place where I was formerly told I breathed att first my lyfe'.[40] It appears that this, too, came to nothing. Nevertheless, these attempts to secure property in Belfast are revealing. That Black III was in contact with figures such as Jones and Mussenden lends weight to Ward's suggestion that his connections to the town and 'interest in its affairs' were sustained by 'business relations'.[41] Moreover, his contact with Donegall's agent, John Gordon, is equally significant, demonstrating that his circle of contacts extended beyond the ranks of Belfast's merchants. But above all, his attempts to secure a property in Belfast following a life spent largely in Bordeaux serve to highlight his continued orientation towards, and association with, the town.

There is no mystery as to why this should have been the case. Belfast was, after all, his birthplace. Added to this, the realities of familial separation, so common among Atlantic families, enhanced the importance of the town.[42] As has been noted, Black III had a large family. His wife, Margaret Black née Gordon, had died in 1749, but thirteen of his fifteen children – John, Isobel,

37 Laus Deo, 22 June 1757 (PRONI, T1073/8).   38 Ibid.; George Benn, *A history of the town of Belfast from 1799 till 1810, together with some incidental notices on local topic and biographies of many well-known families* (London, 1880; repr. Belfast, 2008), pp 115–16, 183–6.   39 Laus Deo, 1 July 1757, 19 July 1757, 10 Aug. 1757, Oct. 1757 and July 1758 (PRONI, T1073/8).   40 Laus Deo, 16 Nov. 1758 (PRONI, T1073/8); Benn, *A history of the town of Belfast from the earliest times*, p. 578 n.1.   41 Ward, 'Black family', 185 n.6.   42 Sarah M.S. Pearsall, *Atlantic families: lives and letters in the later eighteenth century* (Oxford, 2008),

Jane, Robert, Priscilla, George, Joseph, Alexander, Samuel, Esther, James, Thomas and Katharine – survived infancy and made it to adulthood. They were, however, scattered across the eastern Atlantic region, in Ireland, Britain, France and the Isle of Man; as Valentine Jones put it, Black III's family was 'numerous & dispersed'.[43] In such circumstances, Belfast offered a fixed point of reference. It was not, to be sure, the only such location: Dublin, the home of Black III's daughter Jane and her husband Isaac Simon was also important.[44] Indeed, writing in August 1763, Black III described Dublin as 'a proper place & the center of my family correspondency'.[45] Nevertheless, Belfast remained of particular importance to his sense of self. It was, as he put it in August 1757, his 'native place'.[46] In Belfast, he could worship in the church in which he had been baptized and root himself in his familial context in the town's burial ground – as he did in August 1758, when he spent time 'walk[ing] amongst our ancestors' tombs & inscriptions'.[47] That he sought, later that same year, to acquire the lease for the house in which he had been born is quietly telling, as also is the evident pleasure he took when his own children gravitated towards Belfast. Black III's son George had settled in the town by the late 1740s, and his father would later jest that he was 'the chief governor & superintendent of my colonie Belfastienne'.[48] A second son, Sam, had entered the lucrative linen trade in 1758, acquiring 'a bleach green reckoned one of the most compleat of its kind in Ireland' and located a short distance south of Belfast.[49] By 1762, George and Sam had been joined by a third son, Tom, and Black III observed that Belfast was 'pretty well stocked with flourishing & promising branches of our family' and predicted, with perhaps a hint of satisfaction, that 'my George my Sam & Tom will maintain the remembrance of our name'.[50]

II

Despite having spent the better part of his life in Bordeaux, John Black III thus remained closely attached to Belfast and it is against this backdrop that his

pp 26–55.   **43** 'Black family tree' (PRONI, D4457/363); Laus Deo, 14 June 1763 and 20 Aug. 1764 (PRONI, T1073/16); Livesey, *Civil society and empire*, p. 132.   **44** 'Black family tree' (PRONI, D4457/363); Laus Deo, 14 Oct. 1751 (PRONI, T1073/7).   **45** Laus Deo, 24 Aug. 1763 to 12 Sept. 1763 (PRONI, T1073/16).   **46** Laus Deo, 18 July 1757 (PRONI, T1073/8).   **47** John Black III to Robert Black, 1 Sept. 1758, (PRONI, D719/51); Laus Deo, Aug. 1758 (PRONI, T1073/8); Laus Deo, 24 Aug. 1760 (PRONI, T1073/12). For a similar analysis of Black III's relationships with Belfast and Dublin, see Nicholas Canny, 'The Irish colony in Bordeaux, 1757: a representative sample of Irish communities abroad?' in Thomas M. Truxes (ed.), *Ireland, France and the Atlantic in a time of war* (London, 2017), p. 48.   **48** John Black III to George Black, 16 Mar. 1748 and Apr. 1748 (PRONI, D1950/18 and 20); John Black III to George Black, 30 June 1764 (PRONI, D4457/202).   **49** John Black III to Robert Black, 1 Sept. 1758 (PRONI, D719/51).   **50** John Black III to Alexander Black, Oct. 1762 (PRONI, D719/63). For Black III's sons and their place in Belfast, see Gamble,

interest in the improvement of the town should be viewed. Indeed, his interest long predated his letter of July 1765. It has been suggested that the Black family was, by around 1750, 'one of the leading families in the growing city of Belfast, playing an important role in the development of the city landscape'.[51] This is something of an exaggeration. Although the Black family's connections with Belfast can be traced back to the mid-seventeenth century, John Black II had died by March 1726 and in the 1730s and 1740s the family's presence in Belfast was peripheral, and its influence minimal: as James Livesey has put it, 'they were not a locally prominent family'.[52] Black III did, however, seek to play a part, albeit informally, in shaping the development of the town from around the mid-1750s onwards. Writing to his son George in November 1754, for instance, he commented on the construction of a new street in Belfast and remarked that he had 'some time ago' contacted John Gordon and recommended that the Donegall family 'might advantageously employ some share of their soe vastly increased rents in takeing in the north side of the dock and graving bank by a wall towards the channell as far as opposite the rope walk closed in there alsoe by a wall leaving an opening for Warren Street east as far as the channell &c &c.'[53] Four years later, in July 1758, he noted in his journal that he had written a 'humourous letter to Jo Stewart of Balladrain with a plan of my native Belfast which might as [per] my memeoriall att length be so well & usefully improved', and in March 1763 he despatched a letter to London, addressed to 'my townsman Mr Bigger, Lord Donegal's receiver there, proposing some new improvements to our native Belfast &c.'[54] Clearly, Black III did not wish to maintain a passive link with Belfast. Rather, he sought to help shape its future. But what were the influences that informed his proposals for the town's development? And what do those proposals tell us about his view of the world?

In turning to these questions, the first point to note is that Black III's interest in improvement was by no means unusual. As Toby Barnard has demonstrated, 'a zest for improvement gripped many in late seventeenth- and eighteenth-century Ireland.' Deriving ultimately from the mid-seventeenth century, and the activities of a group of surveyors, innovators and writers influenced by Samuel Hartlib, the 'cults and cultures of improvement' are perhaps most readily associated with novel schemes and agricultural advances sponsored by clergymen, reforming landowners and learned societies.[55] But improvement also spread to the 'middling sorts' and impacted on the towns and cities of

'Business community', p. 255; *An Ulster slave-owner*, ed. Wright, pp 22–4. **51** McMinn, 'An engraving of Blamont', 92. **52** Laus Deo, Aug. 1758 (PRONI, T1073/8); Livesey, *Civil society and empire*, p. 130. **53** Quoted in Ward, 'Black family', 179. **54** Laus Deo, July 1758 (PRONI, T1073/8); Laus Deo, 24 Feb. 1763 (PRONI, T1078/16). **55** Toby Barnard, *Improving Ireland? Projectors, prophets and profiteers, 1641–1786* (Dublin, 2008), pp 11, 19–20, 120 and *passim*; Ian McBride, *Eighteenth-century Ireland: the isle of slaves* (Dublin, 2009), pp 6–7; Toby Barnard, *Irish Protestant ascents and descents, 1641–1770* (Dublin, 2004), pp 208–34, 306–29; see also, Livesey, *Civil society and empire*, pp 54–89.

eighteenth-century Ireland.[56] Indeed, as James Kelly reveals elsewhere in this volume, a 'spirit of improvement' was at work in Dublin during the second half of the eighteenth century, eliciting regular public comment in the 1780s.[57] For evidence of Black III's engagement with the culture of improvement we need look no further than his library. One corollary of the attempts that were made to improve Ireland's present was the reappraisal of its past. In some circles, as Barnard has noted, there developed 'a belief that a detailed knowledge of the past would assist towards a better Ireland' and a variety of attempts were thus made, in the eighteenth century, to produce Irish histories.[58] Included in their number were the Physico-Historical Society's surveys of counties Cork, Down and Waterford. Prepared by Walter Harris and Charles Smith, these combined both 'natural and civil history' and sought, as Eoin Magennis has put it, 'to depict an improved Ireland with the potential for greater economic, social and cultural advances'.[59] All three titles were included in the collection of books that Black III despatched to Belfast prior to his departure from Bordeaux in 1751, and it is possible to detect traces of their influence in his journal.[60]

In their surveys, Harris and Smith devoted space to the discussion of standing stones, round towers and other antiquities, and in his journal entries for early 1753 we see Black III casting an antiquarian eye on the landscape, identifying both ancient monuments and sites of more recent historical significance.[61] Early in the year he visited Belfast for the marriage of his son George to Arminella Campbell, and while in the town travelled the short distance to Carrickgfergus where there was an 'old tower said to be built by K. Fergus of Scotland near 2000 years agoe'. On the same Belfast visit, he also travelled south to the Purdysburn home of Hill Wilson, the 'unckle & guardian' of his daughter-in-law, and from there 'went to view a place in that neighbourhood they vulgarly call the gyant's ring.' In a passage which contains echoes of Harris's discussion of the same site in his 1744 survey, *The antient and present state of the county of Down*, he remarked that this was:

> of circular form about 400 paces diameter with a mound of elevated yearth & ditch around it by some said to have been an encampment of the antients or of the invadeing Danes in the centre there stands a circle of large stone on end which supports a kind of round table stone 7 or 8 feet broad conjectured to have been in paganism a kind of altar for sacrifices

56 Barnard, *Improving Ireland?*, p. 167.　57 See Kelly, 'Dublin in an "era of improvement"' in this volume.　58 Barnard, *Improving Ireland?*, p. 90.　59 Ibid., pp 114–17; Eoin Magennis, '"A land of milk and honey": the Physico-Historical Society, improvement and the surveys of mid-eighteenth-century Ireland', *RIA Proc.*, 102C (2002), 199–217 (212 for quote); Walter Harris, *The antient and present state of the County of Down. Containing a chorographical description, with the natural and history of the same* (Dublin, 1744), ii, iv.　60 'List of books sent to Belfast, 15 March 1751' (PRONI, D4457/64).　61 Magennis, '"A land of milk and

offered by their priests or [devoted] to their heathen deities severall urns with ashes & bones of men having been dugg up around in a neighbouring field.[62]

The following May, Black III visited Enniskillen and 'observed that place soe famous in 1689 for the bravery of its inhabitants', and a few weeks later, while travelling from Belfast to Dublin, he passed through Drogheda and 'from the old Dane mount saw the obelisk memorial of King William's passing the Boyne & defeat of K. Ja.s army in 1689' and 'the breach by which O. Cromwell entered & sacked the town with soe much bloodshed'.[63]

History and antiquarianism aside, Black III also appears in his journal in a more overtly improving guise as an enlightened and informed traveller, alert to signs of industry and economic activity. Passing through Antrim in May 1753 he 'saw my L.d Mazarines house' and observed 'large barks with English goods coals &c'.[64] Likewise, in May 1759, he noted approvingly that 'my Sam's bleach green begins greatly to improve with usefull engines', and in September 1760, having visited Newtownards, where his daughter Katharine had settled following her marriage to the merchant Francis Turnly, he characterized it as 'a village of about 2000 inhabitants of weavers'.[65] For Black III, Ulster – or, at any rate eastern Ulster – was synonymous with industry. Writing to his son George, in June 1766, he referred to 'the industrious Ulster part of our Hybernia', and one notable characteristic of his schemes for the improvement of Belfast was his advocacy of enhancements calculated to boost economic activity.[66] As noted above, in his letter to his son George of November 1754, Black III explained that he had earlier contacted the agent of Lord Donegall to propose the improvement of the town's docks. Infrastructural development of this kind would have been of obvious utility to the town's merchants and, indeed, it *was* one of the town's merchants, Thomas Greg, who was to begin the process of improving the docks some fifteen years later.[67] In the same letter, Black III also referred favourably to 'the projected canal' – the Lagan Navigation, which promised to connect Belfast to Lough Neagh – noting that 'I heartily wish it good and speedy success'.[68] His support for this project was no doubt informed by knowledge of an earlier man-made waterway – the eighteen-mile-long canal that had been constructed between 1731 and 1742 in order to link Newry

honey"', 211. 62 Laus Deo, 16 Jan. 1753 (PRONI, T1073/7); Harris, *Antient and present state*, pp 200–2. 63 Laus Deo, 10 May 1753 and 1 June 1753 (PRONI, T1073/7). 64 Laus Deo, 10 May 1753 (PRONI, T1073/7). 'Mazarine' was Clotworthy Skeffington, the first earl of Massereene, the majority of whose lands were located in County Antrim, and whose 'house' was Antrim Castle. Rosemary Richey, 'Skeffington, Clotworthy' in *DIB*, *sub nomine*. 65 Laus Deo, 25 Apr. 1759 (PRONI, T1073/8); Laus Deo, 6 June 1760 and 24 Aug. 1760 (PRONI, T1073/12); Gamble, 'Business community', p. 255. 66 John Black III to George Black, 20 June 1766 (PRONI, D4457/227). 67 Ward, 'Black family', 179 n.5; Benn, *A history of the town of Belfast from 1799 till 1810*, p. 11. 68 Ward, 'Black family',

with Lough Neagh.[69] Certainly, he was familiar with this earlier canal, for he regularly passed through Newry, while *en route* to Dublin, and in 1757 advised his son James, who was then in Ireland, that he could travel 'along the canal' from Newry to Blamont.[70] Moreover, shortly after its opening in 1742, Newry's canal had been surveyed, and its potential benefits enumerated, by Harris in his *Antient and present state of the county of Down*. By the mid-1750s, Harris's prediction that the canal would facilitate a 'thorough trade' had been borne out.[71] Newry had emerged as 'the busiest port in the north of Ireland' and Black III's support for the Lagan Navigation was likely informed by an awareness that the southern town's gain was Belfast's loss.[72]

The encouragement of developments conducive to trade and industry, and a recognition of the potential of the Lagan Navigation, is equally apparent in the July 1765 letter in which Black III discussed his 'anonymous memorial' on the improvement of Belfast. Here, he proposed an appropriate site for a Merchant's Exchange, and highlighted the value of 'the strand north of Warren Street'. This was, he believed:

> the most proper place for ship building & ... for a dry dock to repair ships' bottoms. Alsoe for publick slaughter houses to prepare & salt beef for foreign marketts. Lykewise a fitt place for the timber yards rather than where att present they are south of Anne Street, which might be employed in pleasant dwellings & a quay on the side of My Ladies' Dock which runs & empties itself above bridge into the Lagan & might be a landing place for the goods & gabards goeing & comeing on the Lisburn cannall which it's to be hoped will be made in due time in a very advantageous navigation to & from Lough Neagh.[73]

Such proposals reflected an understanding of the town as an integrated economic space, a site in which trade could thrive and wealth be created. But Black III's vision of Belfast was not solely economic. The town was also a site of sociability and domesticity, and Black III had thoughts as to how it could be rendered more pleasant.[74] Most obviously, clean and orderly streets were desirable. Writing in November 1754, he expressed his 'respectfull esteem' for the town's then sovereign, Stewart Banks, predicting that he would 'recommend the removall of all publick nusances as much as possible ... and the frequent cleaning the

179, 179 n.6; Connolly, 'Improving town', p. 172; Gillespie, *Early Belfast*, p. 160.   **69** Tony Canavan, *Frontier town: an illustrated history of Newry* (Belfast, 1989), pp 79–87; Gillespie, *Early Belfast*, p. 160.   **70** *Bordeaux–Dublin letters*, ed. Cullen et al., p. 98; Canny, 'The Irish colony in Bordeaux', p. 43. There are numerous references to Newry in the journal. See, for just a few examples: Laus Deo, 14 May 1752 and 1 June 1753 (PRONI, T1073/7); Laus Deo, 4 May 1757 (PRONI, T1073/8).   **71** Harris, *Antient and present state*, pp 112–19 (118 for quote).   **72** Canavan, *Frontier town*, p. 87; Gillespie, *Early Belfast*, p. 160.   **73** John Black III to George Black, 18 July 1765 (PRONI, D4457/214).   **74** Gillespie, 'Making Belfast',

streets from rubbish and dunghill before the doors.'[75] If Banks did make such recommendations their impact was limited. By 1765 the state of Belfast's streets remained a problem; 'the square att the north end of Broad Street' was 'a dung hill of nastiness', though Black III continued to praise Banks – 'the best & fittest of magistrates' – who had been appointed, once more, as sovereign. If the town could be cleaner, it could also, in Black III's view, be more carefully planned and ordered. The unpleasant square on Broad Street 'ought to be levelled kept clean & railed about for a public walk' and the so-called 'new buildings', which were, in reality, in a state of dilapidation, 'ought to be thrown down to open up a square of green walks'. More ambitiously, the construction of a thoroughfare 'to open & enter the town on a direct line to the opening of Hercules Street across the North Street unto the new street would give a wholesome opening conveniency to strangers & others' and 'a great conveniency & ornament with a freer open air to the town would be to open a new street in a direct line & the same bredth of Broad Street to Anne Street over the stone bridge'. Improvements of this nature would, of course, be aesthetically pleasing. But they promised other benefits besides. As Black III put it: 'stagnation breeds corruption [and] the more open well aired a populous place is, the wholesomer to its inhabitants'.[76]

Black III's vision of an improved Belfast streetscape, characterized by space, clean streets and enclosed public walks, evokes Peter Borsay's description of England's 'urban renaissance', which brought with it 'a new consciousness of the relationship between buildings' and changing architectural modes. Out went irregularity and the vernacular, and in came 'a uniform domestic architecture', more spacious streets and the square.[77] This prompts the question as to which models Black III drew from when he contemplated the improvement of Belfast. He did not, of course, *need* the examples offered by England's growing towns and cities. By the mid-eighteenth century, developers were constructing broad streets, squares and impressive public buildings in Dublin, a city Black III knew well.[78] That said, he would undoubtedly have been aware of the changing nature of England's urban spaces. In addition to his properties in Bordeaux and County Armagh he also owned a house in London, where developers had led the way in constructing squares in the late seventeenth century.[79] Moreover, he had travelled extensively in England, passing through many of its provincial towns. Returning to Ireland from Bordeaux in 1751 he travelled through the south of the country, following an itinerary which took him from Dover to London (via Canterbury, Rochester and Chatham), and on to Liverpool (via Windsor, Oxford, Woodstock, Blenheim, Bristol, Gloucester, Worcester, Shrewsbury,

pp 124, 156–7.   75 Quoted in Ward, 'Black family', 179–80.   76 John Black III to George Black, 18 July 1765 (PRONI, D4457/214).   77 Peter Borsay, *The English urban renaissance: culture and society in the provincial town, 1660–1770* (Oxford, 1989), pp 60–79 (esp. 60, 63 and 74–5).   78 See Kelly, 'Dublin in an "era of improvement"' in this volume.   79 Laus Deo, 1 Jan. 1751 (PRONI, T1073/7); Laus Deo, 14 Oct. 1763 (PRONI, T1073/16); Borsay,

Whitchurch and Chester).⁸⁰ In 1761, when he toured England with his son Tom, his itinerary was still more extensive. Among other towns, it encompassed Whitehaven ('nott above 100 years old enritched by its coalrice sent to Ireland'), Carlisle, Newcastle, 'old gothick Durham', Darlington, Thirsk, York, Tadcaster, Ferrybridge, Bawtry, Tuckford, Newark, Grantham, London, St Albans, Stratford, Coventry, Warrington and Liverpool.⁸¹

But if Black III would thus have been familiar with the impacts of England's 'urban renaissance', it is equally possible that in considering the improvement of Belfast his thoughts turned to the urban space in which he had spent the greater part of his life: Bordeaux. Certainly, Bordeaux offered striking examples of the sort of 'healthful' spaces that he recommended for Belfast. Beginning in the mid-1740s, its royal intendant, the marquis de Tourny, promoted a process of improvement which would see the construction of impressive boulevards and the spacious and striking *jardin public*, a garden that was comparable with that of the Tuileries in Paris and that would become, in the words of one historian, 'the model for public gardens to the end of the eighteenth century.'⁸² Initially, Black III viewed these schemes with scepticism. In a letter penned in Bordeaux in April 1748 he scoffed at 'our chimerical plans'.⁸³ Nevertheless, by the mid-1750s the impact of Bordeaux's improvements was increasingly apparent and the parallels with Black III's advocacy of wider streets, public walks and the benefits of fresh air following his final return to Ireland in 1757 are, at the very least, suggestive.⁸⁴

III

Whatever influence it had on his schemes for Belfast, Bordeaux provided Black III with a point of comparison. In April 1748, when he referred dismissively to the 'chimerical plans' for Bordeaux's improvement, he did so within the context of a comment on the management of Belfast: 'it's well', he wrote, 'the Donegal family is for encouraging & promoting the interest of the inhabitants which will doe more good than our chimerical plans of streets trophies in honor of the revolution &c'.⁸⁵ Insofar as they related to Belfast, these comments were wide of the mark, for by the mid-eighteenth century the town was suffering from a

---

English urban renaissance, p. 75.   **80** Laus Deo, 14 Oct. 1751 (PRONI, T1073/7).   **81** Laus Deo, 7 Apr. 1761, 8 May 1761 and 21 May 1761 (PRONI, T1073/12).   **82** Richard Cleary, 'Making breathing room: public gardens and city planning in eighteenth-century France' in John Dixon Hunt and Michael Conan (with Claire Goldstein) (eds), *Tradition and innovation in French garden art: chapters of a new history* (Philadelphia, 2002), pp 73–4; Eric J. Jenkins, *To scale: one hundred urban plans* (New York, 2008), p. 32.   **83** John Black III to George Black, Apr. 1748 (PRONI, D1950/20).   **84** Jean-Pierre Poussou, 'The outset and course of the Seven Years War in Bordeaux, 1755–1763' in Truxes (ed.), *Ireland, France, and the Atlantic in a time of war*, p. 129.   **85** John Black III to George Black, Apr. 1748 (PRONI, D1950/20).

period of prolonged proprietorial neglect. Belfast's proprietors, the Donegall family, were long-term absentees and Sir Arthur Chichester, the fourth earl of Donegall, who had come into possession of the Donegall estate as a ten-year-old boy in 1706, and who was considered by some to be mentally deficient, had done little to promote the town's development. Indeed, the Donegall estate was beset by legal complications and by the early 1750s Belfast's inhabitants were growing increasingly anxious at the prospect of their leases expiring without renewal.[86] Black III himself would later observe that 'the Belfastians are under too great discouragements from their landlord's weakness & short leases of dependencey' and it seems highly unlikely that he was unaware of the problems facing the town when he wrote in 1748.[87] How, then, can we account for his rosy assessment of Belfast's proprietors?

It is possible that when praising the Donegall family's management of Belfast Black III was thinking of its earlier contributions to civic life. The fourth earl's predecessor had, for instance, been highly regarded, and in the early eighteenth century the family had provided funding for the town's schoolmaster and for repairs of the Cromac Bridge.[88] However, an alternative explanation is suggested if we consider briefly the formal political life of Belfast. From around the mid-1690s, the town's corporation was dominated by Presbyterian merchants, a state of affairs the Episcopalian Donegall family seemed happy enough to accept. Harmony prevailed until 1704, when the Irish parliament passed the Test Act, making receipt of communion in the established church a prerequisite for public office holders. This led to the resignation of the town's Presbyterian sovereign, David Buttle, but the Presbyterian burgesses held on to their positions and in 1707, seemingly orchestrated by the influential brothers George and James Macartney, elected a Presbyterian, Samuel Ogle, as an MP for the town. In so doing they challenged the authority of the Countess Donegall, who oversaw the Donegall estate during the minority of her son, the fourth earl, and who had put forward an alternative candidate for election, William Cairnes. In due course, the result of the election was challenged in the Irish parliament, which unseated Ogle and clarified that the provisions of the Test Act applied not just to the sovereign, but also to the burgesses, a number of whom consequently resigned and were replaced by adherents of the Church of Ireland.[89]

86 W.A. Maguire, 'A question of arithmetic: Arthur Chichester, fourth earl of Donegall, 1695–1757' in Brenda Collins, Philip Ollerenshaw and Trevor Parkhill (eds), *Industry, trade and people in Ireland, 1650–1950: essays in honour of W.H. Crawford* (Dublin, 2005), pp 32–3, 41, 43–6; Gillespie, *Early Belfast*, pp 151–6. See also Peter Roebuck, 'The Donegall family and the development of Belfast, 1600–1850' in P. Butel and L.M. Cullen (eds), *Cities and merchants: French and Irish perspectives on urban development, 1500–1900* (Dublin, 1986), pp 125–36.   87 *Bordeaux–Dublin letters*, ed. Cullen et al., p. 98.   88 Agnew, *Belfast merchant families*, p. 96; Gillespie, *Early Belfast*, p. 155.   89 Gillespie, *Early Belfast*, pp 152–3; Maguire, 'A question of arithmetic', pp 34–6; Agnew, *Belfast merchant families*, pp 92–4, 96–104.

Superficially, this appears to have been a religious dispute, but as Jean Agnew has demonstrated it was really about power: George and James Macartney, who had arranged the election of the Presbyterian Ogle, were themselves Episcopalians and the events of 1707 in fact marked 'the culmination of a struggle between the Macartneys and Lady Donegall for control over the corporation.'[90] Further clashes would occur in subsequent years, but in 1707 the pattern for the eighteenth-century was set: the corporation's independence had been decisively curbed and Belfast's Presbyterians were excluded from the formal political life of the town.[91]

Viewed in his context, Black III's praise of the Donegall family reads as rather more than a straightforward assessment of the management of Belfast. Instead, his comments hint at an acceptance of proprietorial authority and respect for the traditional, hierarchical social structure embodied in the relationship between landlord and tenants. This hint is reinforced by the evidence of his journal and correspondence. That Black III sought to shape the development of Belfast by forwarding memorials to Donegall's agents is, for instance, significant, reflecting a willingness to work within the constraints of proprietorial bureaucracy, a no doubt frustrating state of affairs for a merchant used to conducting business on his own behalf. Equally significant is his careful cultivation of connections with Donegall's agents. Early in January 1752, having learnt that John Gordon had been appointed as an agent of the estate Black wrote to congratulate him, and by 1757 he was describing Gordon as his 'old worthy friend'.[92] Whether the pair's relationship predated Black III's letter of January 1752 is unclear, but it is known that Black III kept in touch with Gordon and established connections with his successors in the years that followed.[93] Moreover, he also encouraged one of his younger sons, Alexander, to do likewise, writing in March 1764 that he should seek to introduce himself 'to our Belfastian friend M.ʳ Bigger agent for My L.ᵈ Donegal in London'.[94] By this point the fourth earl of Donegall had died – in October 1757 Black III recorded the passing of the 'weak unlamented earle' in his journal – but the Blacks maintained a connection with the fifth earl.[95] Indeed, in March 1763 Black III noted that his son Sam, who was then in London, 'Entertained often with Lord Donegall other nobles & W.ᵐ Clarke his friend there'.[96] Those nobles may have included Lord Hillsborough, for a year earlier, in his letter to Alexander Black, Black III made reference to 'my Sam's friend Hillsborough Lord of the trade'.[97] When we add to this the fact that yet

90 Agnew, *Belfast merchant families*, pp 100–1. 91 Gillespie, *Early Belfast*, p. 153; Agnew, *Belfast merchant families*, p. 104; Maguire, 'A question of arithmetic', p. 36. 92 Laus Deo, 15 Jan. 1752 (PRONI, T1073/7); Laus Deo, 22 June 1757 (PRONI, T1073/8). 93 See notes 36, 37 and 39 above. 94 John Black III to Alexander Black, 14 Mar. 1764 (PRONI, D719/72). 95 Laus Deo, 8 Oct. 1757 (PRONI, T1073/8). 96 Laus Deo, 23 Feb. 1763 (PRONI, T1073/16). 97 John Black III to Alexander Black, 14 Mar. 1764 (PRONI, D719/72). Wills Hill, Lord Hillsborough, was a prominent County Down landowner and politician. He had been installed as president of the board of trade and foreign plantations

another of Black III's sons, George, had by the 1770s become an agent for the colonial administrator and landowner George Macartney a picture begins to emerge of a family respectful of social hierarchy, whose members carefully developed links with traditional authority figures.[98]

There were, of course, perks to be gained from developing such relationships. Black III was well aware that Hillsborough was a potential source of patronage, and both George Black and Sam Black benefitted from their family's connections with the Donegalls (and their own conformity to the established church), with both becoming members of Belfast's corporation – George in 1770 and Sam in 1774 – and serving several terms as town sovereign.[99] For Black III, however, respect for social hierarchy was not purely mercenary. It also reflected a wider conception of society as ordered and presupposed the existence of obligations. On a personal level, Black III was acutely aware of his own social and familial responsibilities. He sought to be a 'usefull member of society', to contribute to his neighbours' 'good' and to 'make a discreet & reasonably equall distribution' of his wealth among his children.[100] 'The happiness of long life & old age consists only in a proper use & improvement of time for the advantage of others for whom we are to provide in acts of benevolence to them & a strict course of virtue in the conduct of our lifes through time unto a blessed immortality', he wrote in January 1761.[101] But all had obligations. Thus, in the July 1765 letter in which he summarized his memorial for the improvement of Belfast, he expressed the hope that Lord Donegall, who was due soon to visit his 'vassall Belfastians', would 'make a proper & good use of the valluable talent committed to him by the Almighty Providence for his own good & others welfare'. Closely aligned to a sense of social obligations was an understanding of society's orders. Belfast was a port town, expanding on the back of its merchants' industry. Such individuals were, in Black III's description, 'publick benefactors', presumably because they created wealth. And there were, of course, the 'sick & distressed', large numbers of whom could be seen on Belfast's streets and who were, in Black III's understanding of society, deserving of charity. Indeed, he considered Belfast fortunate in being served by a clergy 'who preach by their good example of Christian charity as well as by sermon precept'.[102]

In seeking a source for Black III's view of society it is tempting to turn to Bordeaux and, in particular, to his relationship with Montesquieu. Discussing the experience of the Black family against the wider backdrop of empire, Livesey

the previous year, and went on to serve as joint postmaster general and secretary of state for the colonies. In 1789, four years prior to his death, he became the marquess of Downshire. James Kelly, 'Hill, Wills' in *DIB*, *sub nomine*.   98 *An Ulster slave-owner*, ed. Wright, p. 23. 99 Ibid.; John Black III to Alexander Black, 14 Mar. 1764 (PRONI, D719/72); Gamble, 'Business community', p. 255.   100 Laus Deo, 23 Jan. 1751 (PRONI, T1073/7); Laus Deo, 21 Mar. 1757 (PRONI, T1073/8); John Black III to Alexander Black, Oct. 1762 (PRONI, D719/630).   101 Laus Deo, 24 Jan. 1761 (PRONI, T1073/12).   102 John Black III to George Black, 18 July 1765 (PRONI, D4457/214).

has observed that the once-widely dispersed family's world had begun to contract by the 1760s, and that around the same time Black III made increasing use, in his correspondence, of the concept of society that Montesquieu had helped bring into existence. Livesey's particular argument that Black III seized on society when changed circumstances rendered untenable the older idea of 'British cosmopolitanism' that his family had made use of need not concern us here, but what of his suggestion that Black III's 'forty-year friendship with Montesquieu gave him privileged access to the emerging vocabulary of social description'?[103] That Black III prized his relationship with Montesquieu is readily apparent. Writing shortly after he had 'heard the affecting news' of the *philosophe*'s death in February 1755, he lamented that it was 'an irreparable publick loss & to me as he had been my intimate friend these 40 years'.[104] Added to this, it is possible to discern similarities between Black III's understanding of society and that outlined by Montesquieu in *De l'esprit de lois*. For Montesquieu, John Alan Baum has noted, society was comprised of 'a set of interrelated elements'. He emphasized the importance of 'balance' in functioning societies, with the 'various elements or parts interacting the one with the other', and notwithstanding his influence on later generations of reformers and radicals he was, fundamentally, 'a conservative and had no desire to reform the social class hierarchy'.[105] A copy of *De l'esprit de lois* was to be found in Black III's library and it is known that he discussed Montesquieu's work.[106] In January 1758, he was visited at Blamont by the Revd Richard Barton, a Lurgan clergyman and writer with links to the Physico Historical Society.[107] As Black III put it in his journal – in a passage which offers an intriguing glimpse of the retired merchant as savant, disseminating knowledge in provincial Ulster – Barton had learnt of his 'intimacy with the illustrious Presid Montesquieu whose *Esprit de Lois* medal & letters I shewed him'.[108] That Black III's thoughts on society were influenced by Montesquieu is not, then, wholly implausible. Indeed, it is possible to make the case that his characterization of merchants as 'publick benefactors' derived from his friend, for Montesquieu, as Stephen Small has noted, helped to render acceptable the idea 'that commerce leads to general benefit'.[109] But caution is required here. It is equally possible that Black III's view of merchants derived from an alternative source. Intriguingly, in August 1763, he encouraged his daughter Katharine to read numbers 68 and 69 of *The Spectator*, wherein could be found 'an excellent description of the Merch[t]. Exchange London', a

103 Livesey, *Civil society and empire*, p. 149.   104 Laus Deo, Jan. 1755 (PRONI, T1073/8). 105 John Alan Baum, *Montesquieu and social theory* (Oxford, 1979), pp 91–2; Doyle, *Origins of the French Revolution*, pp 87–8, 120–1; Stephen Small, *Political thought in Ireland, 1776–1798: republicanism, patriotism, and radicalism* (Oxford, 2002), p. 257.   106 'List of books sent to Belfast, 15 March 1751' (PRONI, D4457/64).   107 Eoin Magennis, 'A "beleaguered Protestant"?: Walter Harris and the writing of "Fiction Unmasked" in mid-18th-century Ireland', *Eighteenth-Century Ireland*, 13 (1998), 97.   108 Laus Deo, 26 Jan. 1757 (PRONI, T1073/8).   109 Small, *Political thought*, p. 30.

description that included the bold claim that 'there are not more useful members in a Commonwealth than merchants. They knit mankind together in a mutual intercourse of good offices, distribute the gifts of nature, find work for the poor, add wealth to the rich and magnificence to the great.'[110] Here, indeed, we see the merchant depicted as 'publick benefactor'. But whatever might be said of the influence of Montesquieu or *The Spectator*, a more convincing explanation for Black III's understanding of society as hierarchical and underpinned by obligations can be found elsewhere, in his firmly held religious beliefs.

In July 1765, when he expressed the hope that the fifth earl of Donegall would make 'proper & good use of the valluable talent committed to him by the Almighty Providence' Black III did so sincerely.[111] His words reflected both a profound belief in what he described elsewhere as 'the supreme will of kind providence which is ever watchfully Interposing in all our concerns' and a sincere piety evidenced in his journals, which are characterized, as Jean Agnew has noted, by a 'strongly religious tone'.[112] This religiosity might well have derived from Black III's experience in December 1725, when he survived – in his words 'miraculously' – the wrecking of the ship on which he was returning to France from Ireland, where he had visited his failing, bedridden father.[113] Certainly, this experience marked him deeply. Thereafter, he observed an 'annual fast & remembrance' of the event, and in December 1759, having learned of a similar case of 'sea deliverance', involving a ship that had departed Bordeaux and had been feared lost, he was moved to pen an account of it, alongside a relevant passage from the Psalms:

> They that goe down to the sea in ships, that doe business in great watters, these see the works of the Lord, & his wonders in the deep, for he commandeth & raiseth the stormy wind which lifteth up the waves … they cry unto the Lord in their trouble, & he brings them out of their distress.[114]

It is equally possible, however, that Black III's religious convictions pre-dated the dramatic events of December 1725, for he had been raised by a 'pious and worthy father' and 'had by baptism been an infant initiated member of the Christian Church'.[115] Either way, the fact remains that he was, by the 1750s, a deeply religious man who considered it his 'sole ambition … to be doing

110 Laus Deo, 11 July 1763 (PRONI, T1073/16); *The Spectator*, 19 May 1711 (no. 69). 111 John Black III to George Black, 18 July 1765 (PRONI, D4457/214).   112 'Loose bunch of papers' (PRONI, D4457/359); Agnew, *Belfast merchant families*, p. 66.   113 Laus Deo, 14 June 1763 (PRONI, T1073/16).   114 Laus Deo, Nov. 1753 (PRONI, T1073/7); Laus Deo, Dec. 1754 and Dec. 1758 (PRONI, T1073/8); Laus Deo, 16 Nov. 1760 (PRONI, T1073/12); Laus Deo, 17 Nov. 1762 and 10 Nov. 1764 (PRONI, T1073/16); 'Extract of religious prose' (PRONI, D4457/156). Here, and throughout, scriptural passages are reproduced as given by Black III.   115 Laus Deo, 24 Aug. 1760 (PRONI, T1073/12); Laus Deo, 14 June 1763 (PRONI, T1073/16).

good in this my generation according to discretion & the best of that reason & judgement providence has endowed me with &c'.[116]

In denominational terms, Black III is difficult to pin down precisely. Although raised a Presbyterian, he later gravitated towards the established church and defined his beliefs broadly.[117] 'The essentials of J.B.'s religion', he explained, in an undated manuscript fragment, 'are written in the xx of Exodus & in the best theology that was ever preached as is seen in the v & vi vii chap of St Matthew's Gospell'. Encompassing the Ten Commandments (Exodus 20) and Christ's Sermon on the Mount (Matthew 5, 6 and 7) these are, of course, passages foundational to Christian belief and practice, and concern man's behaviour towards his fellow man, and his relationship with God. Alongside this statement, Black III also jotted a reference to 1 Corinthians 13 with the comment 'universal charity', and transcribed a series of pointed lines from Alexander Pope's *Essay on man*:

> for forms of government lett fools contest
> whate'ere is best administered is best
> for modes of faith lett graceless zealots fight
> his can't be wrong who's life is in the right
> all must be false that thwart this one great end
> & all of God that bless mankind & mend – [118]

Overall the impression that emerges is of a man who was much concerned with morality, right behaviour and charity, but who cared little about ecclesiastical niceties. Accordingly, following his return to Ireland from Bordeaux Black III worshipped promiscuously, attending services in both 'church' and 'meeting house' – that is, in both the Church of Ireland and the Presbyterian Church.[119] While in Blamont, his local parish church was Kilmore, where the Revd Dean John Brandreth, a friend of Jonathan Swift, preached 'excellent' sermons on Ephesians 4:25–6 ('wherefore putting away lying, speak every man truth with his neighbours for we are members one of another – be ye angry & sin nott, lett not the sun goe down upon your wrath') and James 3:17 ('butt the wisdom which is from above is first pure then peaceable gentle & easy to be entreated full of mercy & good fruits without partiality & without hypocrisy').[120] However, he also favoured the Revd James Todd by attending services in the Presbyterian

116 Laus Deo, 18 Apr. 1754 (PRONI, T1073/7).   117 Laus Deo, 24 Aug. 1760 (PRONI, T1073/12); Kennedy, 'The journal of John Black', 3.   118 'Small note written by John Black' (PRONI, D4457/334). The lines from Pope are transcribed as Black III gave them. For the original, see Alexander Pope, *An essay on man* (London, 1745), pp 41–2.   119 Black III drew a distinction between the two when writing about a visit to Newtownards in 1760: there were, he noted, '2 meeting houses full & few att Church'. Laus Deo, 24 Aug. 1760 (PRONI, T1073/12).   120 Laus Deo, 24 Aug. 1760 (PRONI, T1073/12); Laus Deo, 29 Aug. 1762 (PRONI, T1073/16); Brett Hannam, *Mullavilly: portrait of an Ulster parish* (Mullavilly,

meeting house at Vinecash and acted as a go-between for Todd and Dr Alexander Haliday of Belfast, the administrator of a support fund – 'the Maxwell of Drum legacy to the poor Presbiterian frontier clergy of Ulster' – from which the Vinecash minister received payments.[121]

When in Belfast, Black III was equally ecumenical. In July 1754, prior to his final return to Ireland, he had written favourably of the Revd Thomas Drennan, minister of First Belfast Presbyterian Church, remarking:

> if the dutys of my station required my abode all the week on the bleak top of the Black Mountain above Belfast I would by the grace of God pass that time in proper devotion & gratitude to Almighty Providence in hopes that on Sunday I might descend into the valley & there enjoy the comfort of a pious lecture & sermon from the Rever.d Mr. Drenan & become one of his good congregation &c.[122]

If such comments suggest a particular attachment to Drennan's ministry, this is not borne out by the evidence of Black III's journal. As was the case in Blamont, whenever visiting Belfast he worshipped in both Presbyterian and Church of Ireland churches, but appears to have been particularly impressed by the ministry of Belfast's Church of Ireland vicar, the Revd James Saurin.[123] Drennan, an associate of Francis Hutcheson, was a well-connected figure in the world of non-subscribing, 'New Light' Presbyterianism – an Irish manifestation of rational dissent, which valued politeness and the improving potential of religion, but which could also, as Ian McBride has noted, be 'carried into the political sphere', where it 'challenged existing political and ecclesiastical structures'.[124] Saurin represented a very different world. Appointed vicar of Belfast in 1747, he was an establishment figure in a town whose Presbyterian majority was excluded from formal political life. He was also a socially engaged minister, albeit one who viewed society hierarchically, believing, as Raymond Gillespie has put it, that 'social inequalities were man-made, but necessary' and that charitable activity, in which he was heavily involved, 'was a social imperative intended to ensure that the temporary, but necessary, distinctions

---

2011), pp 39–42.   **121** Laus Deo, June 1762 (PRONI, T1073/12); Laus Deo, 1764 and 20 Aug. 1764 (PRONI, T1073/16); W.D. Killen, *History of congregations of the Presbyterian Church in Ireland and biographical notices of eminent Presbyterian ministers and laymen* (Belfast, 1886), pp 241–2; see also, for the Maxwell Bequest, Robert Whan, *The Presbyterians of Ulster, 1680–1730* (Woodbridge, 2013), pp 94–5 and, for Haliday, A.T.Q. Stewart, *A deeper silence: the hidden roots of the United Irish movement* (London, 1993), pp 121–2 and *passim*.   **122** Laus Deo, 18 Apr. 1754 (PRONI, T1073/7).   **123** For examples of Black III attending Presbyterian worship in Belfast, see Laus Deo, 24 Aug. 1760 (PRONI, T1073/12); Laus Deo, 17 Nov. 1762, Jan. 1763 and 24 Feb. 1763 (PRONI, T1073/16).   **124** Ian McBride, *Scripture politics: Ulster Presbyterians and Irish radicalism in the late eighteenth century* (Oxford, 1998), pp 41–61 (55 and 60 for quotes); Stewart, *A deeper silence*, pp 67–73, 113–19; A.T.Q. Stewart,

of social order were maintained'.[125] Black III was not, it is important to note, wholly antipathetic to the tradition represented by Drennan. In the late 1730s, he had read the anti-clerical *Independent Whig*, an influential text in the so-called 'commonwealthman' community to which Drennan and the early Irish non-subscribers were closely linked.[126] Nevertheless, by the 1750s and 1760s, Black III's views squared more neatly with Saurin's, and in his journal and correspondence we can catch glimpses of his engagement with the latter's ministry. In August 1758, for instance, it was following 'Church devotion & an excellent sermon by M[r] Saurin', that his thoughts turned 'serious' and he visited the graves of his 'pious & good father' and other relatives.[127] Several years later, in January 1763, 'the worthy M.[r] Saurin' preached on Matthew 5:5 ('blessed are the meek for they shall inherit the earth'), inspiring Black III to note that 'the meek hearted & benevolent are happy in themselves a blessing to society & entails & convey happiness to all about them'. The following March, Saurin delivered yet another 'excellent sermon' – the description recurs – on Matthew 5:16 ('Lett your light so shine before men that they may see your good works & glorify your father which is in heaven'), 'recommending the practice of our holy religion & doing our duty to God & to man'.[128] The formulations employed here – 'a blessing to society'; 'duty to God & to man' – were by no means coincidental, for Saurin made frequent use of the concept of society in his preaching.[129] Whether or not Black III derived his understanding of society from Saurin cannot be said for certain; it is entirely plausible that the two men had arrived independently at a similar worldview. Nevertheless, in Saurin Black III found a minister whose vision of society – embodied in his preaching on charity, duty and social order – he approved, and it was most likely Saurin that he had in mind when he commented, in July 1765, that Belfast was 'happy [...] in having so worthy & rever[d] a clergy'.[130]

IV

Given his religiosity, Black III's attempts to improve society were not limited to his plans for the development of Belfast. On a more modest scale, he encouraged religious belief, morality and virtuous behaviour within his family. At an early

'Drennan, William' in *DIB*, *sub nomine*.   **125** *Preaching in Belfast, 1747–72: a selection of the sermons of James Saurin*, ed. Raymond Gillespie and Roibeard Ó Gallachóir (Dublin, 2015), pp 10, 17–18, 20.   **126** Livesey, *Civil society and empire*, pp 138, 259 n.60; Caroline Robbins, *The eighteenth-century commonwealthman: studies in the transmission, development and circumstances of English liberal thought* (New York, 1968), pp 115–16, 167–9, 173–8; Stewart; *A deeper silence*, pp 91–119.   **127** John Black III to Robert Black, 1 Sept. 1758 (PRONI, D719/51); Laus Deo, Aug. 1758 (PRONI, T1073/8).   **128** Laus Deo, Jan. 1763 and 24 Feb. 1763 (PRONI, T1073/16); see also Laus Deo, 20 Apr. 1763 (PRONI, T1073/16).   **129** Raymond Gillespie, 'Poverty and the making of the Belfast Charitable Society', forthcoming.   **130** John Black III

age, his children were sent from Bordeaux to Aberdeen and Belfast in order
that they might receive an education, 'learn the principles of Christianity' and
become 'habituated ... to a due sense of religion'.[131] These early lessons were
reinforced, in later years, by a drip-feed of paternal advice. In October 1756, for
instance, Black III wrote to his son James, who was then resident in England,
'recommending care of his health & a virtuous course of lyfe ... with as usuall
some morall wise sentiments for the conduct of lyfe'.[132] Two years later, in
June 1758, a letter to George Black contained the information 'that oeconomy
was a principall prudent & necessary virtue', while in November 1759 Thom
Black was advised 'to be sober carefull & virtuous' and 'a morall letter' was
despatched in November 1764, 'recommending to My Allick & James att
London the doing their duty to God to their neighbour & to themselves which
is their surest & best interest'.[133] Beyond the ranks of his own children, Black
III also attempted to inculcate morality and sound religious principles among
his grandchildren. In July 1764 he informed his son George that he had 'taken
frequent opportunities to assure your dear Jacky Black [that is, George's son
John] that to be a good boy & doe his duty to God & to obey his dear Papa &
Mama would bring down a blessing from heaven upon him', and in November
1765 he sent 'a new shorter catechism' to Belfast, recommending that it 'may be
seriously read & in memory retained by my dear Jacky & Letty & Betty & Peggy
Black [the younger members of the family] as it recommends the love of God &
to doe always to our neighbour as we would he should – in lyke case – doe unto
us – as it is summary & substance of the revealed will of God in the law in the
prophet & in the holy Christian gospell'.[134] Ostensibly private, such advice was
of wider public value, for in Black III's mind personal conduct and social good
were closely connected.

Parental and grandparental advice aside, Black III's provision of a printed
catechism points to another means through which he sought to encourage
morality and better society: the circulation of print. Befitting his status as a
successful merchant with interests in improvement, Black III possessed a
varied library. In addition to the titles alluded to above – *De l'esprit de lois*, the
Independent Whig and the Physico-Historical Society's surveys of Cork, Down
and Waterford – his collection included works on Greek and Roman antiquity;
lives of John Milton, William III and Queen Anne; William Camden's influential
Britannia; and the four volumes of Gilbert Burnet's *History of his own times* – an
'undeviatingly Whig narrative', in Barnard's judgment.[135] Among others, these

to George Black, 18 July 1765 (PRONI, D4457/214); *Preaching in Belfast, 1747–72*, ed.
Gillespie and Ó Gallachóir, p. 21.   131 John Black III to Alexander and James Black, 4 June
1767 (PRONI, T2420/2D).   132 Laus Deo, Oct. 1756 (PRONI, T1073/8).   133 Laus
Deo, June 1758 and Oct. 1759 (PRONI, T1073/8); Laus Deo, 10 Nov. 1764 (PRONI,
T1073/16).   134 John Black III to George Black, 26 July 1764 and 8 Nov. 1765 (PRONI,
D4457/203 and 217). For Jacky/John Black, Black III's grandson, see *An Ulster slave-owner*,
ed. Wright.   135 'List of books sent to Belfast, 15 March 1751' (PRONI, D4457/64); Toby

volumes sat alongside a French and English dictionary, an 'Essay on health', ten volumes of 'Mezeray's History of France' and a bestseller of the 1740s in the form of Richard Walter's lavishly illustrated four-volume account of the naval exploits of George Anson.[136] Naturally, devotional material also featured. Black III thought highly of the published sermons of the impeccably Anglican John Tillotson (a former archbishop of Canterbury, and the only writer James Saurin is known to have quoted in his preaching), and his 'favourite author' was the seventeenth-century English jurist Matthew Hale – a figure similar to Tillotson in outlook – whose *Contemplations moral and divine* he was gifted by his father-in-law, Robert Gordon.[137] Reflecting his obvious interest in learning and the printed word, Black III circulated reading material he considered useful within his family. In addition to the catechism already referred to, his grandson John (son of George Black) was supplied with a prayer book, and in 1765 'some instructive good books' were despatched to Bordeaux for the use of John Black IV's children.[138] A year earlier, arrangements had been made to forward 'A dissertation on natural religion and the duties of society' to Bordeaux (for the use of John Black IV), and in August 1763, as has already been noted, his daughter Katharine was urged to read an article on the London exchange, which had appeared in *The Spectator*.[139]

On at least two occasions, moreover, Black III's attempts to circulate printed material extended well beyond the Black family, as he sought to encourage the publication of Belfast editions of works he considered valuable. Writing in his journal in June 1762, for instance, he alluded to a 'printed relation of the execution of Mr Rochette att Toulouse' – Rochette being a Protestant preacher, tried and hanged during an outbreak of 'extreme anti-Protestant excitement' – noting that he had 'caused it be reprinted att Belfast to be dispersed thro the country'.[140] Likewise, in November 1765, in the same letter in which he informed his son George that he was forwarding a catechism for the use of his children, he mentioned a second book which he hoped to see printed in Belfast, explaining:

Barnard, *Brought to book: print in Ireland, 1680–1784* (Dublin, 2017), pp 35, 111; Wyman H. Herendeen, 'Camden, William' in *ODNB, sub nomine*. **136** 'List of books sent to Belfast, 15 March 1751' (PRONI, D4457/64); JoAnne Mancini, 'Siege mentalities: objects in motion, British imperial expansion and the Pacific turn', *Winterthur Portfolio*, 45 (2011), 131–2. **137** John Black III to George Black, 8 Nov. 1765 (PRONI, D4457/217); Laus Deo, Dec. 1756 (PRONI, T1073/8); Laus Deo, 17 Nov. 1762 and Jan. 1763 (PRONI, T1073/16); *Preaching in Belfast, 1747–72*, ed. Gillespie and Ó Gallachóir, p. 12; Barnard, *Brought to book*, pp 219, 304, 319; Alan Cromartie, 'Hale, Sir Matthew' in *ODNB, sub nomine*. **138** Laus Deo, 9 Jan. 1766 (PRONI, T1073/16); *An Ulster slave-owner*, ed. Wright, p. 70. **139** John Black III to George Black, 6 Aug. 1763 (PRONI, D4457/193); Laus Deo, 11 July 1763 (PRONI, T1073/16). **140** Laus Deo, Mar. 1762 (PRONI, T1073/12); David D. Bien, 'The background of the Calas affair', *History*, 43 (1958), 198 (for quote), 202; McBride, *Eighteenth-century Ireland*, p. 314.

th'other day, seeing on the desk of my Issac Simon's compting house, a
little book & seeing on the title page – *An essay upon oeconomy* – a word
that I have always a great regard for as well for the publick as private
utility, I took it up & have read it with pleasure & delight as it contains
lessons which deserve to be seriously considered by persons of all ranks &
conditions for the good of themselves & of society ... I herewith send you
one that I bought att the printers for your's & friends perusall in Belfast
where I believe it has nott yet appeared & which if you please you may
lend to our worthy good friends M^r. Val. Jones with my humble & sincere
respects & if he & you think fitt it may be communicated alsoe to our
good & kind friends Mess^s Joy who, if they think it worth their trouble &
expense, may att their conveniency give it a new Belfast edition & may, I
hope, prove an entertaining moral New Year's gift to some of their choice
friends & customers.[141]

If a Belfast edition of this volume was published, it has left no trace. Nor, despite
Black III's claims to have 'caused it be reprinted', is there any evidence of an
account of the unfortunate Rochette appearing in Belfast, though the case was
known, having been briefly reported by the *Belfast News-Letter* in April 1762.[142]
But whatever the outcome of his attempts to bring them to a wider audience,
the fact that Black III believed that these works merited such efforts remains
striking. His enthusiasm for the *Essay upon oeconomy* requires little explanation:
here was a work that was of obvious utility to a merchant community, a work
that contained lessons valuable both to individual readers and society at large.
But what of the account of Rochette's execution? What value did Black III
see in a work of this nature, and in what ways did it relate to the vision of an
improved Belfast that he outlined in the July 1765 letter with which this chapter
commenced?

For Black III, the value of Rochette's story was twofold: on the one hand,
it was of relevance to discussion concerning the operation of penal legislation
in Ireland; on the other, it drew to mind well-entrenched tropes of Catholic
hostility and intolerance towards Protestantism. As he wrote in his journal, it
would serve 'to shew the persecution that Protestants are exposed to in popish
countrys & that the papists here have no reason to complain of bad treatment'.[143]
Black III's concern with such matters was most likely linked to reports from
Munster, where the activities of the Whiteboys early in 1762 had prompted dark
mutterings of popish conspiracy.[144] He might also, however, have been mindful

141 John Black III to George Black, 8 Nov. 1765 (PRONI, D4457/217). The Joys were the
Belfast printers Henry Joy and Robert Joy. Best known for producing the *Belfast News-Letter*,
which had been established by their father, Francis Joy, in 1737, they also supplied books,
prints and plays. C.J. Woods, 'Joy, Francis' in *DIB, sub nomine*; Barnard, *Brought to book*, pp
89, 311, 315.   142 *Belfast News-Letter*, 6 Apr. 1762.   143 Laus Deo, Mar. 1762 (PRONI,
T1073/12).   144 Jacqueline R. Hill, 'Popery and Protestantism, civil and religious liberty:

of the efforts that some Catholic writers made from the late 1740s to develop what Jacqueline Hill has termed an 'enlightened Catholic' position, which was characterized by an eschewal of anti-Protestant polemic and a 'willingness to accept the results of the Williamite revolution'.[145] Whatever the case, it is clear that Black III considered the penal laws to be defensible and inclined to the rather different 'beleaguered protestant' narrative – a narrative inspired by exaggerated accounts of the horrors of 1641, articulated in the writings of polemical historians (Sir John Temple, above all) and sustained by the sermons preached at services to mark the anniversaries of 5 November 1605 and 23 October 1641.[146] Black III's journal makes reference to one such discourse. On 23 October 1757, he recorded that he 'heard our Rever^d Dean Brandreth preach a moving pathetick sermon on this anniversary of the bloody catastrophy 1641'.[147] No doubt he heard others, but the lessons such sermons sought to convey were well known to him. Indeed, they were matters of lived experience and family tradition. As a child, Black III had listened while a relative – the sister of his grandmother – detailed her family's 'share in the dismall devastations murders & massacres of the heretick usurpers in 1641', and in 1689 the Black family had fled Belfast 'in the dark night' when it was reported, following the break of Dromore, that 'the Irish were coming down, sparing neither age nor sex, putting all to the sword'.[148] The family sailed for Scotland, eventually finding refuge in the Cromwellian-era citadel in Ayr, where a young Black III 'learned the alphabet until Marshall Schomberg arrived in Belfast', at which point they returned home, only to discover their 'house & cellars emptied of all the goods & furniture & the rooms lodging for the sick English soldiers who ashore & abord the transports then in the lough died in great numbers'.[149]

For Black III, as for many Protestants in eighteenth-century Ireland, the turmoil of the seventeenth century was not, then, a matter of distant history. The events of the 1640s and the later Williamite War were long-remembered, and offered durable exemplars of Catholic treachery and animosity. This did not, of course, prevent him from spending the greater part of his adult life in Catholic France.[150] Nor, in 1763, did it bar him from obliging 'Priest Lavertie' – the Catholic parish priest of Kilmore – who sought his assistance

the disputed lessons of Irish history 1690–1812', *Past and Present*, 118 (1988), 122; David Dickson, 'Novel spectacle? The birth of the Whiteboys, 1761–2' in D.W. Hayton and Andrew R. Holmes (eds), *Ourselves alone? Religion, society and politics in eighteenth- and nineteenth-century Ireland* (Dublin, 2016), pp 61–83 (esp. 70, 73); McBride, *Eighteenth-century Ireland*, pp 312–14. **145** Hill, 'Popery and Protestantism', 104–6. **146** Ibid., 100, 106; Barnard, *Irish Protestant ascents and descents*, pp 111–42; S.J. Connolly, *Religion, law and power: the making of Protestant Ireland, 1660–1760* (Oxford, 1992), p. 30; see also Magennis, 'A "beleaguered Protestant"?' and, for further discussion of Black III's Protestant worldview, Livesey, *Civil society and empire*, pp 138–9, 143–4; *Bordeaux–Dublin letters*, ed. Cullen et al., pp 67–8; Canny, 'The Irish colony in Bordeaux', pp 43–4, 48. **147** Laus Deo, 8 Oct. 1757 (PRONI, T1073/8). **148** *Bordeaux–Dublin letters*, ed. Cullen et al., p. 98. **149** Laus Deo, 18 Aug. 1752 (PRONI, T1073/7). **150** Livesey, *Civil society and empire*, p. 143; see also,

in arranging the transfer of a sum of seven guineas to 'young Johnston a scholar att Bordeaux'.[151] But set against this we have the profound mistrust of Catholicism Black III expressed when giving an account, in February 1757, of Robert François-Damian's attempt to kill Louis XV. This, he suggested, was a Jesuit intrigue, motivated by 'their ends of ambition, worldly power & dominion over the minds bodies & estates of men'.[152] Likewise, we have his telling comment, following his final return, later that same year, from Bordeaux to Ireland: 'Escaped from the Egyptian gallick slavery to this my native land of liberty & property'.[153] Despite his long sojourn in the country, Black III considered Catholic France to be unfree. Conversely, Ireland, a Protestant state in which a Catholic majority was legally disadvantaged, was a 'land of liberty'. Black III thus subscribed to an anti-Catholic, Protestant ethos. But how did this worldview inform his vision of Belfast? On the surface, the connections seem to be limited, not least as Belfast's Catholic community remained small until the early nineteenth century.[154] Yet it is worth remembering that in the July 1765 letter in which he summarized the scheme of improvements he had forwarded to the agent of Lord Donegall, Black III did not begin with wider streets, public walks or improvements calculated to encourage economic activity. Rather, he began with the church.[155] In 1765 Belfast's existing parish church was run down. One visitor in the mid-1750s remarked that it was 'a very mean fabric for such a considerable place', and Black III's first proposal for the improvement of Belfast concerned the construction of a new church building.[156] Viewed one way, this recommendation was of religious significance: a new church would, after all, provide a more fitting venue for worship and prayer. However, the parish church was not simply a religious space. It was also a social space and, perhaps above all, a space imbued with political significance, which provided a stage on which social hierarchy could be enacted and corporate ceremony displayed.[157] In his 1823 history of Belfast, George Benn explained how, in years past, members of Belfast's corporation 'repaired to it in great state at the celebration of divine service'. 'The sovereign', he wrote, 'was habited in a scarlet or crimson cloak, and the twelve burgesses in black, preceded by the town sergeants bearing the mace.'[158] In recommending the construction of a

McBride, *Eighteenth-century Ireland*, pp 414–15.   **151** Laus Deo, 24 Aug. 1763 and 12 Sept. 1763 (PRONI, T1073/16); Tomás Ó Fiaich, 'The parish of Kilmore', *Seanchas Ardmhacha*, 23 (2010), 166.   **152** *Bordeaux–Dublin letters*, ed. Cullen et al., pp 74–5, 97; Canny, 'The Irish colony in Bordeaux', p. 43; Christian Ayne Crouch, 'Between lines: languages, intimacy, and voyeurism during global war' in Truxes (ed.), *Ireland, France and the Atlantic in a time of war*, p. 175.   **153** Laus Deo, 24 Apr. 1757 (PRONI, T1073/8); see also Livesey, *Civil society and empire*, p. 139.   **154** See, for example, *Charles Abbot's tour through Ireland & north Wales in 1792*, ed. C.J. Woods (Dublin, 2019), p. 32.   **155** John Black III to George Black, 18 July 1765 (PRONI, D4457/214).   **156** Quoted in Gillespie, *Early Belfast*, p. 132.   **157** Gillespie, 'Making Belfast', pp 146–52.   **158** George Benn, *The history of the town of Belfast, with an accurate account of its former and present state* (Belfast, 1823), p. 112. The exact point at which

new parish church, Black III was proposing the improvement of a building that stood as a physical manifestation of the Protestant character of Belfast's corporate life. His vision of an improved town might, then, have included new streets, buildings and infrastructure, but it was also an implicitly Protestant vision that incorporated older ideas of order and hierarchy.

V

On 17 October 1767, John Black III died. Fittingly, he did so in Belfast, while visiting his son George.[159] Three days later, the *Belfast News-Letter* informed the town of his passing and remarked that he had, following his return to Ireland, 'spent the remainder of his days […] in that unfeigned piety and benignity of heart, which will ever distinguish the real Christian and honest man'.[160] Black III would surely have been pleased with this encomium; having sought during his life to retain his links with Belfast, he was fondly remembered at the time of his death. He would have been equally pleased had he known of some of the changes that occurred in the town during the 1770s and 1780s: as has already been noted, new streets were constructed and new buildings erected, including the Poor House, the White Linen Hall and a new parish church. But other developments would have appeared altogether less favourable to his eyes. The fragility of public order was, for instance, thrown into sharp relief on 23 December 1770 when the Hearts of Steel marched on Belfast to secure the release of a prisoner who had been arrested on suspicion of houghing cattle on the County Antrim lands of the Belfast merchant Thomas Greg.[161] More seriously, new political energies were unleashed by the American War of Independence and the French Revolution. In the age of the Irish Volunteers and the United Irishmen, order and hierarchy were up for debate and old political arrangements were reassessed. In this climate, Belfast's unrepresentative corporation attracted hostile comment: 'we like not this paltry oligarchy the corporation should take the lead, and the more respectable people of Belfast follow as their train-bearers', Alexander Haliday wrote, in July 1787. 'Time was, when the former stood aloof, and we were ever ready, in some such public manner, to mark our respect, not for rank, but eminent public merit.'[162] The implication here is clear: the corporation's

these processions died out is unknown. While Benn noted, in 1823, that the 'practice has long since been discontinued', he also recalled in 1856 that he had 'once heard a very old inhabitant saying that in her youth she had seen members of the corporation proceeding in state […] to the Church in High-street, on some important public occasion.' Ibid., p. 112; G.B., 'Old corporate records of Belfast', *UJA*, 4 (1856), 269–70.   **159** Ward, 'Black family', 187.   **160** *Belfast News-Letter*, 20 Oct. 1767.   **161** James S. Donnelly, Jr., 'Hearts of Oak, Hearts of Steel', *Studia Hibernica*, 21 (1981), 38.   **162** HMC, *Thirteenth report, appendix, part viii. The manuscripts and correspondence of James, first earl of Charlemont. Vol. II – 1784–1799* (London, 1894), p. 58.

members no longer deserved the respect they had previously been accorded and its authority had declined. Added to these developments was the inexorable rise of the town's population and the beginning of a change in its confessional make-up. Belfast's Catholic community would remain numerically insignificant until well into the nineteenth century, but it did expand in the years following Black III's death and the Catholic presence in the town was marked, albeit in an unassuming form, by the opening of St Mary's Catholic church in 1784.[163] By the end of the eighteenth century Belfast had been transformed. But had it been improved? For John Black III, that would have been a different question entirely.

163 Connolly, 'Improving town', pp 175–8.

Presbyterians and Jacobites in County Antrim in 1716: the interplay of local and national politics in early eighteenth-century Ireland

D.W. HAYTON

The cliché 'all politics is local' has a particular resonance in Ireland. Indeed, in a formidable analysis of parliamentary elections in the mid-nineteenth century, Theodore Hoppen argued that 'the parish pump has long been the symbol of the hidden Ireland'. Historians have responded in different ways to this assertion of the 'deep and constant importance' of localism, depending on the particular characteristics of the periods they have studied.[1] While local issues, conflicts and personalities have always had a part to play in Irish politics – as indeed in political life everywhere – the extent to which horizons were restricted has been shown to vary considerably over time. The degree of interaction between local and national politics seems to depend on two principal considerations: first, the nature of the political issues agitating 'public opinion', which may or may not have been widely shared across Irish society and thus readily transferable to a local context; and second, the degree to which popular politicization was facilitated by education, literacy, and the development of the popular press.

This essay will explore the relationship between local and national politics in the early eighteenth century through a case-study of one episode dating from the early months of 1716. Minor disturbances in the parish of Ballentoy, on the north coast of County Antrim, became briefly the centre of attention among the Irish political classes, because of their direct relevance to current debates in parliament. This was a period in which Protestant society was agitated by powerful currents of sectarian antagonism, between the Church of Ireland and Protestant Dissenters. Feelings ran especially high in east Ulster, where Presbyterians were concentrated, and where there was a recent history of conflict – inflammatory pamphlets, legal action taken against Presbyterians in civil and ecclesiastical courts, even outbreaks of mob violence. This had been translated into political terms in c.1698–1704 by the rise of a 'Tory' interest in church and state, which embarked upon parliamentary campaigns to restrict the

This essay is a by-product of research on local politics in eighteenth-century Ireland generously financed by an Emeritus Fellowship granted by the Leverhulme Trust. 1 K.T. Hoppen, *Elections, politics, and society in Ireland, 1832–1885* (Oxford, 1984), p. 437; *idem, The mid-Victorian generation, 1846–1886* (Oxford, 1998), p. 561. The literature is helpfully surveyed in Douglas Kanter, 'Was all Irish politics local? The Portarlington election of 1832 and the structure of politics in 19th-century Ireland', *Parliamentary History*, 33 (2014), 438–52.

civil liberties and political rights of Protestant Dissenters. Soon there emerged in Ireland a form of 'party politics' on English lines, which not only divided the Irish parliament but stretched down into the constituencies and fractured some county and borough communities. Tories cast themselves as the defenders of the established church against the incursions of 'sectaries' and 'schismatics', the heirs of the regicides of the 1640s; Whigs emphasized their own commitment to the maintenance of the Williamite settlement in the face of Jacobite conspiracy and Catholic rebellion.

Local politics was the more easily coloured by the conflict of Whig and Tory interests when the ideological divisions between the parties reflected visible social realities: either the recent expansion of the Presbyterian community following a substantial wave of immigration from Scotland, or the evident survival of the Catholic landed interest despite the Williamite land confiscations and the subsequent enactment of various penal laws. In County Antrim both sets of circumstances obtained: on the one hand the fears entertained by churchmen of Presbyterian aggression, and on the other Protestant nervousness about the continuing influence of a Catholic landed magnate.

Another factor was important in connecting the national and the local: ease of communication between centre and periphery, which enabled party political controversies to penetrate provincial consciousness. Research by Jacqueline Hill and others has already alerted us to the existence of a lively political culture across Ireland in the first half of the eighteenth century, with a focus on questions of national as well as local significance. In particular, David Fleming's work on 'provincial people' in Limerick and Sligo has shown how the increasingly rapid dissemination of information and ideas, mainly through the pamphlet and newspaper press, resulted in local disputes being cast in national terms.[2]

Although, in comparison with England, Irish newspapers were still in their infancy in the early eighteenth century, this relative deficiency was more than made up for by a brisk trade in cheap print, centred on the production of pamphlets and broadsides.[3] There was, moreover, a flourishing associational culture in Irish towns, manifest in the growth of guilds, clubs and societies, and more informally in vigorous social interactions in tavern and coffeehouse.[4] In different ways, the development of the state in post-Revolution Ireland also provided a stimulus to public discourse: in particular, the fact that the Irish parliament was meeting regularly for the first time. Parliamentary sessions

2 D.A. Fleming, *Politics and provincial people: Sligo and Limerick, 1691–1761* (Manchester, 2010), esp. pp 233–4.   3 Robert Munter, *The history of the Irish newspaper, 1685–1760* (Cambridge, 1967); James Kelly, 'Political publishing, 1700–1800' in Raymond Gillespie and Andrew Hadfield (eds), *The Oxford history of the Irish book*, iii: *The Irish book in English, 1550–1800* (Oxford, 2006), pp 215–33; Suzanne Forbes, *Print and party politics in Ireland, 1689–1714* (Basingstoke, 2018).   4 Patrick Walsh, 'Club life in late seventeenth- and early eighteenth-century Ireland: in search of an associational world, *c*.1680–*c*.1730' in James Kelly and Martyn Powell (eds), *Clubs and societies in eighteenth-century Ireland* (Dublin,

provided not only a forum for debate about politics but a place for local interest-groups to bring demands and grievances, which stood more chance of being heard if dressed up in Whig or Tory clothes.

What happened at Ballentoy in 1716, and its aftermath, demonstrates how an apparently trivial incident in a remote corner of Ireland could become a focus for party politics. High Church bishops and Tory politicians in Dublin sought to exploit allegations of the presumptuous behaviour of Presbyterian militiamen in harassing local clergymen in order to influence debates over proposals to modify statutory restrictions on Presbyterian office-holding. This was only the most recent in a series of incidents trumpeted by Tory, and particularly clerical, propagandists, in order to discredit Ulster Presbyterians and forestall the dismantling of the legal provisions that kept Dissenters out of public employment. A close examination will show how events in Ballentoy originated from a combination of national, regional and local circumstances; how the sloganizing of national politics influenced local perceptions; and how far local realities were distorted when they became the subject of national attention.

I

The 'test' clause in the Irish Popery Act of 1704 imposed on every person holding 'an office of profit under the crown' the requirement to take Holy Communion at least once a year in the established church. This provision was designed to purge Protestant Dissenters from government, and from the higher echelons of borough corporations, and was particularly effective in Ulster, where Presbyterians refused to conform 'occasionally'. The 'test' quickly became a major grievance to Presbyterians. Attempts in 1707 and 1709 by English viceroys to secure repeal foundered on the determined resistance of a majority of MPs. Even after the Hanoverian succession in 1714 and the installation in London and Dublin of ministers supposedly sympathetic to Dissent, a mission from the General Synod of Ulster to the new lord lieutenant, Sunderland, was fobbed off with vague promises.[5]

The Jacobite rising in Scotland in 1715–16 seemed to give Presbyterians the opportunity they needed to press again for the removal of the test, at least in so far as it affected their capacity to join in the defence of the Protestant establishment. By law a Presbyterian could not take up a commission of array – empowering him to muster the inhabitants of a district – or a commissioned rank in the militia. Presbyterians themselves seem to have felt that they could not serve in the militia at all. The formation of independent volunteer companies at times of threatened Jacobite invasion shows both the willingness of Dissenters to take up

2010), pp 36–49.   5 D.W. Hayton, 'Presbyterians and the confessional state: the sacramental test as an issue in Irish politics, 1704–80', *Bulletin of the Presbyterian Historical Society of Ireland*, 26 (1997), 25–6.

arms and their fear of prosecution.[6] But it was in any case unlikely that, without commissioners of array or officers of their own persuasion, Presbyterians would be embodied in the militia; gentlemen belonging to the established church were naturally wary of arming and drilling Dissenters.[7]

It was against this background that during the summer of 1715, with a gathering crisis in Britain, and a decision by the Irish government to array the militia, a meeting of influential Presbyterians in Belfast asked the Ulster Whig politician William Conolly to transmit to the lords justices a memorial declaring their determination 'to come forward in defence of their religion and liberties' by serving in the militia, and requesting immunity from prosecution. Conolly not only endorsed the petition but proposed that prominent Presbyterian gentlemen be added to the commissions of array.[8] Then in December 1715 Sir Gustavus Hume, another Presbyterian sympathizer, was given leave by the Irish House of Commons to bring in 'heads' of a bill (the first stage in the preparation of legislation under the evolved Poynings' Law procedure) to exempt Dissenters from prosecution for serving.[9] Nothing came of this order, but instead the House of Commons incorporated into the heads of a bill for the security of the king's person clauses indemnifying Dissenters who had already made themselves liable to prosecution.[10] Tories in the Irish House of Lords responded with their own measure, identical to the House of Commons' bill except that it omitted the clauses relating to the test, setting the stage for a confrontation between the two houses.[11]

The lords justices, the duke of Grafton and the earl of Galway, were in a difficult position. When passed, heads went to the Irish privy council, where, according to Poynings' Law, they could be amended before being engrossed and transmitted to England. The British privy council might impose further amendments before a bill was returned to be considered by the Irish parliament, which could then only pass or reject it. Grafton and Galway did their best to secure a compromise. The privy council merged the two sets of heads into a single bill, and in February 1716 councillors discussed the issues at length, eventually accepting provisions to indemnify Dissenters in respect of their militia service during the rebellion, and to permit them to serve in the militia for the future, but restricting a further clause, relating to service in the regular army, for the duration of the rebellion. What was noticeable in these proceedings was the fact that even some Whig peers resisted softening the law and among

6 Jim O'Donovan, 'The militia in Munster, 1715–78' in Gerard O'Brien (ed.), *Parliament, politics and people: essays in eighteenth-century Irish history* (Blackrock, County Dublin, 1989), pp 33–5.   7 Neal Garnham, *The militia in eighteenth-century Ireland: in defence of the protestant interest* (Woodbridge, 2012), pp 20–1.   8 J.S. Reid, *History of the Presbyterian Church in Ireland* ..., rev. W. D. Killen (3 vols, Belfast, 1867), ii, 67; William Conolly to lords justices, 9 Aug. 1715 (TNA, SP 63/373/70).   9 'Papers relating to the Irish clauses' (BL, Add. MS 61640, f. 95).   10 Garnham, *Militia*, p. 26.   11 Grafton to James Stanhope, 15 Feb. 1715/16 (TNA, SP 63/374/99).

the bishops 'Low Churchmen', like William King of Dublin, were as vehement in defence of the test as their 'High Church' colleagues.[12] So vigorous was the reaction of churchmen in general that ministers were requested by loyal Whigs in Ireland to amend or remove the offending clauses when the bill came to Whitehall, in order to avoid 'breaking the king's friends' in Ireland.[13]

High Churchmen spared no pains to convince both houses of the Irish parliament of the dangers inherent in allowing Dissenters to serve in the militia. William Tisdall, vicar of Belfast, whose pamphlet, *A sample of true-blew Presbyterian loyalty...*, published in 1709, had sparked a 'paper war' with various Nonconformist ministers, repeatedly returned to the subject in his diatribes against Presbyterians.[14] It was his contention that Presbyterians' supposed loyalty to the crown was bogus: the evidence of history, especially in the 1640s, demonstrated their profound antipathy to monarchy. Their attitude to the militia, and their behaviour when embodied in militia troops, were key elements in Tisdall's argument. *A sample of true-blew Presbyterian loyalty* ... reminded readers of the outcome when the Presbyterians' 'loyal predecessors ... wrested the power of the militia' out of the hands of King Charles I.[15] Two subsequent pamphlets, in 1712 and 1713, drew attention to what Tisdall represented as the Presbyterians' cynical refusal to participate in the militia array necessitated by the Jacobite invasion scare of 1708, on the pretext of fear of prosecution but with a view to claiming immunity. This was further proof of the essentially bogus nature of Presbyterians' loyalty: in a crisis their first thought was to try and extort concessions for themselves. Not surprisingly, perhaps, he took his evidence from his own neighbourhood in east Ulster, publishing letters from Church of Ireland gentlemen in Antrim and Down who were magistrates and commissioners of array.[16]

The situation in 1715 was different. Presbyterians had been emboldened by the successful transition to a Hanoverian dynasty and a Whig government in Whitehall and Dublin. In common with Irish Protestants more generally, they were also driven to a higher pitch of alarm by the events surrounding the Jacobite invasion of Scotland in 1715: not only had troops landed, but a series of high-profile defections of Tories to the Pretender's cause, most notably the former Irish viceroy, Ormond, and Queen Anne's English secretary of

---

12 Grafton and Galway to Stanhope, 24 Feb. 1715/16 (TNA, SP 63/374/105–6); Galway to Stanhope, 16 Mar. 1715/16 (SP 63/374/147). 13 Henry Maxwell to [Stanhope], 16 Mar. 1715/16 (TNA, SP 63/374/89); J.A. Froude, *The English in Ireland in the eighteenth century* (3 vols, London, 1906), i, 429–30; forecast for division on unamended security bill (TNA, SP 63/374/94). 14 For Tisdall, see the entries in *DIB* (online edition: www.dib.ie); and *ODNB* (online edition: http://www.oxforddnb.com). 15 William Tisdall, *A sample of true-blew Presbyterian loyalty, in all changes and turns of government* ... (Dublin, 1709), p. 22. 16 William Tisdall, *The conduct of the Dissenters of Ireland, with respect both to church and state* ... (Dublin, 1712), pp 32–9; *idem*, *A seasonable inquiry into that most dangerous political principle of the kirk in power* ... (Dublin, 1713), pp 24–6.

state, Bolingbroke, seemed to indicate treachery at the heart of the political establishment. In 1715 Presbyterians no longer stood aloof from the militia array, but joined in large numbers, in troops that were mustered and officered by their co-religionists.

Tisdall now changed his line of argument, or, rather, reverted to the line he had taken in *A sample of true-blew Presbyterian loyalty* ..., pointing to the malign consequences of Presbyterian participation in the militia. The possibility of a relaxation of the test was in the forefront of his mind. A pamphlet published in November 1715, and directed at the 'nobility and gentry' of Ireland, argued against statutory interference. Tisdall accused Presbyterians of accepting places as commissioners of array and encouraging their co-religionists to serve in defiance of the test, in order that afterwards they might press the case for repeal on the strength of having risked prosecution by participating in the defence of the realm. As always, his suspicions focused on 'teachers and elders', by whom the 'common people' were 'wholly governed'.[17] The evidence came from County Antrim, where he claimed the four militia troops were primarily officered by Dissenters. Three of the colonels, Sir Robert Adair, Archibald Edmonstone and Clotworthy Upton, were Presbyterians,[18] and Upton in particular had instructed his tenants against betraying conscience in order to qualify.[19] The way the colonels and their officers conducted themselves showed 'the palpable danger of arming the Dissenters of Ireland with any degree of civil or military power'. Presbyterians had declared that 'they would be commanded by none but those of their own persuasion'. They had told commissioners of array they would not serve under churchmen and threatened violent resistance if compelled. Elsewhere they had contrived to exclude churchmen from their troops. The sinister implications of arming none but Presbyterians in a parish scarcely needed elaboration.[20]

II

At the very point at which tensions were at their highest in parliament over the security bill, another incident came to public notice which, as far as Tisdall was concerned, and those who shared his fear and loathing of Ulster Presbyterian 'teachers and elders', seemed to be conclusive proof of the perils involved in tampering with the test.[21] On 16 March 1716 the archbishop of Armagh,

---

17 William Tisdall, *The case of the sacramental test, stated and argu'd* ... (Dublin, 1715), preface and pp 33, 35.   18 For Adair, Edmonstone and Upton, see *HIP*, iii, 56; iv, 107–8; vi, 454–5; Robert Whan, *The Presbyterians of Ulster, 1680–1730* (Woodbridge, 2013), pp 60, 62, 64, 68, 94–7, 127–8, 173, 181.   19 Tisdall, *Case of the sacramental test* ..., pp 31–2, 34.   20 Ibid., pp 43, 54–6.   21 The story is told in detail in W.J. Roulston, *'The insolence of Dissenters'? Religious controversy in Ballintoy in 1716* (Ballintoy Archaeological and Historical Society, 2018), drawing heavily on the printed report of the assizes judges.

Thomas Lindsay, and the bishop of Down and Connor, Edward Smyth, submitted a memorial to the lords justices drawing attention to complaints made by some of Smyth's diocesan clergy in north Antrim of 'great hardships', on account of having their houses searched 'as disaffected persons' and firearms removed which were necessary for self-defence.[22] According to the memorial, the searches had been undertaken in and around Ballentoy in February 1716, by armed bands of Presbyterian militiamen.

The clergymen subjected to these indignities were James Smyth, rector of Ballentoy, John Martin his curate, and Geoffrey Fanning of Benvarden, all of whom provided written statements. According to this evidence, Fanning's house was the first to be searched, on Wednesday, 1 February, allegedly by a body of armed Presbyterians acting under the orders of the high constable of the barony. Three days later, on the Saturday, 'a great number' of militiamen, accompanied by Captain Hugh Boyd of Ballycastle, came to Ballentoy House, where Smyth was living, 'to search for arms, and to take up suspected persons' believed to be hiding there. The house belonged to Archibald Stewart, rector of Ramoan, and was the residence of Stewart's brother Alexander. The troops found no one to arrest, but took away various weapons, including fowling-pieces. They also visited the curate, 'broke open his doors, and searched his house, and carried away in triumph an old gun he kept for his defence'. When Smyth protested he was told that the order had come from some justices of the peace, who claimed to have evidence of 'several suspected persons being concealed' in Ballentoy House. Then a week later, on Saturday, 11 February, the sub-sheriff, accompanied by James Porter, a local Presbyterian minister, and thirty armed men, paid a second visit to Martin with the intention of seizing his son, George. They failed to make an arrest, but on the following Monday George Martin appeared at Ballymoney, together with 'another relation of his' living nearby, and John Martin gave bail for them to appear at the next assizes.[23]

Lindsay and Smyth were among the leaders of the High Church party among the bishops, and clearly intended to use this information to advance their case against the security bill.[24] Smyth probably heard of the incident through James Smyth, who was both his cousin and brother-in-law. Before the memorial was presented James was writing regularly to the bishop with details of 'the sufferings of the clergy and church people in our county' and 'materials

---

22 *The report of the judges of assize, for the north-east circuit of Ulster; upon a memorial given in to the lords justices of Ireland ...* ([Dublin], 1716 [henceforth *Report*]), pp 3–4; Lord Brodrick to [Thomas Brodrick], 15 Apr. 1716 (*Anglo-Irish politics, 1680–1726: the correspondence of the Brodrick family of Surrey and County Cork*, ed. David Hayton and Michael Page (2 vols so far, Oxford, 2019–20), ii, 128).   23 *Report*, pp 5–8; James Smyth to William Smyth, 6 Feb. 1715/16 (NLI, MS 41,582/2).   24 There are other copies of the depositions in Marsh's Library, MS Z.3.1.1., no. xii, possibly from the papers of Archbishop King of Dublin, another strong opponent of any relaxation of the sacramental test.

necessary to represent our case to the government'.[25] But there could also have been supplementary sources of information, in particular William Tisdall, whose ear was always to the ground, and the fourth Viscount Massereene, a strong Tory who was also Bishop Smyth's brother-in-law. Massereene's sister was married to the Catholic earl of Antrim, the ground landlord of those involved in the disturbances. Alexander Stewart of Ballentoy House was Antrim's land agent and seneschal.[26]

The lords justices passed the memorial to the judges for the north-east circuit, Lord Chief Justice John Forster, a former Speaker of the Irish House of Commons, and his colleague in common pleas, James Macartney. It soon became clear that any investigation by Forster and Macartney would have to be very carefully handled. Not only were both men Whigs, but Macartney, the son of a Belfast merchant, had many Presbyterian connections even though himself a member of the Church of Ireland.[27] The Irish lord chancellor, Lord Brodrick, a man who despite his Whig principles had limited sympathies for Ulster Presbyterianism,[28] persuaded the lords justices that the chief secretary should send a firm letter to both judges setting out the seriousness of the allegations and requiring a very thorough examination. At the same time, Bishop Smyth was to be reassured that the memorial would be followed up with due diligence. Neither Lindsay nor Smyth were privy councillors, but their allies on the council were making hay with the case. As Brodrick reported, during discussions in council 'we heard ... more than once of the insupportable difficulties and oppressions the churchmen lay under in the County of Antrim'.[29]

The assizes began at Carrickfergus on 28 March. Before the grand jury was sworn, Forster, as the senior judge, informed those present of the charges made in the memorial, adding that he and his colleague

> had received particular directions from the lords justices to inform themselves so fully of the facts as to be able to lay a true state of it before them at their return, as well as to execute the law against such as should be found offenders. He told the sheriff it was his duty to return a good and sufficient grand jury and acquainted those who were witnesses of the facts set forth in the memorial or attended to justify the truth of the matters laid to the charge of those who are complained against in it, that if any men were returned on the grand jury concerned in the matters alleged in the memorial or against whom any cause of exception to be on the grand jury should be offered, the court was ready to hear what should be objected ...

25 James Smyth to William Smyth, 15 Mar. 1715/16 (NLI, MS 41,582/2).   26 George Hill, 'The Stewarts of Ballintoy ...', *UJA*, 6 (1900), 160–1.   27 Jean Agnew, *Belfast merchant families in the seventeenth century* (Dublin, 1996), pp 233–5.   28 S.J. Connolly, *Religion, law and power: the making of Protestant Ireland, 1660–1760* (Oxford, 1992), p. 168.   29 *Anglo-Irish politics*, ed. Hayton and Page, ii, 129.

Archibald Stewart, whom Bishop Smyth had commissioned 'to prosecute this complaint', quickly objected against Hugh Boyd, William Moor, one of the justices of the peace who had authorized the searches, Moor's son, and Clotworthy Upton.[30] But the end result was still a jury with a Presbyterian majority: ten out of the 17 jurors are identifiable as Presbyterians and the seven churchmen included Clotworthy Upton's brother Hercules, who had only recently conformed.[31]

Stewart asked for a short postponement to enable him to summon witnesses, and in the meantime tried to backtrack on two of the charges that had been made: he was now convinced that the minister, Porter, had no hand in the events, and thought that the mention of Porter's name in the memorial had 'proceeded from some mistake of the bishop'; indeed, Stewart was anxious not to proceed at all in relation to the search of Ballentoy House, which he did not feel was 'of such consequence as to receive so solemn an examination'. But the judges were insistent that their orders required an examination of every allegation. The court proceedings eventually took place on the 31st. William Tisdall joined Stewart in the courtroom, having 'come thither to assist his brethren the clergy', and was allowed to question the witnesses, even though counsel had been retained 'on both sides'. The bishop was represented by Richard Nutley, a former judge notorious for his high-flying, possibly Jacobite, sentiments.[32]

The hearing did not begin well for Stewart, since two of the churchmen on the jury, the foreman, John Itchingham Chichester, MP, and 'French John' O'Neill of Shane's Castle, 'declared their surprise, that the matter contained in the memorial, could have happened in that county without the knowledge or privity of any of them' and that 'the Dissenters in their neighbourhood were very quiet and peaceable in their behaviour to those of the established church'. Worse was to come: the examination of witnesses enabled the affronted clergy to add more detail about their ill-treatment, but at the same time revealed errors and exaggerations in the depositions, and enabled the introduction of evidence of the extreme political views of some of those involved, notably Fanning and the younger Martin. Archibald Stewart was also forced to admit that no 'Dissenting

30 *Report*, pp 10–11, 13; *Anglo-Irish politics*, ed. Hayton and Page, ii, 130. 31 The presbyterians were: Henry Dalway (Whan, *Presbyterians*, pp 77, 127, 174), James Wilson (Thomas Witherow, *Historical and literary memorials of Presbyterianism in Ireland (1623–1800)* (2 vols, London, 1879–80), ii, 1–7), George Portis (*Historic memorials of the first Presbyterian church of Belfast* … (Belfast, 1887), p. 70), John McMaster (*Records of the General Synod of Ulster* … (3 vols, Belfast, 1890–8), i, 427), Alexander Harper (Whan, *Presbyterians*, p. 135), James Crafford (Witherow, *Memorials*, ii, 1–7), Alexander Dalway (*HIP*, iv, 3), Nicholas Thetford (*Historic memorials of the first Presbyterian church*, 70; cf. Agnew, *Belfast merchant families*, p. 102), St John Johnston (*Historic memorials of the first Presbyterian church*, p. 75) and Joseph Bigger (Whan, *Presbyterians*, p. 111). For Hercules Upton see Whan, *Presbyterians*, p. 62). Lord Chancellor Brodrick reported that the jury was composed of 'nine churchmen and eight … Dissenters' (*Anglo-Irish politics*, ed. Hayton and Page, ii, 130). The jury is listed in Co. Antrim grand jury presentment book, 1711–21 (PRONI, ANT4/1/1). 32 For Nutley, see F. Elrington Ball, *The judges in Ireland, 1221–1921* (2 vols, London, 1926), ii,

teachers' were involved, not even Porter, who was actually on good terms with Martin and had only attended 'to serve some friends of his who were taken up', including one 'Lieutenant Stewart', presumably a relation of the family at Ballentoy House. The grand jury could find nothing to justify the assertions in the memorial, and their report represented a complete defeat for the bishops: the searches had been undertaken in accordance with due legal process; there had been no systematic harassment of clergymen; and no Presbyterian ministers had been involved.[33]

In June the judges' report was published, along with the original memorial, the depositions, a summary of the court proceedings, and the conclusions of the grand jury. This was the material that had been submitted to the lords justices.[34] No place of publication was given, or printer named, but it was clearly a Dublin production, and printed either at the instigation of government, to put an end to public discussion on a potentially explosive issue, or by supporters of a partial repeal of the test. It was certainly used by one of Tisdall's enemies, the Dublin Presbyterian minister Joseph Boyse, as evidence that the complaint was 'utterly groundless and unreasonable'.[35] Interestingly, there was a London reprinting, with a more elaborate and tendentious title, beginning *The insolence of the Dissenters against the establish'd church; exemplified in a memorial given in to the lords justices ....* The fact that the printers, John Baker and Thomas Warner, were closely connected to Daniel Defoe and to the Huguenot newswriter Abel Boyer, would suggest that the title was heavily ironic, and intended to undermine the claims of over-excitable Tories.[36]

At first Lindsay and Smyth seem to have intended to take the matter further, by bringing the matter before the Irish House of Lords, but they seem to have opted for discretion and let the matter lie.[37] In fact, they did not need to take further action, because the amended security bill fell in the House of Commons. Frustrated of their hopes, those who had promoted the cause of indemnity had to make do with two resolutions of the lower house, one praising Dissenters who had taken militia commissions and the other declaring that anyone who in future should initiate a prosecution for the taking of a commission contrary to the test clause 'is an enemy to King George and the Protestant interest, and a friend to the Pretender'. This seems to have had the effect of deterring prosecutions, though no legal indemnity had been passed.[38]

39, 72; *HIP*, v, 365–6.   33 *Report*, pp 12–32; *Anglo-Irish politics*, ed. Hayton and Page, ii, 131–2.   34 *Anglo-Irish politics*, ed. Hayton and Page, ii, 128–34, 151.   35 [Joseph Boyse], *Remarks on a pamphlet publish'd by William Tisdall, D.D. and intituled, The case of the sacramental test stated and argued* (Dublin, 1716), preface.   36 H.R. Plomer, *A dictionary of the printers and booksellers who were at work in England, Scotland and Ireland from 1688 to 1725* (Oxford, 1922), pp 14–15; Paula Backscheider, *Daniel Defoe: his life* (Baltimore, MD, 1989), p. 595; M.E. Novak, *Daniel Defoe, master of fictions* (Oxford, 2001), pp 457–8. Baker had printed Defoe's *Review*, and was currently printing Boyer's *Political state of Great Britain*.   37 *Anglo-Irish politics*, ed. Hayton and Page, ii, 151.   38 J.C. Beckett, *Protestant*

III

The febrile political atmosphere in County Antrim in the winter of 1715–16 was a product of local circumstances as well as the anxieties engendered by developments in national and international politics. The trepidation of Whig and Presbyterian interests in and around Ballentoy, and their belief that high-flying Tory clergymen were active Jacobites, reflected attitudes that could be found in the correspondence of politicians in Dublin, and indeed across the country. But religious demography meant that animosities between churchmen and Presbyterians were especially intense in the north-eastern counties. The crisis over the Hanoverian succession saw frequent outbreaks of violence. In 1714 Presbyterian meeting-houses were attacked, while Presbyterian booksellers had their wares confiscated.[39] At the parliamentary election in 1715 a Sacheverellite mob assaulted Whig voters at the poll for knights of the shire for Antrim, and there were also reports of the intimidation of Whig voters in the borough of Newry.[40] Two years later, in Armagh, there would be a full-scale riot when Presbyterians armed with knives and hatchets confronted two Tory magistrates notorious for prosecuting Dissenters.[41]

The epicentre of this sectarian conflict seems to have been in the south of County Antrim, and adjoining parts of County Down, where Presbyterians were thickly settled, and economically and politically powerful. All the evidence cited by Tisdall to support his arguments about Presbyterians and the militia had been drawn from the area around Belfast. It was the country he knew best, of course, but it was also where Presbyterians were most populous and prosperous. The trading economy of Belfast and Carrickfergus was dominated by wealthy Presbyterian merchants and a strong Presbyterian 'middling sort' of shopkeepers and craftsmen. Even more dangerous, politically, as far as the established church was concerned, was the relative concentration of Presbyterian landed proprietors in south Antrim and Down, headed by the Upton family, who in 1716 provided both the county's MPs. (The long-term decline of the small Presbyterian gentry class, pushed towards conformity by the effects of the test clause, was not yet apparent.)[42] According to Tisdall, the Uptons not only mobilized their own tenants in the 1715 general election but also received the votes of Presbyterians on other estates, 'spirited up' by ministers to defy their landlords' recommendations.[43] The strength of the Presbyterian interest in this

Dissent in Ireland, 1687–1780 (London, 1948), pp 72–4; Garnham, *Militia*, p. 30. **39** W.D. Killen, *History of the congregations of the Presbyterian Church in Ireland* ... (Belfast, 1886), p. 167; Reid, *Hist. Presbyterian Church*, iii, 55; Samuel McSkimin, *The history and antiquities of the ... town of Carrickfergus*, ed. E.J. M'Crum (2nd ed., Belfast, 1909), p. 76. **40** D.W. Hayton, 'Irish Tories and victims of Whig persecution: Sacheverell fever by proxy', *Parliamentary History*, 31 (2012), 80–1; *CJI* (2nd edn.), iv, 143–50. **41** Examinations, 17 Mar. 1717 (PRONI, T808/14937). **42** On the Presbyterian gentry in general, see Whan, *Presbyterians*, ch. 2. **43** Tisdall, *Case of the sacramental test*, pp 48–9.

area produced in turn a vigorous reaction from churchmen: the hottest Tories in the county were to be found in the hinterland of Belfast and in the Lagan valley. In particular, Brent Spencer of Lisburn (one of the defeated Tory candidates for the county in 1715) and Westenra Waring, sheriff of Antrim in 1712 and Down in 1713, had become notorious in Queen Anne's reign for their unrelenting pursuit of Presbyterian ministers whose theological scruples prevented them from taking the oath of abjuration as required by law.[44]

The situation in Ballentoy was significantly different. There was certainly a Presbyterian presence, and a congregation established close by, at Dunluce. But the local Presbyterian population was relatively small. A list dating from 1734 of the householders in the barony of Cary, which ran along the north coast from Dunluce to Torr Head, numbered 217 churchmen and only 63 Dissenters (together with 42 Catholics).[45] Dunluce congregation was small and poor, regularly berated by its presbytery for failing to pay the minister's stipend or other moneys owed, and being obliged to shift its place of meeting from time to time for the greater convenience of members.[46] The men who conducted the searches in 1716 were of necessity drawn from a much wider area, from the environs of Ballycastle and indeed from as far afield as Ballymoney, some fifteen miles to the south. They did not include any substantial Presbyterian landowners, for there were none in the vicinity. Only one of the Presbyterians mentioned in the depositions can be identified as a man of property: David Snell of Ballymoney, described in a lease as a merchant (possibly a shopkeeper) and given the status of 'gent.'[47]

By contrast, the Church of Ireland community in Ballentoy itself seems to have been thriving, at least to judge by the parish vestry book, which shows evidence of extensive repairs and reconstruction to the church being undertaken at around this time, including the building of a gallery, the installation of a new font, the recasting of the bell and the repair of the belfry.[48] When Archibald Stewart became rector in 1718 he was able to consent to the separation of Rathlin Island from the parish, in spite of the loss of tithe income involved.[49] It was all very different from the uphill struggle faced by Tisdall in Belfast, competing with two substantial Presbyterian congregations, and deprived of his

---

44 Beckett, *Protestant Dissent*, pp 64–9; Agnew, *Belfast merchant families*, pp 74–5. **45** Groves transcripts (PRONI, MIC15A/88). **46** Typescript copy of the minute book of the presbytery of Route, 1701–6 (Presbyterian Historical Society of Ireland). In 1702 the congregation requested permission to move the meeting house a few miles away to Bushmills (ibid., p. 32). In later years it was variously located at Dunluce, Bushmills and Billy (*A history of congregations in the Presbyterian Church in Ireland, 1610–1982* (Belfast, 1982), pp 255–6). The presbytery, Route, was itself relatively unimportant: it did not send either elders or ministers to the General Synod of Ulster even though it came under the synod's authority (*General Synod Records*, i, 330). **47** *Report*, pp 14–15; leases 1729, 1736 (PRONI, Antrim papers, D2977/3A/3/2/10/66, 72). **48** Vestry book *c.*1712–90 (PRONI, T679/68). **49** *The state of the case of Raghlin* ([1720]). I am grateful to Dr Andrew Sneddon for providing me with

'house money' (the urban equivalent of tithe) by the refusal of Dissenters to pay.[50]

But while the Presbyterian community in and around Ballentoy was relatively small, and the position of the established church and its clergy relatively comfortable, there were other, specifically local, reasons why tensions were running high between Presbyterians and churchmen, and between Whigs and Tories. Even if many clergymen in the north of Ireland were unfairly tarred with Jacobitism, it remains the case that each of the individual ministers searched in 1716 – Smyth, Martin and Fanning – had a justified reputation as a high-flyer.[51] In Martin's case this was guilt by association. Nothing was said against him personally. But evidence was given to the grand jury that his son 'drank the duke of Ormond's health last winter at Bushmills and in other places', after Ormond's flight to join the Pretender in France.[52] According to another witness, Fanning proposed a similar health in December 1715, in politically mixed company, describing Ormond as 'one of the best peers that ever was in the kingdom'. The 'common repute in the country' was that Fanning was disaffected.[53] As for Smyth, although no accusation was made against him in open court, his private correspondence nevertheless shows a man driven by powerful Tory opinions and allegiances, who wrote of his hopes that the new Whig ministry would fall; was delighted that Oxford University had decided to honour the former lord chancellor of Ireland, Sir Constantine Phipps, whom Whigs excoriated as a crypto-Jacobite; bemoaned the fact that 'the Presbyterians have now the power'; and campaigned vigorously for Tories to be returned to the Irish parliament and for High Churchmen to be elected to convocation.[54]

Behind these high-flyers, however, stood a far more sinister figure: Randal MacDonnell, fourth earl of Antrim, one of the few Catholic landowners to have survived the Williamite revolution with his patrimony intact. Antrim, who was then living at Ballymagarry, near Dunluce, had a huge estate, encompassing several baronies.[55] It is a fair assumption that he was at least sympathetic in principle to the Jacobite cause, and the geographical position of his house would have afforded every opportunity to communicate with Jacobites in Scotland.[56] While his estate papers show that his tenants spanned the religious and political

this reference.   **50** Agnew, *Belfast merchant families*, pp 72–4.   **51** John Leathes to William Leathes, 15 Jan. 1715/16 (Suffolk Record Office, Ipswich, De Mussenden Leathes papers, HA 403/1/6).   **52** *Report*, pp 23, 29.   **53** Ibid., p. 16.   **54** James Smyth to William Smyth, 13 Nov. 1714, 14 Nov. 1715, 6 Feb., 15 Mar. 1715/16 (NLI, MS 41,582/2).   **55** *Richard Pococke's Irish tours*, ed. John McVeigh (Dublin, 1995), pp 41, 43; Roulston, '*Insolence of Dissenters*', p. 2.   **56** Hector MacDonnell, 'Jacobitism and the third and fourth earls of Antrim', *The Glynns*, 13 (1985), 50–4; Éamonn Ó Ciardha, *Ireland and the Jacobite cause, 1685–1766: a fatal attachment* (Dublin, 2002), pp 115, 123, 181. There is a scrap of supporting evidence in HMC, *Stuart MSS*, iii, 316, a letter from a Jacobite whom Antrim had helped to leave Ireland. Having twice been placed in preventive detention by government in 1716, Antrim eventually took himself off to France (*Saturday's Post*, 6 Oct. 1716).

spectrum, the fact that the Stewarts of Ballentoy House were so closely connected to him, as were the McNaughtens of Benvarden, Fanning's parish, identified the local clergy firmly with the Antrim interest.[57]

The extent to which Antrim's wealth and presumed influence alarmed some contemporaries is clear from a letter sent at the end of December 1715 to the English secretary of state, James Stanhope, by a Lieutenant H. Lynn, an officer in Count Maurice Nassau's regiment, who was on leave in his native County Antrim. He may tentatively be identified as Hugh Lynn or Linn (d.1731), a Belfast Presbyterian.[58] Lynn warned Stanhope that Antrim was 'the most considerable papist in the nation', 'those of his party' were constantly writing letters to Scotland and supplying provisions to the rebels there, and that during 1714 Antrim had entertained a prominent Highland Jacobite at Ballymagarry. The whole area was in fact a nest of rebels: there were only three magistrates 'in all this quarter', of whom two were clergy and therefore suspect, while 'those of the greatest eminency in this country are either Tories or papists, all having a dependence on that lord'.[59]

The Dublin government was already alert to the danger, however, and took action even before Stanhope could pass on the information. On Saturday, 21 January, the earl of Antrim went down to Dublin. The following morning he was taken from his bed by a file of musketeers, and brought to Dublin Castle, where he was imprisoned, along with other Catholic peers and gentlemen, as a precautionary measure, a move which would have confirmed the belief of Lynn and those who thought like him that Antrim was indeed a traitor.[60] While the other 'state prisoners' were soon released, the earl remained incarcerated for two months.[61]

The atmosphere was made more frenetic by reports of Jacobite agents in the district enlisting men for the Pretender's service.[62] One, named as 'Andrew MacCook', escaped by shooting dead one of the party despatched to arrest him, and fled to Scotland in a boat belonging to Alexander Stewart. That he had taken the boat without permission, according to James Smyth, and moreover was a Presbyterian, did nothing to dispel the popular impression that this was further evidence of the treasonable activities of the Stewarts. The discovery of a quantity of MacCook's goods in an outbuilding at Ballentoy House – food and

57 Leases, 1716, 1720 (PRONI, D2977/3A/3/1/ 61, 66). The noted physician Alexander McNaughten, whose address was given as Benvarden in these leases, seems to have had 'a closet' in Fanning's house in 1716 (*Report*, p. 15). Alexander's father John (d.1700) had been one of the commissioners of supply for County Antrim appointed under the Supply Act passed by the Jacobite parliament in Dublin in 1689 (John Bergin and Andrew Lyell (eds), *The acts of James II's Irish parliament of 1689* (Dublin, 2016), p. 14). 58 Mortgages, 1708, 1714 (Registry of Deeds, Dublin, 1/430/295; 13/210/5616); *Historic memorials of the first Presbyterian church*, p. 89. 59 Lynn to Stanhope, 27 Dec. 1715 (TNA, SP 63/373/212). 60 *Evening Post*, 31 Jan.–2 Feb. 1716. 61 *Weekly Journal*, 14 Apr. 1716. 62 Roulston, '*Insolence of Dissenters*', p. 7.

other materials that could be construed as supplies intended for the Jacobite army across the water – confirmed the connection between the fugitive and the earl of Antrim's seneschal and suggested that MacCook was operating as a go-between with the Scottish rebels.[63]

The dynamics of local politics may also have played a significant role in heightening tensions in the district around Ballentoy in 1716. This had little to do with the conflict of parties, or the uneasy relationships between the various landed interests in the county. Instead it concerned the ambition of one particular individual, Hugh Boyd. He led the raids on Ballentoy House and on Martin's residence, on each occasion looking for 'suspected persons', and accompanied the sub-sheriff and 'about thirty of the militia … to search the lord of Antrim's house'.[64] The search party at Ballentoy House also included a 'Mr Jackson' (probably Richard) of Drumawillin, the townland on which Boyd resided.[65]

There are several possible explanations for Boyd's enthusiasm. He may have entertained designs of acquiring property from the Antrim estate, should it be possible to prove the earl guilty of treason.[66] That Archibald Stewart was rector of Boyd's home parish of Ramoan could have been a further source of friction. Finally, he would have been concerned to demonstrate his loyalty to the new regime. Boyd is familiar to historians as a gentleman entrepreneur, who developed the collieries at Ballycastle and spent money on improving the town. His political career is less well known.[67] He was the son of a clergyman, and like most of the neighbouring gentlemen was a tenant of Lord Antrim.[68] In April 1713 he had served as foreman of the county grand jury that made a presentment praising the Treaty of Utrecht and denouncing those, who by 'artful misrepresentations' of the peace terms, were showing themselves enemies to the queen and the church.[69] How far Boyd had previously embarked in the Tory interest is unclear, but no young man aspiring to a public career would have found it difficult to judge the direction of the prevailing political winds after 1714, especially in County Antrim.

Since the death of Queen Anne the balance of power within the county had shifted dramatically. Not only had Whigs taken both shire seats, the party had also regained control of the county grand jury, whose membership was dominated by Whigs and Presbyterians. Alexander Stewart of Ballentoy, who

63 *Report*, pp 20, 23, 26, 28. MacCook's identity and occupation remain a mystery. He was possibly related to Alexander McCook, a butcher in Ballymoney granted a lease on the Antrim estate in 1738 (PRONI, D2977/3A/2/10/104A). The goods seized by the militia comprised 'ten barrels of beef, sixteen casks of butter, two boxes of candles, of about two hundred pound weight, one hundred weight of cheese, and one hundred weight of soap'.   64 *Report*, pp 6–7, 21, 23, 26–9.   65 Ibid., p. 23; Richard Jackson to Michael Ward, 9 Mar. 1724 (PRONI, Castle Ward papers, D2092/1/1/, p. 98); lease, 1720 (ibid., D2977/3A/2/1/27A).   66 For evidence of his continuing hostility to the Antrim interest, and his attempts to prise away lands from the estate, see George Hill, *An historical account of the MacDonnells of Antrim* … (Belfast, 1873), p. 366.   67 *DIB*.   68 Leases, 1709 (PRONI, D2977/3A/2/1/22–3).   69 PRONI, ANT4/1/1, *s.v.* 12 Apr. 1713.

had twice served as foreman in 1712–13, was not empanelled again until 1720.[70] With the exception of the Skeffingtons, Viscounts Massereene, the magnate families who had provided the backbone of the Tory interest in the county were also shifting towards a more conciliatory position. This much is clear from the proceedings of the grand jury in 1716, for the two gentlemen who made decisive interventions against the complainants, John Itchingham Chichester and John O'Neill, were both from families which had previously been strongly committed to the Tory cause. Thus the dynamic of politics both nationally and locally required Boyd to prove his Whig credentials, and the security crisis in the winter of 1715–16 furnished him with the opportunity.

The depositions show Boyd as determined but polite. However, a letter from James Smyth, written in September 1716, casts him in a very different light, and suggests that Boyd may himself have been the moving force behind the events of the previous winter. If accurate, it depicts Boyd as a man of a violent and unpredictable temper, possibly acting under considerable strain. Smyth recounted how some time earlier in the year (he does not specify the date, only that it occurred 'when Lord Antrim was in the country') he and one of the Stewarts had encountered Boyd on the road near Ballycastle. This was the man, Smyth said, who had 'bred all the disturbance in our country', and 'had encouraged many false informations against our family'. For a time, Boyd followed the same road. Stewart upbraided him 'for his threatening him among the country people, and accusing him [Stewart] of high treason (for which he was taken up) and neither he nor any of his accomplices appearing against him at the assizes'. Boyd at first seemed 'very meek and humble' in the face of this onslaught, but then, wrote Smyth, 'galloped up to me, and there begun to abuse Mr Stewart heavily, calling him traitor, and assuring me he both believed and could prove him guilty of high treason'. Smyth called Boyd a rascal, and rode off, upon which Boyd

> drew out his pistol at me, but soon returned it upon cousin Stewart's coming up. Soon after this I returned to the company, to prevent ... a quarrel ... and when my back was turned he again cocked his pistol at me. Mr Stewart, enraged at this usage, alighted from his horse, and made the fellow get off also, but he was glad to mount again upon my coming up. I then confirmed my old title of rascal to him, and argued the baseness of his mind and his actions, upon which he often asked mine and Mr Stewart's pardon ... The fellow seemed very penitent, but we refused him, and his last words were, I thank God we part in peace and friendship, and kissed Mr Stewart at parting ... But the devil I believe has not left him ...[71]

70 PRONI, ANT4/1/1.   71 James Smyth to William Smyth, 14 Sept. 1716 (NLI, MS 41,582/2).

As an example of the interplay of national and local politics, the Ballentoy episode presents a range of complex interactions. Public discourse about the case was framed in the context of national politics. Prominent figures on either side of the debate over the test were keen to exploit the story. At first, Tories saw the chance to prove the danger of putting weapons into Presbyterian hands; then, when the grand jury investigation had dismissed the allegations, it was the turn of those in parliament who were hoping to force through concessions to make capital.

At the same time, there was a strong local dimension. Tisdall's original pamphlet campaign had been stimulated by the pressure of Presbyterian expansion in eastern Ulster, and more particularly by the evident strength of Presbyterian interests in Antrim and Down, not just in boroughs like Belfast, but in county elections. Similarly, Presbyterian hostility towards the Church of Ireland hierarchy arose not just from the association of High Church clerics with the activities of Tories in government and parliament under Queen Anne, but from what was perceived as the persecution of Presbyterian ministers and their congregations by lay magistrates and ecclesiastical courts.

Strictly speaking, this was a regional rather than a parochial context, not something for which the 'parish pump' could properly serve as an emblem. But there was also a very specific, and very narrow, local context, deriving from the peculiar conditions of the north Antrim coastal communities. Unlike the south of the county, Presbyterians in and around Ballentoy were neither powerful nor aggressive, and the established church was not embattled and defensive. There are fragments of evidence to suggest that relations between churchmen and Presbyterians may have been good, not least the friendship between the curate, Martin, and the Presbyterian minister, Porter. But the lack of discretion shown by clergy in their cups was enough to make Whig observers believe that these men were Jacobites. The clinching factor may have been the looming presence of the earl of Antrim. Even though Antrim had far more Protestant than Catholic tenants and sub-tenants, it was easy to assume that he was secretly promoting the cause of the Pretender, especially when the countryside was disturbed by a rural crime wave. The elusive 'MacCook' may or may not have been a Jacobite, but his nefarious activities stoked fears of a Catholic uprising. Finally, there is the question of the part played by Hugh Boyd, an excitable character with a point to prove.

This combination of circumstances produced the controversial narrative which was brought on to the national stage. But at the same time the north Antrim clergy and their tormentors were not entirely inward-looking: their political views were determined by awareness of events in the wider world. Whig and Presbyterian suspicions of the earl of Antrim did not arise from his behaviour as a landlord; High Church antagonism towards Dissenters did not arise from anything that the small and troubled congregation of Dunluce might have done. In the early eighteenth century, popular attitudes and responses, even in a remote corner of rural Ireland, were heavily influenced by the conflicts, and the rhetoric, of national politics.

'The common opinion of the town': rumour and rancour in provincial Ireland, 1758

TOBY BARNARD

The parliamentary politics of Ireland between 1692 and 1800 have been clarified greatly by recent investigations. The members elected and the characteristics of their constituencies have been inventoried; so too, the laws, whether merely proposed or enacted.[1] The careers of notable parliamentarians, ranging from William Conolly in the earlier decades of the eighteenth century to Henry Flood, John Foster, John FitzGibbon and Sir Edward Newenham in the later, have been recounted.[2] Furthermore, a succession of episodes during which the Dublin parliament was unusually active, vociferous and divided have been analysed.[3] Also, the pressures from outside the parliament building on College Green, whether through physical assaults, invasions of the chamber or through extra-parliamentary petitions and demonstrations, have been charted.[4] Notable among these insights are those provided by Jacqueline Hill, with her focus on turbulent Dublin.[5]

I am grateful to David Fleming, David Hayton and Jimmy Kelly for comments on earlier versions of this essay.   **1** *HIP*; D.W. Hayton, *Ruling Ireland, 1685–1742: politics, politicians and parties* (Woodbridge, 2004); D.W. Hayton, J. Kelly and J. Bergin (eds), *The eighteenth-century composite state: representative institutions in Ireland and Europe, 1689–1800* (Basingstoke, 2010); James Kelly, *Poynings' Law and the making of law in Ireland, 1660–1800* (Dublin, 2007); Queen's University Belfast, Irish legislation database (https://www.qub.ac.uk/ild/).   **2** Patrick Walsh, *The making of the Irish Protestant ascendancy: the life of William Conolly, 1662–1729* (Woodbridge, 2010); D.A. Fleming and A.P.W. Malcomson (eds), *'A volley of execrations': the letters and papers of John FitzGibbon, earl of Clare 1772–1802* (Dublin, 2005); A.C. Kavanaugh, *John FitzGibbon, earl of Clare: Protestant reaction and English authority in late eighteenth-century Ireland* (Dublin, 1997); James Kelly, *Henry Flood: patriots and politics in eighteenth-century Ireland* (Dublin, 1998); James Kelly, *Sir Edward Newenham, MP, 1734–1814* (Dublin, 2004); A.P.W. Malcomson, *John Foster: the politics of the Anglo-Irish ascendancy* (Oxford, 1978); A.P.W. Malcomson, *John Foster (1740–1828): the politics of improvement and prosperity* (Dublin, 2011); A.P.W. Malcomson, *Nathaniel Clements: government and the governing elite of Ireland, 1725–75* (Dublin, 2005); Sean Murphy, 'Charles Lucas and the Dublin election of 1748–1749', *Parliamentary History*, 2 (1983), 93–111; Sean Murphy, *A forgotten patriot doctor: Charles Lucas, 1713–1771* (Centre for Irish Genealogical and Historical Studies, 2011 available at http://homepage.eircom.net/~seanjmurphy/epubs/lucaspatriot.pdf) [accessed 9 Sept. 2021].   **3** James Kelly, *Prelude to Union: Anglo-Irish politics in the 1780s* (Cork, 1992); Eoin Magennis, *The Irish political system, 1740–1765* (Dublin, 2000); Patrick McNally, *Parties, patriots and undertakers: parliamentary politics in early Hanoverian Ireland* (Dublin, 1997); M.J. Powell, *Britain and Ireland in the eighteenth-century crisis of empire* (Basingstoke, 2003).   **4** James Kelly, *Food rioting in Ireland in the eighteenth and nineteenth centuries* (Dublin, 2017); P.J. Jupp and E. Magennis (eds), *Crowds in Ireland, c.1720–1920* (Basingstoke, 2000).   **5** J. Hill, *From patriots to unionists: Dublin civic*

The older picture of a torpid and venal minority remote from and usually indifferent to the needs of their constituents, let alone the generality of the population, has been refined. Nevertheless, despite the evidence of public spirit and useful industry, both collectively and of individual MPs, the traditional stereotype cannot be jettisoned completely. It is still easier to ascribe self-interest rather than altruism to parliament and to municipal corporations. This essay attempts neither further rehabilitation of the institution and its activists nor the reinstatement of earlier, hostile assessments. It concerns itself chiefly with the process and issues that came into play during one parliamentary by-election: at Dungarvan in County Waterford early in 1758. It is based on documentation that has rarely survived, a poll book in which were recorded the names of voters with the frequent and sometimes lengthy doubts that were expressed about their eligibility to vote.[6] This evidence prompts some reflections on relationships within mid-eighteenth-century Irish communities, and how electoral contests offered an outlet for tensions, maybe exacerbating them.

So far as is known, Dungarvan is the only urban constituency during the eighteenth century for which a detailed record of the challenges presented to would-be voters has come to light. The habit of candidates, or their agents, in listing the names of their likely backers was frequent. Indeed, it occurred at Dungarvan in 1703.[7] Reports of how electors voted were also compiled, as for Limerick city in 1731 and 1761 and for the county in the latter year, and sometimes printed.[8] The grounds for objecting to electors are set out at length in at least a couple of county constituencies for which poll books are extant. In counties, the challenges were overwhelmingly based on either the authenticity of the forty-shilling freehold or religious affiliation, usually of a wife. Undue influence through bribery was also a common charge.[9] The petitions prepared for the parliamentary committee of privileges and elections focused on these malpractices. Some were published as leaflets; others, including that relating to

politics and Irish Protestant patriotism, 1660–1840 (Oxford, 1997). 6 NLI, MS 43807/3. I am grateful to John Bergin for making a copy of the document and to David Fleming and Luke Hartigan for transcribing it. References to the poll book hereafter are simply by the number of the entry. 7 T.C. Barnard, 'Considering the inconsiderable: electors, patrons and Irish elections, 1659–1761' in D.W. Hayton (ed.), *The Irish parliament in the eighteenth century: the long apprenticeship* (Edinburgh, 2001), p. 114; H.F. Kearney, 'A handlist of the voters of Maryborough, 1760', *IHS*, 9 (1954), 53–82. 8 'The poll taken the 16. Day of Septemb. 1725' [Clonakilty, County Cork] (Chatsworth, Lismore MS 36/24); Limerick city poll book, 1731 (BL, Add. MS 31,888); County Limerick poll book, 1761 (NLI, MS 16,093); Limerick city poll book, 1761 (NLI, MS 16,092); *A complete list of the gentlemen, clergy and freeholders … who voted at the election for knight of the shire in the county of Limerick* (Limerick, [1768]); T.C. Barnard, *Brought to book: print in Ireland, 1680–1784* (Dublin, 2017), pp 61–2; Barnard, 'The Irish parliament and print, 1660–1782' in Clyve Jones and James Kelly (eds), *Parliament, politics and policy in Britain and Ireland, c.1680–1832: essays in honour of D.W. Hayton, Parliamentary History*, 33:1 (2014), 110–13; D.A. Fleming, *Politics and provincial people: Sligo and Limerick, 1691–1761* (Manchester, 2010), pp 82–3. 9 Poll book, County Clare, 1745 (TCD, MS 2059); 'A county election in 1761', *JLAHS*, 6 (1925–8), 27.

the Dungarvan election of 1703, were entered into the journal of the House of Commons, and subsequently included in its printed *Journals*.[10]

I

The larger political context for the competition at Dungarvan is provided by the acrimonious disagreements in parliament between those who adopted an avowedly patriotic stance, upholding what they identified as Ireland's interests, and those obedient to the distant British government. These rifts widened during the 1750s, most dramatically when, late in 1753, a Money Bill was narrowly rejected. Thereafter, if the political temperature cooled, it remained volatile. The agitation in Dublin reverberated into the provinces, with patrons and members of parliament from south Munster to the fore.[11] Indeed, two of the leading protagonists were deeply rooted in the region. Henry Boyle served as Speaker of the Irish House of Commons between 1733 and 1756, and undertook to manage government business in parliament until, early in the 1750s, he swung his political weight against the Dublin Castle administration. Part of Boyle's power derived from the sizeable squadron of clients and followers that he commanded, centred on south Munster where his principal seat – Castlemartyr – lay. By birth a junior member of the Boyle dynasty, the largest proprietors in south Munster, because resident and skilful he had been able to cultivate much of the Boyle interest in the area and turn it into a solid electoral base. In 1756, he was elevated to an earldom (of Shannon) and granted a generous pension. In consequence, his hitherto formidable powers as a parliamentary manager declined, although his son continued to mobilize what remained of the phalanx. However, the uncertainties about Boyle power, which had extended as far as Dungarvan, improved electoral opportunities for others.

Important in the Shannon dominance were the boroughs created for and still owned, at least partly, by the senior branch of the Boyles, earls of Cork and Burlington. For over a generation, the Cork and Burlingtons had been habitually absent from Ireland, leaving oversight of their valuable estates to agents on the spot and – to some degree – to their kinsman at Castlemartyr. However, these arrangements ended in 1753 when Lord Burlington died. His heir – although not to his titles – was a daughter. Her marriage to the son of the third duke of Devonshire (and his eventual successor as fourth duke) delivered a valuable fiefdom, together with its potential parliamentary seats, to the English magnates. The Devonshires might live in England, but even before the inheritance, they were heavily involved in Ireland. Father and son each acted as lord lieutenant

10 Barnard, 'The Irish parliament and print', pp 105–6; *CJI*, ii, 323, 381–3; iii, 472.   11 Hayton, *Ruling Ireland*; J.R. Hill, '"Allegories, fictions and feigned representations": decoding the money bill dispute, 1752–6', *ECI*, 21 (2006), 66–88; Magennis, *The Irish political system*.

of Ireland: from 1737 to 1744 and 1755 to 1756. Indeed, the future fourth duke visited both Lismore and Youghal in 1755.[12]

As well as having a proprietorial interest in maintaining authority over whom their boroughs sent to parliament, as governors of Ireland the Devonshires would hardly welcome the return of representatives obstructive to the king's business. Yet, remote from the constituencies and relying on the reports and efforts of their deputies, it was hard to keep tight control. Townspeople had long chafed against orders regarded as too dictatorial and insensitive to local wants. Other landowners who had industriously been carving out enviable estates of their own, often at the Cork and Burlingtons' expense, were keen to add parliamentary seats to their quiver. Accordingly, it was an increasing struggle to uphold what was regarded as the hereditary right to determine who sat for the Boyle boroughs. In 1758, the Lord Chancellor cautioned Devonshire that voters in his boroughs might be coming to prefer resident rather than absentee candidates.[13] Furthermore, the challenger at Dungarvan in 1758 told a rival, 'these boroughs were not any longer to be considered as they formerly had been, an appendix of the Burlington estate, for that the case was now quite altered'.[14] Specifically, another observed that the situation in Dungarvan was 'very ticklish'.[15]

Matters were further complicated, first by Shannon's independent line and then by his apparently weakening grip. In consequence, the Devonshires were encouraged to consider alternatives who offered to manage their parliamentary concerns more effectively. Two of the third duke's daughters had married into an Irish family, the Ponsonbys, with great ambitions to oust Shannon from his political supremacy. The Ponsonbys, although based in County Kilkenny and further north, had been encroaching steadily onto Boyle territory and could be expected to use parliamentary elections to dispute the Boyles' hegemony.

These rivalries could be used by those with smaller and local ambitions. They also encouraged voters if not to set a price on their support then to extract benefits, either for the larger community or just for themselves. In this unstable situation, by-elections, occurring unpredictably but regularly, were hotly fought. During the 1750s, the relative strength of the Boyles and their aggressors had been tested: in Cork city (in 1751) and then at Tallow, Dungarvan, Lismore and Youghal. Dungarvan's, Lismore's and Tallow's electorate included pot-wallopers, in addition to the more commonly entitled forty-shilling freeholders. The Burlingtons' agent interpreted this as being synonymous with the Protestant householders within the bounds of the manor.[16] Only eleven Irish

---

12 Hartington to Lady Burlington, 5 June 1755 (Chatsworth, Devonshire letters, 260.139). 13 J. Bowes to Devonshire, 3 Oct. 1758 (Chatsworth, Devonshire letters, 442.20). 14 Lord Boyle to Devonshire, 4 Feb. 1758 (Chatsworth, Devonshire letters, 351.3). 15 J. Ponsonby, paper on Irish constituencies [1758] (PRONI, T 2158/1601). 16 W. Conner to W. Abdy, 25 Feb. 1755 (Chatsworth, W. Conner letter-book, 1749–58).

constituencies accorded votes to pot-wallopers.[17] The qualification enfranchised all possessed of a hearth of their own on which they could boil a pot, so long as they had resided there for at least six months before the poll.[18] This condition, potentially a wide one, led to disputes as to whether or not individual electors lived independently even when they shared the same premises, or whether they were just lodgers ('inmates'). In support of claims to entitlement, liability to and payment of the hearth tax might be adduced. As a last resort, if the true situation could not be established, the accommodation was inspected. Otherwise, the questions raised during the Dungarvan poll in 1758 resembled those frequent elsewhere: proof of having a freehold of sufficient value; confessional affiliation of the elector or his spouse; malpractices by officials, especially the returning officer and sheriff.[19]

The information afforded by the poll book shifts the focus away from the manoeuvres of the prosperous propertied seeking the status and rewards of a parliamentary seat. It gives no insight into voters' attitudes towards the issues of the day. Instead, it offers glimpses into their circumstances and the enforced intimacies of small-town life. It would be anachronistic to apply later standards of privacy to communities accustomed to live hugger-mugger. Yet, the public nature of the polling, stretching over several winter days in the presence not only of the voters or would-be voters, but also of potential witnesses and mere bystanders, was intimate, sometimes oppressively so. Participants were under the glare of the two competing grandees by whom they had been entertained recently and to whom promises of support may have been made. Before turning to the unexpected detail from the poll book, it is necessary to set out the more conventional view of the tussle as seen through the perspectives of strangers to the town who – at best – alighted only briefly for the duration of the poll.

II

The vacancy was caused by the death on 4 January 1758 of one of the two members, Robert Roberts. A writ was quickly issued, and the election occurred over four days late in January 1758. The candidates were Sir William Osborne and Robert Boyle Walsingham. The latter was elected, receiving forty-seven votes to Osborne's forty. Osborne was reported to have given up the poll 'as the election has been very tedious and continued a long time'. In fact, he had

---

17 *HIP*, ii, 111 (twelve pot-walloper seats); J.L. McCracken, 'Irish parliamentary elections, 1727–68', *IHS*, v (1947–8), 228 (eleven pot-walloper seats).   18 *HIP*, ii, 111–14.   19 Poll book, County Armagh, 1753 (NLI, Genealogical Office, Dublin, MS 443 and PRONI, T 2768/1); Poll book, County Cavan (PRONI, T1522); Poll book, County Clare, 1745 (TCD, MS 2059; 'A county election in 1761', 27).

not given up: he was determined 'to be as vexatious as possible'.[20] Twice he petitioned the House of Commons to void the return, but did not succeed.[21]

The contest had been expected for at least a year on account of Roberts's deteriorating health. In anticipation, Osborne prepared the ground. His principal seat was near Clonmel, but he had aspired to become knight of the shire for Waterford (as his father had before him). Lacking sufficient leverage to defeat the Beresfords in the county, he turned his sights on the borough of Dungarvan. He had property there and resorted to the common practice of multiplying freeholds, thereby enfranchising more of his tenants. He sought in vain the endorsement of Lady Burlington for his candidature. He was also rumoured to be contemplating a pact with a substantial landowner in the district, Thomas Carew.[22] Furthermore, he appeared in the town, where he treated voters.[23] Despite these stratagems he was deemed 'remarkably close' [that is, reserved] and 'his stiffness among the lower rank of people prevents his being popular'.[24]

In contrast, the manager of the campaign for the successful Boyle Walsingham, his eldest brother, Lord Boyle, was reputed to be popular in the town. This offset one obvious disadvantage of Boyle Walsingham, on which Osborne traded: his absence on service in the British navy. He would soon sail across the Atlantic with Boscawen's fleet to take Louisburg from the French. Viscount Boyle and Boyle Walsingham were sons of Lord Shannon, and the elder had been a member for Dungarvan since 1749. The Boyles also had been expecting Roberts to die, and, early in 1757, the succession was discussed.[25] The dowager Lady Burlington insisted that it must remain a Boyle possession – Roberts, first elected in 1735, had been Burlington's principal agent. But, with her own husband dead, and the Devonshires' acquisition of his Irish and English properties, it was no longer she alone who could nominate. Also, the long-serving agent in the region, William Conner, was jittery about the loyalties of Dungarvan's electors. Both the size of the electorate and the Boyles' limited holdings in the area meant uncertainty about the outcome. Conner also

20 Lord Boyle to Devonshire, 4 Feb. 1758 (Chatsworth, Devonshire letters, 351.3); W. Conner to Sir W. Abdy, 31 Jan. 1758 (Chatsworth, W. Conner letter-book, 1749–58); Revd E. Lyndon to? W. Conner, 17 Feb. 1758 (Chatsworth, Lismore MS 36/143). 21 *CJI*, vi, 85–6, 180, 190–3. 22 W. Conner to Sir W. Abdy, 4 Feb. 1757 (Chatsworth, W. Conner letter-book, 1749–58); Sir W. Osborne to Devonshire, 16 July 1757, Lord Boyle to same, 4 Feb. 1758, W. Conner to same, 17 Aug. 1759, 2nd Lord Shannon to R.B. Walsingham, 16 Jan. 1766 (Chatsworth papers, PRONI, T1536, 1571, 1615, 1652). 23 W. Conner to Sir W. Abdy, 16 Jan. 1757, 23 Apr. 1757 (Chatsworth, W. Conner letter-book, 1749–58). 24 Sir W. Abdy to J. Usher, 3 July 1746 (NLI, MS 13,252/3); W. Conner to Sir W. Abdy, 4 and 25 Feb. 1755 (Chatsworth, W. Conner letter-book, 1749–58); Sir W. Osborne to Devonshire, 16 July 1757 (Chatsworth, Devonshire letters, 498.0); Barnard, 'Considering the inconsiderable', p. 116. See M. Bodkin, 'Notes on the Irish parliament in 1773', *PRIA Proc.*, 48C (1942), 216. 25 Sir W. Abdy to W. Conner, 9 Jan. 1757; W. Conner to Sir W. Abdy, 16 Jan. 1757, 4 Feb. 1757

foresaw the objection that would be raised against the Boyle candidate as an absentee unfamiliar with the town. In the event, Lady Burlington overruled that reasonable reservation.

Nor did the history of previous contests comfort the anxious. True, it was said that the election in 1749 had been 'cheap and easy'.[26] But reaching back to that of Roberts in 1735, it was remembered that it had cost Burlington £1000.[27] Earlier, there had been contestation in 1727, but most cautionary and still vividly recalled was the tumult in 1703.[28] Then, the high sheriff as returning officer was accused of malpractices, with a troop of militia brought to the poll, not just to intimidate but to vote. In all, it was reported that over 500 votes had been cast.[29]

Immediately after the Boyle victory in 1758, it was reckoned that Lord Boyle had spent fifteen days in Dungarvan and disbursed £600. Osborne had not given so many public treats, but was believed to have lavished an equivalent sum, because 'tis thought he purchased many votes, and paid dear for them'.[30] By comparison with the fracas of 1703, proceedings in 1758 looked more orderly. Rather than the poll being adjourned to the spacious churchyard, it now took place in the 'decent' sessions and market house.[31] There was no obvious military presence. Perhaps most dramatically, the number recorded as voting – eighty-seven – was less than 20 per cent of the 1703 total. The contraction of the electorate is partly explained by the absence of any influx of 'foreigners' and militia-men. But probably the greater impact can be traced to the disenfranchisement of Catholics.

A sense of physical proximity is palpable, especially as would-be voters came forward under the gaze of the two protagonists, Lord Boyle, standing in for his sailor sibling, and Osborne. The latter arrived well-prepared. He (or his clerks) produced and read out the report of the parliamentary committee on the 1703 Dungarvan election and a resolution of the House of Commons from 1731 banning revenue officers from meddling in parliamentary elections.[32] The statute against clandestine marriages was also invoked.[33] If the manorial court and other legal hearings were held regularly in the same room, it might well have been furnished with essential works of reference, such as the published statutes and journals of the House of Commons, and possibly handy digests such as Bullingbrooke's *Abridgement*, to which appeals were made.[34] The bevy of clerks in attendance presumably offered legal guidance. Also present for some

(Chatsworth, W. Conner letter-book, 1749–58). **26** W. Conner to Sir W. Abdy, 7 Feb. 1748[9] (Chatsworth, W. Conner letter-book, 1749–58). **27** W. Conner to Sir W. Abdy, 25 Feb. 1755 (Chatsworth, W. Conner letter-book, 1749–58). **28** *CJI*, iii, 472. **29** *CJI*, ii, 323, 377, 381–3; Barnard, 'Considering the inconsiderable', pp 113–16; *HIP*, ii, 342. **30** W. Conner to Sir W. Abdy, 31 Jan. 1758 (Chatsworth, W. Conner letter-book, 1749–58). **31** Charles Smith, *The antient and present state of the county and city of Waterford* (Dublin, 1746), p. 89. **32** *CJI*, iv, 30. **33** No. 39, Lancelot Hamilton. **34** Barnard, *Brought to book*, pp 51–3; Barnard, 'The Irish parliament and print', pp 107–10; Edward Bullingbrooke and J. Belcher, *An abridgement of the statutes of Ireland* (Dublin, 1754).

of the time were the incumbent of the parish church, Revd Edward Lyndon, the parish clerk, and a hearth-tax collector. An interpreter would be called on for those who spoke no or little English.[35]

Osborne interrupted more often than did Boyle. It was he who asked of a revenue officer, 'if it not be the common opinion of the town' that his wife was a Catholic. Again he made the same appeal, to 'the common undoubted opinion of the town' to a second voter.[36] Yet, when Boyle was trying to establish that another would-be elector was a lodger rather than a pot-walloper, Osborne complained about 'hear say evidence'.[37] The returning officer presided, and here – as in the past – argument arose. The duty fell to William Conner, the Burlingtons' long-serving Munster agent, by virtue of his being also seneschal of the manor of Dungarvan. The latter entitlement was disputed, it being alleged that Conner had already surrendered the seneschalship to another.[38] In addition, it was objected that Conner as a Bandonian was ignorant about the place, as well as partial to the Boyles. Although judged to be 'strictly an honest man', even his employers conceded that Conner 'always made himself disagreeable to the people'.[39] Such cavils made for a rancorous atmosphere from the outset. And the contestation continued and sometimes flared over the next days. Conner complained that one spectator 'crowded behind him', and looked over his notes so that he was 'incommoded in the execution of his office'. The offender at first refused to withdraw and used menacing language towards the seneschal. Only the intervention of one of the candidates persuaded the disrupter to leave. At least two participants were reckoned to be drunk.[40]

The grounds on which an individual's right to vote were queried included the most frequent source of uncertainty in other constituencies, the enjoyment of a forty-shilling freehold. Familiar too from other contests was confessional affiliation, especially of spouses. Particular to Dungarvan was the pot-walloper entitlement. Uniquely the allowance of the six votes of attorneys in the manor court was challenged. When upheld, it was thought to have decided the election for Boyle.[41]

35 Andrew Kennedy; no. 18, John Jones.   36 No. 38, William Block; no. 39, Lancelot Hamilton.   37 No. 37, Samuel Clerke.   38 No. 1, Thomas Barbon; W. Conner to Sir W. Abdy, 22 Dec. 1753, 8 May 1758 (Chatsworth, W. Conner letter-book, 1749–58); *CJI*, vi, 85, ccii, ccxxxv, ccxliii; David Fleming, 'Dungarvan potwallopers' (unpublished lecture delivered to Group for Irish Historic Settlement, Dungarvan, May 2018); Edward Keane, P.B. Phaire and T.U. Sadleir (eds), *King's Inns admission papers, 1607–1867* (Dublin, 1982), p. 19; Smith, *Waterford*, pp 34, 69.   39 H. Cavendish to Devonshire, 27 Aug. 1757 (Chatsworth, Devonshire letters, 363.13); W. Conner to Sir W. Abdy, 5 July 1757, 24 Mar. 1758 (Chatsworth, W. Conner letter-book, 1749–58); 2nd Lord Shannon to R.B. Walsingham, 16 Jan. 1766 (PRONI, Chatsworth papers, T3158/1652); T.C. Barnard, *A new anatomy of Ireland: the Irish Protestants, 1641–1770* (New Haven and London, 2003), pp 46, 228, 229; *HIP*, iii, 466–7.   40 No. 14, John Connor; also no. 4, John Kennelly.   41 2nd Lord Shannon to Robert Boyle Walsingham, 16 Jan. 1766 (Chatsworth papers, PRONI, T3158/1652); Poll book, nos 41–6. Only four of them are recorded in Keane et al. (eds), *King's Inns admission papers*.

The need to furnish unimpeachable evidence if an elector was challenged could be inconvenient. Supporting documentation applied not just to the type and value of leases but to claims of conformity to the established Protestant Church of Ireland. One brusque response to the demand for written certification to be brought on the next day was a negative, 'for having a multiplicity of papers' it was impossible.[42] Less ingenious but as plausible were expressions of forgetfulness regarding precise dates or the present whereabouts of particular documents. From time to time, the presiding seneschal would rule that a line of questioning was irrelevant or inadmissible. Allegations made in the open court might have practical consequences if conformity to the established Protestant church was disproved, since with it vanished the right to a freehold tenure. Perhaps more insidious was the loss of reputation for those who were defamed. Supposed marriages and paternity might be impugned.[43] At least one who was quizzed, David Coughlan, when suspected of being a Catholic, voiced these worries. 'Mr Coughlan said that disquisition or enquiry tended to hurt his property & might be injurious to him being done in a public court which he should be heard of in another place'.[44] There was no obvious redress once such rumours had been uttered. Acrimonious elections, which abounded in eighteenth-century Ireland, left scars on participants beyond the transient elation or dejection of partisans for the rival candidates.

III

The Disenfranchising Act of 1728 confined voting in parliamentary elections to those who were communicant members of the established Church of Ireland.[45] In addition, and probably more fertile for uncertainty, was a requirement of Protestant conformity of voters' wives. Doubts on this score took up a considerable amount of time at Dungarvan. Conformity was proved if there was a record of public recantation, as prescribed by the liturgy of the Church of Ireland, certification of receiving the sacrament at least once a year according to the Protestant rite or, better still, legal enrolment of conversion.[46] However, because the last was costly, necessitating the services of an attorney or lawyer, it was frequently overlooked. Even those who claimed to have gone through the complete procedure could not always produce the supporting documentation.[47]

42 No. 26, David Coghlan. 43 No. 7, Robert Tuttey. 44 No. 26, David Coghlan. 45 1 Geo II, cap. 9; James Kelly, 'Sustaining a confessional state: the Irish parliament and Catholicism' in Hayton, Kelly and Bergin (eds), *The eighteenth-century composite state*, p. 60; J.G. Simms, 'Irish Catholics and the parliamentary franchise', *IHS*, 12 (1960–1), 28–37 reprinted in Simms, *War and politics in Ireland, 1649–1730*, ed. D.W. Hayton and G. O'Brien (London and Ronceverte, 1986), pp 225–34. 46 T.C. Barnard, 'Churchwardens' accounts and the confessional state in Ireland, *c*.1660–1800' in Valerie Hitchman and Andrew Foster (eds), *Views from the parish: churchwardens' accounts c.1500–c.1800* (Newcastle-upon-Tyne, 2015), pp 109–20. 47 No. 3, Charles Griffis; no. 9, Will Morrisson; Andrew Kennedy

For lack of incontrovertible legal proof, eligibility had to be determined by oral testimony. In a few cases, it was supplied by the incumbent of the parish, Edward Lyndon, or by the parish clerk.[48]

Lyndon stated plausibly that he recognized the regular worshippers in his church. 'All the Protestants that lived long enough in the parish to be known by their parish minister who had so numerous a flock he believes he knows'. But he added, 'that those who appear as occasional Protestants that come but once or twice a year to church, he does not know'.[49] Although Lyndon became vicar of Dungarvan only in 1756, he had served as curate there since 1742.[50] More generally the state in Ireland placed weighty responsibilities on incumbents as local agents of central government. In addition to knowing by sight regular worshippers, lists were compiled of those liable to the various church rates and dues, although in this matter the parish clerk was more likely to be asked to supply the information. Furthermore, registers of christenings and marriages were maintained that might settle arguments. But when Lyndon was asked to produce the latter, to decide a claim, he demurred. Irritably, he declared that only the bishop had the authority to order such an inspection.[51]

The statutory public recantation might have been made but not certified. There were suspicions that some, knowing that an election was imminent, hurried to qualify themselves by appearing to convert. This ploy was probably adopted by William Morrison, but his legalized conversion, duly enrolled, took place a few days after the by-election. At least two other examples, of belated recantations and registrations of electors, are known: presumably they hoped to validate their votes retrospectively.[52] Equally telling was the revelation that Patrick Condon was often at Mass 'til Lord Boyle came to town' to prepare for the contest.[53] These opportunistic conversions help to explain sudden jumps in the totals.[54]

For want of written documentation, the court fell back on the spoken. There must be doubt about the trustworthiness of some testimony. Memories were fallible and the opportunities to pursue grudges tempting.[55] Ignorance or vagueness, feigned perhaps, was expressed sometimes about the confessional affiliation of a wife.[56] In contrast, John Collins insisted that he had never heard that his wife was a 'papist', 'nor would he marry her if she was'.[57] Once or twice, a witness's statement about religious practice was angrily disputed, causing

---

(also interpreter); no. 5, Thomas Green; no. 19, Thomas Walsh; no. 20, Henry Kneal; no. 26, David Coghlan; no. 47, Dennis Dunn. **48** No. 3, Charles Griffis; no. 5, Edward Boate; no. 32, James Foley; Casey, no. 8, Nat Brabins. **49** No. 32, James Foley. **50** Henry Cottton, J. B. Leslie, W.H. Rennison and I. Knox, *Clergy of Waterford, Lismore and Ferns* (Belfast, 2008), pp 82, 317. **51** No. 32, James Foley. **52** No. 9, Will Morrison; no. 17, Matthew Bull; no. 19, Thomas Walsh; Fleming, 'Dungarvan potwallopers'; E. O'Byrne, *Convert rolls* (Dublin, 1981), pp 27, 204, 277. **53** No. 20, Patrick Condon. **54** David Dickson, *Old world colony: Cork and south Munster, 1630–1830* (Cork, 2008), p. 274. **55** No. 31, George Smyth. **56** No. 18, John Jones; no. 20, Henry Kneal. **57** No. 35, John Collins.

uproar in the courtroom. Inadvertently, habits of worship were revealed: less constrained than has often been supposed in provincial Ireland during the 'penal era'.[58] An extreme example was William Morrison, a wheelwright. It was remembered that he 'turned from mass to church from church to mass and from mass back again to church'.[59] Thomas Lyndon acknowledged that he had been raised as a Catholic, but, at the age of nine, he had been adopted by a clergyman and apprenticed. Since then, embracing Protestantism, he had not attended Mass. Indeed, at this time he was serving as a church-warden. Even so, Osborne sought – in vain – to have him disqualified as a 'papist'.[60] With another elector, when it was suggested that his wife might be a 'papist', he first answered that 'her name was Protestant'. Then it was conceded that 'she never was at mass but out of curiosity'. However, another witness volunteered that he had seen the woman at Mass ten times.[61] The Catholic Martin Hore recounted how Richard Hamitt had been raised as a Protestant until his father converted to Catholicism. Hore had seen Hamitt, doing his duty 'as other papists', and not at a festival. Another witness disclosed that one Sunday when a high Mass was celebrated 'there were a good many Protestants there'.[62] Curiosity was used to explain why others had gone to Mass. A fellow apprentice attested how, thirty years before, he saw Luke Martyn 'shoulder to shoulder with me, hearing mass', five or six times. Martyn had performed the usual devotions, but had not received the sacrament. The witness firmly rejected the idea that Martyn was a Catholic.[63] Similar 'curiosity' also excused some County Clare voters who had been spotted at Catholic worship in the mid-eighteenth century.[64]

   In default of the vicar and clerk, more subjective reports had to be trusted. Witnesses attested to having seen a would-be voter or his wife either at Protestant worship or at Mass.[65] The frequency of these sightings and how long ago they had occurred were sometimes hazy. Of John Kennelly, for example, a witness claimed that he had seen him at Mass twenty times in the previous fifteen years. Yet it was also said that Kennelly went to the Protestant church on 'sermon days'.[66] One of the most substantial Catholic property-owners in the town, Martin Hore, was sometimes appealed to, although he declared himself 'no scholar' and therefore unable to recall exact times. Nevertheless, he remembered seeing Isaac Jordon at the Abbeyside Catholic chapel, 'performing his duty in the manner Papists do', on twenty occasions. Jordon was also exposed as having children 'by different girls'.[67] Hore informed on a fisherman, Matthew Bull, whom he had encountered at confession in the sacristy of the chapel.[68]

58 For hints that this was so in Dublin: T.C. Barnard, 'A saint for eighteenth-century Dublin? Father John Murphy' in Salvador Ryan and Clodagh Tait (eds), *Religion and politics in urban Ireland, 1500–1750: essays in honour of Colm Lennon* (Dublin, 2016), pp 231–2.   59 No. 9, Will Morrison.   60 No. 13, Thomas Lindon.   61 No. 40, Thomas Casey.   62 No. 15, Richard Hamitt.   63 No. 47, Luke Martyn.   64 Poll book, County Clare, 1745 (TCD, MS 2059, ff 64v., 80v., 95v.).   65 For example, no. 38, William Block.   66 No. 4, John Kennelly.   67 No. 39, Isaac Jordon. For Hore, Fleming, 'Dungarvan potwallopers'.   68 No. 17, Matthew Bull.

IV

To be accepted as a pot-walloper, the existence of a separate household of at least six months duration was required. Thereby a beam of light was shone briefly into the domestic arrangements of the humble. Makeshifts, mobility and squalor are disclosed. In claiming to be a pot-walloper, John Connor asserted that he rented the whole of the lower part of a house, but occupied only one room, in which he had his own furniture and could boil his own pot. The sole entrance through 'the street door' was shared.[69] A hearth-money assessor and collector was consulted over the claim of Joseph Faulkner that he had separate accommodation within his father's house near the strand. It was observed, 'there is no upstairs in the house, [it] is small, and [he] wondered how they could all live in it'. It had only a single hearth and chimney; the family ate together at one long table. The son earned a livelihood by fowling, but the father was a rope-maker. The parent when interrogated insisted that the son lived in the front part of the house, sometimes with a brother. There were said to be four pots altogether in the property. One had been seen being used for cooking fish, but in the others tar was boiled when needed in the chandlery. Another witness, who had been in the house lately, declared that the part claimed as separate by the son looked derelict, 'and appeared to be neither fit for pigs & neither had tables and chairs or any visible thing for a Christian to make use of'. Postle, the parish clerk, had recently toured the premises, concluded that what was described as a second dwelling was an empty out-building without a chimney. It was conceded that the town contained cabins without chimneys in which cooking-pots were boiled. Gratuitously the inspector added that 'he never saw the family go decent as to their clothing', other than one son. The wrangling went on inconclusively until the seneschal adjourned the electoral court to the following morning. Overnight the punctilious Conner visited the Faulkners' home. He concluded that, notwithstanding the presence of a small iron pot, the second dwelling was uninhabited. The younger Faulkner had also tried to simulate a bed in the space but had not deceived Conner, who disallowed the former's claim as a pot-walloper. From the contemptuous comments on the Faulkners' way of living they might be thought to be on the margins of the community, and yet they were given a lengthy hearing in the court.[70]

When the circumstances of 'Captain' Thomas Casey were enquired into, it was disclosed that, despite being a boatman for the customs, he was mired in debt. He had lodgings rather than his own house. Casey's difficulties may have been 'common opinion' around the neighbourhood, but they were aired afresh. More positively, as a sign of the extent of the Dungarvan franchise, is the situation of James Hogan. William Roch, 'gent', attested that he had hired Hogan as 'a menial servant' on wages of £3 annually. At the same time, Hogan

69 No. 14, John Connor.   **70** No. 38, Joseph Faulkner.

rented a house in the town where his wife and children were living. Hogan's right to vote was upheld.[71]

Otherwise, there are few insights into the occupational structure of the port. It had built up a profitable coastal carrying trade primarily to Dublin, but it was badly affected by the crop failures and resulting dearth in 1757.[72] The local depression may have prompted an agent to advise Lady Cork and Burlington to offer interest-free loans to Dungarvan trades-people.[73] Among the few voters whose occupations were specified are to be found a carrier, a rope-maker and chandler, a mariner, and a 'sportsman'.[74] Evidence from the parish vestry minutes supplements the sparsity in the poll book, and strengthens the impression that the householder franchise allowed the middling sorts of artisans and traders and even the humble to participate in elections.

V

The role of women in these events looks peripheral, and, at first glance, negative; the main exception is Lady Burlington, who had decreed that a Boyle – her husband's not her family – must be returned *vice* Roberts. (She died later in the same year.)[75] In addition, it was her daughter who through marriage carried the Boyle inheritance, including parts of Dungarvan, to the Devonshires. Among electors, if a wife was demonstrated to be a Catholic, then the husband was disenfranchised. However, women were consulted by the court. Usually they were asked to corroborate either the confessional affiliation of other women or the tenurial status of claimants, sometimes because they were themselves the proprietors of the property being scrutinized. Otherwise they were consulted as observant neighbours. Or were they just busy-bodies who repeated rumours?

With the corporation of Dungarvan long extinguished, the sittings of the manorial court and attendant courts of record, along with the meetings of the parish vestry, allowed inhabitants to gather and discuss shared concerns. Parliamentary elections that occurred unpredictably but regularly added opportunities. Candidates, as well as treating lavishly, might promise more solid and permanent benefits. Ensuring a better water supply was the most obvious and urgent need, and in this matter parliament did assist. Improving the harbour, building barracks and reviving depressed trade were other pressing needs for which the town might turn to candidates as well as nearby landowners for help.[76]

71 No. 38, James Hogan.   72 Earl Grandison to A. Mason, 30 Apr. 175 (PRONI, Villiers-Stuart MSS, T3131/B/7/37, formerly at Dromana, County Waterford, now in Boole Library, University College, Cork); Dickson, *Old world colony*, pp 221–2.   73 W. Conner to Sir W. Abdy, 13 Dec. 1757 (Chatsworth, W. Conner letter-book, 1749–58).   74 No. 32, James Foley.   75 Lord Boyle to W. Conner, 5 Jan. 1758 (Chatsworth, Devonshire letters, 351.0); same to Devonshire, 4 Feb. 1758 (ibid., 351.3).   76 Petition from Dungarvan, 25

The crowding together in the winter of 1758 of those keen to vote added to the opportunities for social exchanges and friction that the sessions of the manor and other courts, church-going, market- and fair-days and recreation by the shore routinely afforded. How stratified by income, confession, education and attitudes the people of the town and its surroundings were cannot be retrieved with any confidence. As both a port and a staging post on the way from Cork to Waterford, Dungarvan was hardly introverted. The soldiery stationed in barracks often spiced up local society; assocational, cultural and even commercial activities remain to be rediscovered in any detail. The town had not yet become a centre of printing, relying instead on what Cork, Waterford and Dublin published and distributed. When a native of Dungarvan, the apothecary Charles Smith, compiled and had published in 1746 an account of County Waterford, only four townspeople subscribed: Conner's deputy and successor as seneschal, Thomas Barbon; Parson Lyndon; a revenue officer; and Thomas Carew, a future member of parliament.[77] In contrast, at least twenty-six inhabitants including the vicar, five women and petty officials were drawn into a network of subscribers for a tale of Protestant morality republished nearby in 1752.[78]

The participatory nature of elections in Dungarvan, with the unusually wide franchise, gave voters potential power over their aspiring representatives. Conner, overseeing the affair on behalf of the Boyles, had noted recently in another of their boroughs that 'most of the woolcombers and other tradesmen' were preparing to resist dictation 'in hopes of getting something thereby'.[79] And yet, for all the ferocity of the documented contests, members were selected from a narrow elite of propertied Protestant grandees. If there were differences of outlook among the competitors over the larger matters of the day – the treatment of Catholics and Protestant dissenters, the relationship between Ireland and Britain, the roles of the military and burgeoning bureaucracy, the impact of continental warfare – they found no echo in the proceedings of 1758.[80] Even in comparison with other heated by-elections of the decade, at Armagh and Navan, lofty principles were missing at Dungarvan, or at least from the available documentation. Only the vicar, Lyndon, identified Osborne's backers with 'the blues' pitted against 'friends of the House of Burlington'. Lyndon had his own reasons for upholding a deference which was dwindling among his parishioners.[81] Whatever principles might be in play, they are concealed behind

---

June 1727 (Chatsworth, Lismore MS 36/29); W. Conner to Sir W. Abdy, Dublin, 13 Dec. 1757 (Chatsworth, W. Conner letter-book, 1749–58); *CJI*, vi, 85, ccii, ccxxxv, ccxliii; vii, 44, 53; Smith, *Waterford*, p. 90.   **77** Smith, *Waterford*.   **78** C. McCarthy, *The fair moralist; or, Love and virtue: a novel* (n.p., 1752); see Barnard, *Brought to book*, p. 338.   **79** W. Conner to Sir W. Abdy, 23 Dec. 1756 (Chatsworth, W. Conner letter-book, 1749–58).   **80** W. Conner to Sir W. Abdy, 15 Apr. 1757 (Chatsworth, W. Conner letter-book, 1749–58); E. Lyndon to ? W. Conner (Chatsworth, Lismore MS 36/143).   **81** D.A. Fleming, 'Patriots and politics in Navan, 1753–5', *IHS*, 36 (2008–9), 502–21; Eoin Magennis, 'Patriotism, popery and politics in the Armagh by-election of 1753' in A.J. Hughes and William Nolan (eds),

a commentary confined to the clash of competing personalities. Not until he was settled permanently in England did Boyle Walsingham write of defending 'the Whig interest of Ireland'.[82]

VI

Captain Boyle Walsingham would be returned again for Dungarvan at the general election in 1761. The activism of Lord Boyle earned him the more prestigious seat of County Cork. His place as Boyle Walsingham's partner was taken by a Thomas Carew. A well-estated local, Carew had been rumoured as a possible ally for Osborne in 1757, but no alliance had materialized. Instead, acknowledging Carew's weight in the constituency, he was paired with Boyle Walsingham and was returned unopposed in 1761.[83] At the same time, William Conner received the reward for which he had long angled, at last overcoming the reservations of those who thought he lacked 'an election turn'. He sat briefly for his native Bandon.[84] Meanwhile, Osborne had been elected elsewhere. But at the next election in 1768, Boyle Walsingham retired, while remaining a member at Westminster, to which he had first been returned thanks to his wife's family a few days following the original Dungarvan contest. Now he expressed opinions that he had never had the chance of sharing with the Dungarvan voters: 'for my part, I as much detest a Tory as if I had been suckled out of the first glass that was ever filled to the glorious and immortal, etc'.[85] Osborne, in tandem with Carew, now took the Dungarvan seats. Lord Boyle, succeeding as earl of Shannon in 1764, proved energetic in protecting and extending the traditional family interests.[86]

The careers of the Dungarvan members of parliament can be reconstructed, albeit in the case of Carew in the barest outline. Boyle Walsingham, inactive in the

Armagh: history and society (Dublin, 2001), pp 485–504; C.F. McGleenon, *A very independent county: parliamentary elections and politics in County Armagh, 1750–1800* (Belfast, 2011), pp 38–83. **82** R.B. Walsingham to Shannon [31 Feb. 1764] (PRONI, Shannon papers, D2707/A/1/10/44). **83** Sir W. Osborne to Devonshire, 16 July 1757 (PRONI, Chatsworth papers, T3158/1536); Lord Boyle to same, 4 Feb. 1758 (ibid., T3158/1571); W. Conner to same, 17 Aug. 1759 (ibid., T3158/1615); 2nd Lord Shannon to R.B. Walsingham, 16 Jan. 1766 (ibid.,T3158/1652). **84** H. Cavendish to Devonshire, 27 Aug. 1757 (Chatsworth, Devonshire letters, 363.13); W. Conner to Sir W. Abdy, 5 July 1757, 24 Mar. 1758 (ibid., W. Conner letterbook, 1749–58); R.B. Walsingham to Lord Boyle [2 Dec. 1760] (PRONI, Shannon papers, D 2707/A/2/4/1); Rev. T. Dawson to Devonshire, 30 Apr. 1761 (Chatsworth papers, T3158/1635; 2nd Lord Shannon to Robert Boyle Walsingham, 16 Jan. 1766 (Chatsworth, T3158/1652); Barnard, *New anatomy*, pp 46, 228, 229; *HIP*, iii, 466–7. **85** R.B. Walsingham to Shannon [31 Feb. 1764] (PRONI, Shannon papers, D2707/A/1/10/44). **86** T.C. Barnard, '"Petticoat government"? Dingle during the 1770s', *JKAHS*, 2nd ser., 18 (2018), 89–97; Barnard, 'Carberians invade Dingle between 1776 and 1797', *Skibbereen Historical Journal*, 14 (2018), 61–6; Hewitt (ed.), *Lord Shannon's letters to his son*; *HIP*, iii, 248–51; J. Quinn, 'Boyle, Richard, 2nd earl of Shannon' in *DIB*, pp 736–7.

Fig. 1 Captain Robert Boyle Walsingham by Nathaniel Hone (private collection).

Fig. 2 Dungarvan port in the 1820s (Ulster Folk and Transport Museum).

Dublin assembly, was praised for independence and integrity at Westminster.[87] The momentary burst of illumination from the poll book fades and with the ensuing darkness, it is not clear if it was a preview into a valley of squinting windows. Had not almost all the records of the Irish law courts in the eighteenth century been burnt, destroying the anecdotes and assertions of witnesses and deponents, instead of darkness there would be brilliant light. Captain Robert Boyle Walsingham was portrayed dashingly in his naval rig and in a heroic posture by Nathaniel Hone (Fig. 1). He would be drowned in 1779 when his ship was caught in a hurricane in the West Indies.[88] In the 1820s, a naïve artist depicted work-a-day scenes in and around Dungarvan (Fig. 2).[89] Here, perhaps, can be seen some whose forbears participated in the events of 1758. Yet, the later images notwithstanding, the shabby crew of Faulkners whose cabin by the sea and unkempt appearance repelled neighbours have no visual memorial, only an entry in the 1758 poll book.

87 John Brooke, 'Boyle Walsingham, Robert' in L.B. Namier and John Brooke (eds), *History of parliament, 1754–90* (3 vols, London, 1964), iii, 603–6. 88 Anne Crookshank and Desmond FitzGerald, Knight of Glin, *Ireland's painters, 1600–1940* (London and New Haven, 2002), p. 102; Brooke in *History of parliament*. I am grateful to William Laffan for further information about the portrait. 89 W.H. Crawford, 'Provincial town life in the early nineteenth century: an artist's impressions' in B.P. Kennedy and R. Gillespie (eds), *Ireland: art into history* (Dublin and Niwot, 1994), pp 43–59.

Jacqueline R. Hill

Publications to 2021 (excluding book reviews)

BOOKS

R.V. Comerford, Mary Cullen, Jacqueline Hill and Colm Lennon (eds), *Religion, conflict and coexistence in Ireland: essays presented to Monsignor Patrick J. Corish* (Dublin, 1990).

Jacqueline Hill and Cormac Ó Gráda (eds), *Austin Bourke, 'The visitation of God'? The potato and the Great Irish Famine* (Dublin, 1993).

Jacqueline Hill, *From patriots to unionists: Dublin civic politics and Irish Protestant patriotism, 1660–1840* (Oxford, 1997).

Colm Lennon and Jacqueline Hill (eds), *Luxury and austerity: Historical Studies XXI, papers read before the 23rd Irish Conference of Historians* (Dublin, 1997).

J.R. Hill (ed.), *A new history of Ireland;* Vol. 7: *1921–84* (Oxford, 2003).

Jacqueline Hill and Mary Ann Lyons (eds), *Representing Irish religious histories: historiography, ideology, and practice* (Cham, 2017).

ARTICLES AND CHAPTERS

1975

'Nationalism and the Catholic Church in the 1840s', *Irish Historical Studies*, 19:76, pp 371–95.

1980

'The intelligentsia and Irish nationalism in the 1840s', *Studia Hibernica*, 20, pp 73–109.

'The Protestant response to repeal: the case of the Dublin working class' in F.S.L. Lyons and R.A.J. Hawkins (eds), *Ireland under the Union: varieties of tension: essays in honour of T.W. Moody* (Oxford), pp 35–68.

1981

'Artisans, sectarianism and politics in Dublin, 1829–48', *Saothar: Journal of the Irish Labour History Society*, 7, pp 12–27.

1982

'The politics of privilege: Dublin Corporation and the Catholic Question, 1792–1823', *Maynooth Review*, 7, pp 17–36.

1984

'National festivals, the state and "Protestant ascendancy" in Ireland, 1790–1829', *Irish Historical Studies*, 24:93, pp 30–51.

1986

'Religion, trade and politics in Dublin, 1798–1848' in P. Butel and L.M. Cullen (eds), *Cities and merchants: French and Irish perspectives on urban development* (Dublin), pp 247–59.

1988

'Popery and Protestantism, civil and religious liberty: the disputed lessons of Irish history, 1690–1812', *Past & Present*, 118, pp 96–129.

1989

'Religious toleration and the relaxation of the penal laws: an imperial perspective, 1763–1780', *Archivium Hibernicum*, 44, pp 98–109.
'The meaning and significance of "Protestant ascendancy", 1787–1840' in *Ireland after the Union: proceedings of the second joint meeting of the Royal Irish Academy and the British Academy, London 1986* (Oxford), pp 1–22.

1990

'The legal profession and the defence of the *ancien régime* in Ireland, 1790–1840' in Daire Hogan & W.N. Osborough (eds), *Brehons, serjeants and attorneys: studies in the history of the Irish legal profession* (Dublin), pp 181–209.

1993

'1641 and the quest for Catholic emancipation, 1691–1829' in Brian Mac Cuarta (ed.), *Ulster, 1641: aspects of the rising* (Belfast), pp 159–71.
'The politics of Dublin Corporation, 1760–1792' in David Dickson, Dáire Keogh and Kevin Whelan (eds), *The United Irishmen: republicanism, radicalism and rebellion* (Dublin), pp 88–101.

1995

'Corporate values in Hanoverian Edinburgh and Dublin' in S.J. Connolly, R.A. Houston and R.J. Morris (eds), *Conflict, identity and economic development: Ireland and Scotland, 1600–1939* (Preston), pp 114–24.

'Ireland without Union: Molyneux and his legacy' in John Robertson (ed.), *A union for empire: political thought and the British union of 1707* (Cambridge and Washington DC), pp 271–96.

1997

'Biblical language and providential destiny in mid-eighteenth-century Irish Protestant patriotism' in Judith Devlin and Ronan Fanning (eds), *Religion and rebellion: Historical Studies XX, papers read before the 22nd Irish Conference of Historians* (Dublin), pp 71–83.

'Dublin Corporation, Protestant dissent, and politics, 1660–1800' in Kevin Herlihy (ed.), *The politics of Irish dissent, 1650–1800* (Dublin), pp 28–39.

1998

'The Act of Union' in Mary Cullen (ed.), *200 years of resonance: essays and contributions on the history and relevance of the United Irishmen and the 1798 revolution* (Dublin), pp 47–53.

2000

'Corporatist ideology and practice in Ireland, 1660–1800' in Sean J. Connolly (ed.), *Political ideas in eighteenth-century Ireland* (Dublin), pp 64–82.

2001

'Irish identities before and after the Act of Union', *Radharc: the chronicles of Glucksman Ireland House at New York University*, 2, pp 51–73.

'Convergence and conflict in eighteenth-century Ireland', *The Historical Journal*, 44:4, pp 1039–63.

'Politics and the writing of history: the impact of the 1690s and 1790s on Irish historiography' in D. George Boyce, Robert Eccleshall and Vincent Geoghegan (eds), *Political discourse in seventeenth- and eighteenth-century Ireland* (Basingstoke), pp 222–39.

'The shaping of Dublin government in the long eighteenth century' in Peter Clark and Raymond Gillespie (eds), *Two capitals: London and Dublin, 1500–1840* (Oxford), pp 149–65.

2002

'Protestant ascendancy challenged: the Church of Ireland laity and the public sphere, 1740–1869' in Raymond Gillespie and W.G. Neely (eds), *The laity and the Church of Ireland, 1000–2000: all sorts and conditions* (Dublin), pp 152–69.

2003

'Dublin after the Union: the age of the ultra Protestants, 1801–22' in Michael Brown, Patrick Geoghegan and James Kelly (eds), *The Irish Act of Union: bicentennial essays* (Dublin), pp 144–56.

2006

'"Allegories, fictions and feigned representations": decoding the money bill dispute 1752–6', *Eighteenth-Century Ireland: Iris and dá chultúr*, 21, pp 66–88.

2007

'The 1847 general election in Dublin city' in Allan Blackstock and Eoin Magennis (eds), *Politics and political culture in Britain and Ireland, 1750–1850: essays in tribute to Peter Jupp* (Belfast), pp 41–64.
'Making sense of mixed descent: English and Irish genealogy in the memoirs of an Irish loyalist, Ambrose Hardinge Giffard (1771–1827)' in Bruno Tribout and Ruth Whelan (eds), *Narrating the self in early modern Europe*. Peter Lang European Connections series, 23 (Bern), pp 277–91.

2008

'The language and symbolism of conquest in Ireland, c.1790–1850', *Transactions of the Royal Historical Society*, 6th series, 18, pp 165–86.
'National festivals, the state and "Protestant ascendancy" in Ireland, 1790–1829' in N.C. Fleming and Alan O'Day (eds), *Ireland and Anglo-Irish relations since 1800: critical essays* (London), pp 33–54 (originally published in *Irish Historical Studies*, 24:93 (1983), pp 30–51).

2009

'Art imitating war? *Observe the Sons of Ulster Marching Towards the Somme* and its place in history', *Études Irlandaises*, 34:1, pp 37–52.
James McGuire and James Quinn (eds), *Dictionary of Irish biography* (11 vols, Cambridge, 2009–18). Entries on:
'Alexander, Sir William (1743–1822)'
'Binns, John (1730?–1804)'
'Dunn, James (1700–73)'

'Giffard, John (1746–1819)'
'Gregg, Tresham Dames (1800–81)'
'McDowell, Robert Brendan (R.B.) (1913–2011)'
'Scully, Denys (1773–1830)'

2010

'"Carrying the war into the walks of commerce": exclusive dealing and the southern Protestant middle class during the Catholic emancipation campaign' in Fintan Lane (ed.), *Politics, society and the middle class in modern Ireland* (Basingstoke), pp 65–88.
'The Church of Ireland and perceptions of Irish church history, *c.*1790–1869' in Terence Dooley (ed.), *Ireland's polemical past: views of Irish history in honour of R.V. Comerford* (Dublin), pp 9–31.
'Loyal societies in Ireland, 1690–1790' in James Kelly and Martyn J. Powell (eds), *Clubs and societies in eighteenth-century Ireland* (Dublin), pp 181–202.

2011

'Whitley Stokes senior (1763–1845) and his political, religious and cultural milieu' in Elizabeth Boyle and Paul Russell (eds), *The tripartite life of Whitley Stokes (1830–1909)* (Dublin), pp 14–28.

2013

'Lord Mayor Thomas McKenny and Catholic emancipation, 1818–19' in Lisa-Marie Griffith and Ruth McManus (eds), *Leaders of the city: Dublin's first citizens, 1500–1950* (Dublin), pp 98–106.
'Daniel O'Connell's top hat' in W.E. Vaughan (ed.), *The Old Library, Trinity College Dublin, 1712–2012* (Dublin), pp 210–12.

2014

'Loyalty and monarchy in Ireland, *c.*1660–1840' in Allan Blackstock and Frank O'Gorman (eds), *Loyalism and the formation of the British world, 1775–1914* (Woodbridge), pp 81–102.

2016

'Dublin Corporation and the levying of tolls and customs, *c.*1720–*c.*1820' in Michael Brown and Seán Patrick Donlan (eds), *The law and other legalities of Ireland, 1689–1850* (Abingdon), pp 187–208.
'Oaths and oath taking: the civic experience in Dublin, 1660–1774' in Salvador Ryan and Clodagh Tait (eds), *Religion and politics in urban Ireland, c.1500–c.1750: essays in honour of Colm Lennon* (Dublin), pp 193–209.

2017

'Laying the nineteenth-century foundations: contributions from a Catholic and Protestant scholar in the 1820s' in Jacqueline Hill and Mary Ann Lyons (eds), *Representing Irish religious histories: historiography, ideology, and practice* (Cham), pp 53–67.

2019

'Plan S: the implications for history journals, researchers and learned societies' in *History Ireland*, 27:5, pp 8–9.

2021

'John Giffard: self-serving sycophant?' in Terence Dooley, Mary Ann Lyons and Salvador Ryan (eds), *The historian as detective: uncovering Irish pasts* (Dublin), pp 180–2.

BIBLIOGRAPHICAL RESOURCES

Jacqueline Hill (ed.), *Writings on Irish history, 1984* (Dublin, 1986).

Irish History Online

Since 2003, Jacqueline Hill has overseen the management of Irish History Online (IHO) and is currently convenor of the IHO Management Committee. IHO was established as an online database in 2003 at the National University of Ireland Maynooth with funding from the Irish Research Council for the Humanities and Social Sciences (IRCHSS). The database was developed in association with the Royal Historical Society Bibliography of British and Irish History between 2003 and 2009. Since January 2010 the two projects have operated separately. IHO is now hosted by the Royal Irish Academy Library, Dublin, and is updated regularly. The database has now exceeded 110,000 entries for publications on Irish historical topics, and it continues to expand.

Index